CRAZY TALK
A Study of the Discourse
of Schizophrenic Speakers

COGNITION AND LANGUAGE
A Series in Psycholinguistics

Series Editor: **R. W. Rieber**

CRAZY TALK: A Study of the Discourse of Schizophrenic Speakers
Sherry Rochester and J. R. Martin

CLINICAL PSYCHOLINGUISTICS
Theodore Shapiro

PSYCHOLOGY OF LANGUAGE AND LEARNING
O. Hobart Mowrer

A Continuation Order Plan is available for this series. A continuation order will bring delivery of each new volume immediately upon publication. Volumes are billed only upon actual shipment. For further information please contact the publisher.

CRAZY TALK
A Study of the Discourse
of Schizophrenic Speakers

Sherry Rochester
Clarke Institute of Psychiatry
Toronto, Ontario, Canada
and
J. R. Martin
The University of Sydney
Sydney, New South Wales, Australia

Plenum Press · New York and London

Library of Congress Cataloging in Publication Data

Rochester, Sherry.
  Crazy talk.

  Includes index.
  1. Schizophrenics — Language. I. Martin, J. R., joint author. II. Title. [DNLM:
1. Schizophrenic language. WM203.3 R676c]
RC514.R56   616.8'982   79-11978
ISBN 0-306-40236-X

© 1979 Plenum Press, New York
A Division of Plenum Publishing Corporation
227 West 17th Street, New York, N.Y. 10011

Printed in the United States of America

Preface

This book is a study of discourse—the flow of talk—of schizophrenic speakers. Our goal is to understand the processes which account for the ordinary flow of talk that happens all the time between speakers and listeners. How do conversations happen? What is needed by a listener to follow a speaker's words and respond appropriately to them? How much can a speaker take for granted and how much must be stated explicitly for the listener to follow the speaker's meanings readily and easily?

Each time we ask these questions, we seem to have to go back to some place prior to the "ordinary" adult conversation. This time, we have tried reversing the questions and asking: What happens when conversation fails? Prompted in part by an early paper by Robin Lakoff to the Chicago Linguistics Society and by Herb Clark's studies of listener processes, we wondered what a speaker has to do to make the listener finally *stop* making allowances and stop trying to adjust the conversational contract to cooperate. This inquiry led us to the schizophrenic speaker. When a listener decides that the speaker's talk is "crazy," he or she is giving up on the normal form of conversation and saying, in effect, this talk is extraordinary and something is wrong. We thought that, if we could specify what makes a conversation fail, we might learn what has to be present for a conversation to succeed.

We intended to study the conversations of schizophrenic patients with clinicians who decided, at some point, that the conversations violated enough of the rules of ordinary conversation that the speakers must be crazy. There were so many unknowns involved in this study, however, that we again stepped back and tried to formulate a procedure for studying this "crazy talk." We wanted to do two things, hopefully at the same time. We wanted to sample speech which clinicians considered "crazy" or incoherent, and we wanted to do this fairly systematically, sampling from a variety of situations and studying groups of speakers who were roughly comparable. We wanted, that is, to conduct a broad-based naturalistic study with as much experimental rigor as we could muster.

Accordingly, over the past five years, our research has focused on analyses of the "talk" of schizophrenic patients and normal subjects in a variety of situations. For the most part, we have concentrated on descriptions of schizophrenic speakers who are considered "thought disordered"—whose speech is so confusing to the examining clinician that the speaker is said to be unable to think clearly. We began by trying to describe the hesitations that accompanied coherent and incoherent texts, in order to study the cognitive processes that underlay the production of such texts. During this time, there were two of us: Sherry Rochester, a research psychologist, and Sharon Thurston, a linguist, both working at the Clarke Institute of Psychiatry at the University of Tornonto. We spent some time trying to formulate a way of going beyond the hesitation data to describe the talk and to account for its incoherence.

To our frustration, almost all the available approaches seemed to be rooted within the sentence. There were, however, some attempts to study the narrative that were encouraging. In addition, there were analyses from the Prague School of Linguistics which stretched beyond the sentence to a concern for whole pieces of talk—for texts and paragraphs and discourse.

At this point, we were joined by Jim Martin, a graduate student at the Centre for Linguistic Studies at the University of Toronto. Martin was interested in Halliday's models of language in a social context and introduced these to the rest of us. The present book is based on the analyses that Martin subsequently developed and that were tested and analyzed by Rochester.

The book falls into two parts. The first part is an introduction to the problem of studying schizophrenic speakers. It is not a review of literature, in the sense that the results of studies are presented and their methodology criticized. Rather, it is an attempt to analyze the assumptions that have guided research in this field over the past sixty years.

The second part is a research study in which we present the results of a series of analyses that began with Halliday and Hasan's (1976) cohesion analyses and grew to be detailed examinations of the ways in which schizophrenic and normal speakers introduce new information and presume old information. Chapter 2 describes the speakers and situations in which they speak and gives an overview of the speech samples. Then, beginning with Chapter 3, various analyses of the discourse are presented. In Chapter 3, we describe analyses of cohesion in discourse and report the findings for schizophrenic speakers who are considered "thought disordered" and "nonthought disordered" and for normal speakers. Chapter 4 introduces several more detailed analyses, all of which are designed to study how speakers introduce new participants into their discourse and how they presume the existence of old participants. Chapters 5 and 6 present these analyses in detail.

In Chapter 7, we summarize the results of the analyses and consider how these results bear on theories of schizophrenic language and speech which either seem promising or have been given a great deal of attention in the recent literature. Finally, we offer some speculations as to which of the current theories seems best supported by the present data.

We owe many debts to the generosity and hard work of several people. Professor Alexander Bonkalo and Dr. Mary Seeman served many long hours as clinical judges, viewing about 100 hours of videotape each and then sharing their impressions with us. Professor Pierre Léon and Dr. Phillip Martin very kindly allowed us to use their pitchmeter and other facilities of the Phonetics Laboratory of the University of Toronto. Michael Dobrovolsky, Henry Pollard, Margaret Sparshott, Sharon Thurston, and Judith Rochester were among the graduate students of linguistics and psychology who served as our coders and frequent advisors. Judith Rupp conducted the entire cartoon task descriptions, and her industry and goodwill were an invaluable part of our efforts. Cathy Spegg, Ron Langevin, and Penny Lawler also served as generous advisors and colleagues.

The research would have not been possible without adequate testing facilities and funding, and for these we are indebted to our sponsoring organization. Since 1973, the studies have been supported by the Scottish Rite Schizophrenia Foundation and by the Clarke Institute of Psychiatry Research Fund. In addition, the Clarke Institute has provided us with considerable office and laboratory space, with videotaping facilities, computer time, and a profound latitude in pursuing our research goals.

Thomas Oltmanns, Nancy Andreasen, Mary Seeman, Elaine Chaika, Joseph Jaffe, and Robin Hunter reviewed earlier versions of the manuscript with great care. Stanley Feldstein reviewed the entire manuscript, commenting with his usual perspicacity and humor. The book is much improved for all their efforts. Throughout all the stages of the writing of this book, Mitas Ongtengco has played a major role — supervising the subjects, administering the budget, and cheerfully typing and retyping the manuscript.

We are indebted to Michael Halliday and Ruquiya Hasan for their insights into the nature of text and its relation to context and lexicogrammar, which will be evident from our many references to their work. Our debt to H. A. Gleason, Jr., is less obvious, since relevant parts of his thinking remain unpublished. We gladly acknowledge his many hours of helpful discussion. It was, in fact, through one of Gleason's students, Waldemar Gutwinski, that we first became interested in cohesion and its application to szhizophrenic discourse.

Finally, we are most grateful to the many subjects who participated in these studies and who so kindly allowed us to examine their talk. The fees they were paid could not possibly compensate them for the time and goodwill they brought to their task.

SHERRY ROCHESTER
Toronto, Canada

J. R. MARTIN
Sydney, Australia

Contents

Chapter 5

Presenting Information in Texts 119

Chapter 6

Presuming Information from the Culture and from the Situation .. 139

1

Thought Disorder and Language Use in Schizophrenia

> It is frequently observed that though schizophrenics use proper words and produce reasonably well-formed sentences, one is unable, after having heard a series of such sentences, to comprehend what has been said. (Pavy, 1968, p. 175)

Schizophrenic speakers sometimes fail to produce coherent discourse. This is the theme of the present monograph, and in this first chapter we introduce the notion of discourse failures and provide a background to the study. Discourse failures (see Section I) occur when the listener cannot follow the speaker, even though the speaker is using familiar words in generally well-formed sentences. These failures do not always occur in the productions of schizophrenic speakers, but when they do, they are regarded as "one of the most outstanding characteristics of schizophrenic thinking" (Cameron, 1938b, p. 2).

It was the prominence of discourse failures in the diagnosis of schizophrenia that led Pavy (1968) to comment: "It may be that the best linguistic theory for work with schizophrenic speech will involve samples of language larger than a sentence"; and to suggest that "the formal analysis of discourse . . . might provide insights which an analysis restricted to sentences would not yield" (p. 175).

In Section I, we discuss the centrality of discourse failures to the original definition of schizophrenia and examine how these failures have come to be termed "thought disorders." We argue that the notion of "thought disorder" has been and still is an elusive and difficult concept to study, and we attempt to trace the effects of this concept on the investigation of schizophrenics' language.

In Section II, we explore the premises underlying studies of lan-

1

guage use in schizophrenia. Though there have been many reviews of the experimental work in this field in recent years, there have been no overviews of the assumptions underlying these studies and no summaries of the recent, exciting descriptions by linguists and asphasiologists. The premises of experiments and naturalistic studies in the field are outlined, and some of the problems associated with these premises are discussed.

Finally, in Section III, we consider the study of discourse failures or "thought disorders" in light of the premises that have been adopted by students of schizophrenic language. The central issue, we suggest, is whether one should pay attention to schizophrenia or to language. Our option is for the detailed study of language use—in particular, discourse production—by schizophrenic speakers. Its study occupies the remainder of this monograph.

I. Discourse Failures and the Schizophrenic Speaker

A. "Schizophrenia" and Discourse Failures

The term "schizophrenia" was coined, in part, to describe discourse failures. In 1911, Eugen Bleuler reported his experience of being a confused listener in the presence of incoherent speakers. He described listening to patients whose speech was difficult to comprehend, where, "fragments of ideas are connected in an illogical way to constitute a new idea," and where "new ideas crop up which neither the patient nor the observer can bring into any connection with the previous stream of thought" (1950, p. 9). These disruptions in the patient's discourse Bleuler took to be indications of a "splitting" of psychic functions, the "schizo" of schizophrenia.

Although Bleuler regarded thought and speech as distinct constructs,[1] those who followed him often treated speech as a direct reflec-

---

[1] If one reads carefully, it is clear that Bleuler did not regard speech as a mirror image of thought. He notes, for example, that a speaker may appear confused when only the "manner of expression" is obscure. In such a case, "logical transitions may be assumed to exist" (1950, p. 21). And elsewhere he observes that a "gap in associations" in the speaker's thoughts may be bridged in speech by grammatical forms. In this case, speech which appears to be reflecting coherent thoughts is, in fact, only simulating them. Thus, the patient's speech may be confusing while the thoughts are logical; or the thoughts may be unconnected while the speech is linked through grammatical forms. Speech is one thing, Bleuler seems to be saying, and thought another; and though the two often meet, they are not inseparable.

tion of cognition. From about the middle 1930s until the present day, schizophrenic patients who have failed to speak coherently have been said to show "thought process disorder" or "formal thought disorder." They have rarely been described in terms of their "discourse failures" or "language disorders" or "communication disorders."

This tendency to infer disordered thought from disordered speech has caused many problems and obscured some interesting issues, as we shall see presently. In recent years, several workers have commented on the confusion which results from assuming that speech is isomorphic to thought (e.g., Andreasen, in press-b; Chaika, 1974a,b; Lecours & Vanier-Clément, 1976; Seeman, 1970; and Singer & Wynne, 1963). But there is a second step that makes the matter even more complicated.

To say that a speaker is incoherent is only to say that one cannot understand that speaker. So to make a statement about incoherent discourse is really to make a statement about one's own confusion as a listener. It is therefore just as appropriate to study what it is about the listener which makes him or her "confusable" as it is to study what it is about the speaker which makes him or her "confusing." The focus of study depends simply on the direction of attribution.

Historically, the direction of attribution has been from clinician to patient. So when a clinician experiences confusion in the presence of a patient, as Bleuler and so many after him did, it is natural to look to the patient's behavior for an explanation of that confusion. Sensitive clinicians treat themselves as measuring instruments which detect difficulties and then signal that something is amiss in the environment. For example, a clinician might experience a headache or at least a sense of bewilderment in the presence of certain speakers and infer that some aspects of the speaker's behavior are responsible for this experience.

This inferential tradition is valuable because it relies on the profound sensitivity of native members of a culture—a sensitivity linguists and psycholinguists are very far from capturing at the present time. But it is also a troublesome tradition, for it obscures the inferential status of many of the clinician's observations. In particular, it obscures two inferences: (a) the assessment of "thought disorder" is based on an inference from talk not thought; and (b) "talk failures" are inferences based on the listener's experience of confusion. In the first inferential step, one is moving from the speaker's utterance to his or her thoughts, and the issue is: To what extent is speech a reflection of thought? In the second inferential step, one is proceeding from the listener's experience of confusion to attribute confusing behavior to the speaker. The issue here is: To what extent is the speaker's utterance responsible for the listener's confusion?

There is one more complication in this process. It occurs because the second inference (from listener to speaker) was originally made by Bleuler in 1911 and has been reified in the ensuing years. Bleuler attempted to account for his experience of confusion in several ways, suggesting that his patients' discourse was "vague and wooly" and full of "loose associations" and "long silences" and "rhyming words"; that it was "haphazard" and "bizarre" and "lacking in goals." Most of these are behaviors that Bleuler presumed were disruptive to his own comprehension. One does not know whether all were actually disruptive; whether some were more disruptive than others; whether there were other behaviors which might have confused Bleuler but were not mentioned; or whether those behaviors would be confusing to other listeners. In short, we do not *know* that Bleuler's list describes behaviors which actually are disruptive and confusing to listeners. We only know that Bleuler suspected these behaviors as the sources of his confusion.

It is the largely uncritical acceptance of Bleuler's list as truth rather than speculation that makes it a problem. As a result of this enduring acceptance and the supportive (but equally speculative) observations of later writers, there are actually two ways in which today's clinicians make inferences of thought disorder. Thought disorder is said to exist if (*a*) the listener (a clinician) feels confused and cannot follow what the speaker (a patient) is saying; and/or (*b*) the listener observes that the speaker is producing discourse which contains events described by Bleuler and later observers in their efforts to explain their own confusion. The inferential status of thought disorder is not different in (*a*) and (*b*). Rather, in (*a*) clinicians rely on their own experience, and in (*b*) they rely on the experience and inferences of others. In both cases, a double inference is being made: from the listener's experience to the speaker's utterance, and from the speaker's utterance to the speaker's own cognition.

B. Defining "Thought Disorder"

The double inference behind the designation of "thought disorder" makes a stubborn tangle for young clinicians hoping to learn its meaning. In one popular modern textbook, for example, thought process disorder is said to be "manifested by irrelevance and incoherence of the patient's verbal productions." The manifestations can range from "simple blocking and mild circumstantiality to total loosening of associations as in word salad" (Freedman, Kaplan, & Sadock, 1976, p. 1333).

The definition is evidently vague, but what is even more frustrating

Figure 1. Imaginary conversation between student and textbook writer.

is that it is circular. As it stands—and the above definition is typical, not exceptional—the definition suggests that thought disorder can be inferred from speech events. But if one pursues the definitions of these speech events, one is led back to a description of thought disorder. For example, "loosening of associations" is defined not in terms of discourse events but in terms of cognition. "In the loosening of association," the reader is told, "the flow of thought may seem haphazard, purposeless, illogical, confused, abrupt, and bizarre." The same circularity is true with "circumstantiality" which "is a disorder of association in which too many associated ideas come into consciousness because of too little selective suppression" (Freedman *et al.*, 1976, p. 385). As the perplexed student observes in Figure 1, thought disorder is when talk is incoherent. And talk is incoherent when the thought is disordered.

C. "Thought Disorder" and Schizophrenia

> The potential payoff of success in understanding schizophrenic thought disorder is great. Schizophrenia is the most massive unsolved puzzle in the whole field of psychopathology, and thought disorder is schizophrenia's most prominent symptom. A true understanding of the nature of the thought disorder might illuminate the nature of schizoprenia itself. (Chapman & Chapman, 1973, p. ix)

"Thought disorder," as we have suggested, is a central concept in the diagnosis of schizophrenia. For most clinicians, the assessment of "thought disorder" is based on inferences from the discourse of patients. Because the inferential status is not explicit, many young (and old) clinicians find the diagnosis of thought disorder mystifying and attempt to dispose of it by resorting to lists of phenomena given by Bleuler or presented in textbooks. As we have argued, using these lists does not change the inferential status of the construct. Nor, as we have just seen, is it much help in picking out just what it is that makes a discourse incoherent.

Students and young clinicians are not the only ones inconvenienced by the problematic status of "thought disorder." Investigators from several different areas find the construct's shifting definition an impediment. It complicates the efforts of clinical investigators who wish to describe the onset and remission of schizophrenic symptoms. It limits the work of those who propose that schizophrenia involves some dysfunction of the left hemisphere, especially the left temporal lobes (e.g., Flor-Henry, 1976; Gruzelier, 1978). And for a long time the elusive construct has both attracted and hindered those who hypothesize that schizophrenia may involve an episodic aphasia (cf. Benson, 1973; Chaika, 1974a).

Why, if "thought disorder" is potentially so valuable to a variety of workers, have we had no systematic descriptions of the discourse failures on which this designation is based? Or, to put this another way, why has "thought disorder" been described in terms of thought-based rather than language-based variables?

The short answer to this question is that clinicians seeking to describe language use in schizophrenia have not noticed the inferential status of their own descriptions and have relied on metaphors to convey their experiences. Experimenters, on the other hand, have tended to produce studies which were methodologically rigorous but which in no way captured the complexity of the phenomenon they were trying to study. The longer answer is that research into language use in schizophrenia has been a microcosm of psycholinguistics. When the psychology of language flourished, as it did in the period from about 1870 to 1920, Bleuler presented his epoch-making descriptions of language use in schizophrenia. And when these studies declined and virtually disappeared in North America from about 1920 until the 1960s, the study of language use in schizophrenia languished as well. In the following section we discuss some of these trends.

II. Studies of Language Use in Schizophrenia and Their Premises

"What are you working on these days?"
"Language and schizophrenia."
"It's a graveyard." (Overheard conversation, Toronto, 1973)

The study of language use in schizophrenia has not been a happy enterprise. Every major reviewer in the last decade has observed that there is no adequate theory of why schizophrenic speakers produce aberrant discourse. And, though most reviewers argue otherwise, we believe that there is also a lack of satisfactory data. In this section, we try to suggest why, after some fifty years of effort, promising models and adequate data are still lacking in this field.

A. The Reviewers

There is no promising model of language use in schizophrenia, and every reviewer in the last decade has commented on this fact. Harold Vetter, for example, after publishing several books and articles reviewing psychopathological language, observed that "even by the most pragmatic

criteria, the results of forty years of research on schizophrenic language
. . . have proven to be quite disappointing." What we know after all this
effort, he continues, is mainly "the rather obvious fact that schizophrenics often differ strikingly from normal persons in what they talk about
and how they talk about it" (Vetter, 1968, p. 25).

David Pavy, in an important and comprehensive review of the field
published in the same year, noted cautiously that "modern investigators
of speech in schizophrenia are to be commended for their experimental
rigor." Nevertheless, "one must conclude that we are far from specifying
the nature of verbal disorder in schizophrenia" (Pavy, 1968, p. 171).

Perhaps the most elegantly phrased observation was made by Bren-
dan Maher in a careful and patient review of the host of experimental
studies from the 1930s into the early 1960s. He writes that, in the attempts
to specify the nature of verbal disorder in schizophrenia, "hypothesis
struggles with hypothesis in a conflict in which new contenders enter the
field but the defeated never retire" (Maher, 1966, p. 433).

The gloomy consensus is that there has been little progress, if any, in
experimental studies of schizophrenic language use and no generally accepted formulations of why schizophrenic speakers produce aberrant
discourse. Experiments have been unsuccessful, it is suggested, because
they have not led to theories that are both testable and relevant to the
confusing productions of the schizophrenic speaker.

It is also implied by some observers that, though there is a lack of
theory, there are more than enough data. We disagree. Rather, there
seems to be (a) a very broad base of data from clinical observations that is
speculative and essentially metaphorical, and (b) a very narrow base of
experimental observations (e.g., statistical summaries of word class occurrences, listener's responses to individual sentences) that are not representative of language use in schizophrenic patients. In the next section,
we suggest that the lack of promising theoretical models is related to the
lack of broadly based, systematic observations. In the absence of a theory
of language use, it seems, observations are constrained. And in the absence of adequate data, fruitful theories are not developed.

B. Studies of Language Use in Schizophrenia: The Early Premises

Although experimental studies of language use in schizophrenia
have been reviewed extensively, the reviews have been either summaries
of the literature or methodological critiques. In addition to those cited
above, there is a comprehensive methodological critique by Chapman &
Chapman, 1973; a valuable review of the European literature by Bär, 1976;

and a review of some clinical observations and theories by Reed (1970). Very little has been attempted in the way of an examination of the premises in the field. In the following discussion, we pursue this examination.

1. A Microcosm of Psycholinguistics. The study of language use in schizophrenia is a poor stepchild of the development of psycholinguistics. It is, to use Titchener's (1905) term, a "microcosm, perfect to the last detail," exemplifying the course of development of psycholinguistic concepts and methods.

From about 1920 until the 1950s psycholinguistics in North America was almost nonexistent. Those who studied language said that they studied "verbal behavior." They took their methods and concepts from those who studied white rats and other domestic animals in laboratories and modified them slightly to fit the behavior of college undergraduates in laboratories. As we indicate below, the concern at this time was to treat language use as a behavior "just like any other behavior."

Though it can hardly be said that those who studied "verbal behavior" were concerned with language use, they *were* concerned with the specification of normal processes. To the extent that language use was a normal process, therefore, it was interesting. These workers were not concerned with the use of language by schizophrenic patients, or with other groups which seemed aberrant in their functioning. Thus, the study of schizophrenic speakers was neglected by those who had a particular interest in language.

Clinicians, on the other hand, were intrigued by their patients' perplexing discourse and, by the 1920s, were attempting to study these productions with some care. But these observers were often primarily concerned with the personality of their schizophrenic patients and with the cause of the schizophrenia. For them, language was an epiphenomenon to be used to understand other, presumably more basic, issues. Again, the language use of schizophrenic speakers was neglected.

Ultimately it was the clinicians who attempted to study the productions of schizophrenic patients by borrowing methods and concepts from their experimental colleagues. The exuberant discourse of schizophrenic speakers was thus squeezed into a behavioristic framework—and the fit was not a good one.

In retrospect, there seems to have been little alternative to the practice of using behavioristic techniques to study the remarkable productions of schizophrenic speakers. As we have suggested, experimentalists were not interested in aberrant language functioning, and clinicians were not particularly interested in language use. In fact, the last point is not quite correct. Several clinicians were fascinated by their patients' use of language, but the reports they produced were almost impossible to use in the experimental frameworks of the time. The clinical accounts relied on evocative descriptions of thinking "which tends to stick to everything it touches" (Cameron, 1938b, p. 29), or which is like a "train which becomes derailed" (Kraepelin, 1919) or like an onion coming unpeeled (Storch, 1924). The descriptions were so elusive and so unsystematic that most of those who attempted experiments were unable or unwilling to grapple with them (a notable exception is Cameron, 1938a,b, 1944).

So perhaps it was inevitable that a full appreciation of the schizophrenic's discourse was neglected. But what is surprising or at least disconcerting to recognize in this retrospective view is the fact that clinicians were no less enthusiastic than experimentalists in adopting the behavioristic approach. With awesome certainty, experienced clinicians assured their readers that, though the methods being used might appear to be "a naive or sterile approach to the complexity of language," in fact the tabulations of grammatical categories and cumulations of word frequencies were revealing significant information about the schizophrenic speaker's use of language (Lorenz & Cobb, 1954, p. 665). Although the techniques "may appear somewhat stilted and oblique," another respected clinician and his colleague assured their audience, counts of the number of different words used by schizophrenic speakers offer "a significant and fascinating approach to the study of mentation in psychotic conditions" (Whitehorn & Zipf, 1943, pp. 831–832).

If the clinical investigators had insisted on the primacy of natural language data—which they did not, and if the experimentalists had been willing to listen—which they almost certainly were not, then things might have been different. The productions of the schizophrenic speaker might have revealed the stunning inadequacy of behavioristic principles to deal with natural language. It would have been evident, as it finally was to Lashley in 1948, to Chomsky in 1957, and to most psycholinguists by the middle 1960s, that reducing language use to a matter of conditioning "treats only the simplest 1% of the psycholinguistic problem" (Miller, 1962), and that our crucially important human skill in conversing with each other is largely ignored by the reduction of language use to conditioned habits.

2. The Early Premises. In large part, the reticence of the clinical investigators and the indifference of the experimentalists seem to have been due to the assumptions of the behavior theory paradigm that prevailed from about 1920 until the 1960s in North America. These assumptions were so powerful, Robert Lockard (1971) has observed, that they functioned "mainly as beliefs beyond confirmation." They were so widely accepted and formed so coherent a view of the world that "individual investigators and even whole disciplines were unable to break out of the framework provided" (p. 170).

The study of the psychology of language was no exception. From a profound interest in natural language processes in the late 19th century, psychologists turned to conditioning studies with animals by about 1920. And linguists, following Leonard Bloomfield (1933), developed an anti-mentalistic, taxonomic approach to language. Throughout North America and Europe, in both psychology and linguistics, there was an orientation away from studies of the production and comprehension of natural language and toward prescriptions for segmenting, classifying, and counting behaviors and speech elements (cf. the valuable account of this period by Blumenthal, 1970).

By about 1950, the study of "verbal behavior," like the enterprise of psychology itself, had worked itself into a very narrow scientific position. Lockard's (1971, p. 169) comment about comparative psychology in this period is appropriate to the study of "verbal behavior" as well: the discipline had ignored all but a tiny fraction of the behavior it purported to study and had incorporated an elaborate set of premises about behavior into a dogmatic tradition.

The premises underlying the study of "verbal behavior" in 1950 are important to us here. They were influential into the early 1960s in the study of normal language processes and, in the study of schizophrenic language processes, are widely accepted even today.

Some of the premises about language which would generally have been accepted in 1950 are as follows:

1. Language use is learned behavior. Its full complexity is developed through the combining of stimulus–response connections.
2. Biology is of little interest in the study of language.
3. There is nothing unique about the use of language. An underlying equivalence exists between natural language behavior and other behaviors (e.g., motor behavior, rote learning).
4. The best way to study language is to study how words are used.

These premises, as we have said, were influential into the 1960s in many psycholinguistic endeavors (cf. the discussion of these issues by Reber, 1973). But by 1965, after an acrimonious series of debates, it was clear that the behavioristic approach to language processing had been rejected in North America. Fodor's (1965) logical critique of neo-behaviorist explanations of language marks the culmination of attacks on what had been "a most strongly established approach to language in the English-speaking world" (Blumenthal, 1970, p. 181).

The study of language use in schizophrenia, however, has lagged behind. At the time of the present writing in the end of the 1970s, many investigators are still adhering to the premises outlined above, and critics are still using these premises as the basis from which to evaluate experiments. For example, in Chapman and Chapman's (1973) review of studies on schizophrenic thought disorder (perhaps the most comprehensive and careful critique of experimental studies in schizophrenia published to date) there is a firm adherence to these premises. There is no concern for the fact that of the 200 or so studies reviewed that require verbal responses from the patients, perhaps three succeed in capturing the central issue of thought disorder. The issue which has been central historically and which is critical at present is this: How or why does the schizophrenic speaker produce language which is so confusing to listeners? This, as we suggested in the introduction, became confounded into: Why is the language of the schizophrenic speaker so confusing? And from that into: Why is the thought of the schizophrenic patient so confused? It is this last question which Chapman and Chapman consider, neglecting the more elementary ones.

Every reviewer cited thus far, with the exception of Pavy, falls prey to the attraction of the behavioristic principles that were once so powerful in the study of "verbal behavior." These principles are inappropriate and often misleading in several ways. In order to discuss some of their difficulties, we focus on studies conducted after 1960 and divide the studies into planned experiments and naturalistic research.

C. Experimental Studies and Their Premises

Experimental studies that require "verbal responses" from schizophrenic patients can be further divided into (1) investigations of information processing capacities, and (2) investigations of psycholingustic abilities.

1. Investigations of Information Processing Capacities. Originating perhaps with the work of Weckowicz and Blewett in 1959 (cf. Chapman & Chapman, 1973, Ch. 13), there have been over 100 studies through the last two decades in which "verbal responses" were used as measures of the schizophrenic patient's ability to attend to "stimuli." The stimuli were sometimes words presented in isolation or in lists, and sometimes target words presented in sentences. Occasionally, patients were presented with strings of words in which attempts were made to vary the amount of "information" or redundancy. In addition, there have been perhaps another 20 experiments devoted particularly to memory for lists of words (cf. review by Koh, 1978; and Traupmann, 1975).

These studies have been extensively reviewed by several writers and we need not summarize them again. However, let us consider one that can serve as an example for discussion. Chapman, Chapman, and Daut (1976) report a study in which chronic schizophrenic patients are given two multiple-choice subtests. The patients are asked to read a series of statements of the following form:

> Mark the statement or statements which tell what a *book* is often like.
> (a) You read it. ("strong meaning response")
> (b) It has a back. ("weak meaning response")
> (c) It's edible. ("irrelevant alternative")
> (d) None of the above.

The study was designed to follow up a number of earlier studies in which it appeared that chronic patients would choose the "strong meaning response" whether it was appropriate or not, whereas normal subjects would choose that response only when it fit the sentence frame. In the present experiment, the investigators presented a second series of statements which resembled the first but which, instead of having a strong and a weak meaning response, had two weak meaning responses. They were attempting to test the hypothesis proposed by Cromwell and Dokecki (1968) that schizoprenics neglect weak meaning aspects of words only in situations in which a strong aspect of meaning is present. In a carefully controlled experiment, the investigators found no difference in the patients' responses to the two types of statements. They conclude that their findings lend no support to the hypotheses, and the most likely explanation is "a schizophrenic defect in the screening of their potential responses for appropriateness" (Chapman et al., 1976, p. 39).

This study and many others like it are tempting sources of inference about language use because they suggest that schizophrenic patients have some difficulty using context in their interpretation of discourse. However, there are two difficulties with studies of "verbal responses" like this one: they do not inform us about actual language use, and they may mislead us about information processes. Let us consider these problems in turn.

a. Language Use. Studies that require patients to respond in terms of a single word may be tapping specific skills and not a general ability to use semantic information. In this task, as in word association experiments, the subject's response is likely to involve stages in which (1) the subject must "understand" the stimulus; (2) and "operate" on the meaning of the stimulus; and (3) produce a response. Clark (1970) argues that it is the unique second stage that sets tasks of this sort apart from situations in which natural language is used. In having to choose between several printed sentences in the multiple-choice task, or in having to associate to or discriminate between target words in word association experiments, the subject is asked to engage in a selection process which may be unrepresentative of ordinary language operations.

There is some support for this assertion. In three experiments, tests that required responses to single words or target words seemed to tap specific information rather than processing abilities. Boland and Chapman (1971) and Rattan and Chapman (1973) demonstrated that normal adults give "schizophrenialike" responses when they do not know the correct answer in multiple-choice tests. That is, they choose words that are similar to the test word, or sound like it, or occur with it in some contexts. And Stolz and Tiffany (1972), in a related study, report that adults make word choices just as children (and schizophrenics) do when the frequency of occurrence of the word is low. In general, studies which restrict themselves to the meanings of words that are isolated or are presented in multiple-choice or discrimination tasks are studying "verbal behavior" in unusual situations. In extrapolating from such tasks, one must be careful to limit generalizations to these unrepresentative kinds of language use.

   b. Information Processing. To say that a set of experiments is unrepresentative of natural language use means that one cannot characterize the listener's behavior in ordinary situations. However, it need not mean that such studies are uninformative. Very many studies have been predicated on the assumption that verbal responses are just as appropriate as any other responses to test hypotheses about selective attention, discrimination, and recognition processes in schizophrenia.

There are several reasons for arguing, however, that "verbal behavior" studies provide the wrong sort of evidence from which to infer information processing operations. First, and most seriously, observations of "verbal behavior" are only very tangentially connected to the information processing constructs used for their explanation. This was not always so. In the early 1950s, psycholinguists often tried to formulate the operations of speakers and hearers in terms of the redundancy in language. The development of information measures in communications theory offered a formal way of discussing language performance, and grammatical structures were seen as the basis for establishing sequential constraints in language. Grammar was what made words more predictable. So knowledge of the rules of English was seen as allowing one to reduce the range of possible completions for sentences, like "The bright ——— shone for ——— first time ——— three days."

Sequential constraints were studied with procedures developed by Miller and Selfridge (1950) and by Taylor (1953). By the 1960s, these procedures were adopted and used widely in studies of schizophrenic "verbal behavior." However, although the techniques themselves might be useful as an approximate measure of structure when nothing about the underlying processes is postulated (cf. Olson & Clark, 1976, p. 38), the models underlying these techniques are not appropriate models of language users. Chomsky's formal demonstrations of the inadequacy of statistical conceptions of language structure (1957; 1965) and the joint discussions of such demonstrations by Chomsky and Miller (1963; Miller & Chomsky, 1963) have shown the limitations of such models. As a result of these demonstrations, the analysis of linguistic strings based on information theory is no longer an acceptable means of representing the language user.

But without such a model, there is no set of intermediate steps between the behavior of the language user and information processing models of the sort proposed in studies of schizophrenic patients. Thus, although investigators argue vigorously about which information processing construct is the correct one in any given study of "verbal behavior," all such arguments are, in fact, highly speculative and probably unproductive.

A second problem in these studies is the difficulty in specifying which "information process" is being measured. For example, if one presents patients with pairs of words to be discriminated, one may be studying discrimination processes, or linguistic abilities associated with semantic knowledge, or some complex combination of discrimination and language processes. If one assumes that verbal responses are not different from responses in other systems, then this will not be a problem. However, if one questions this assumption, then it is difficult to know how to interpret a host of studies that rely on verbal responses. In particular, 90% of the 20 studies of memory published since 1960 use words or sentences as the items to be remembered. And an additional 5% present spatial patterns but rely on exceedingly complex verbal instructions.

Consequently, while it may appear that quite a bit is known about schizophrenic memory processes, in fact we know only about verbal memory for words. We are ignorant of how schizophrenic subjects remember faces and locations, and rhythms and intonation patterns, and music. By not distinguishing "verbal" from nonverbal responses, there is a danger of interpreting the available data too broadly and overlooking observations that are essential to understanding the system under study.

A third difficulty is presented by the use of a task in which one may be demanding a special skill from the subject, instead of a general process. As we mentioned, one probably cannot extrapolate from the experimental results to patients' language comprehension in everyday situations. The problem with regard to information processes is related, but a little different. Because the tasks are unrepresentative of normal processing, they may demand a skill from the subjects which is irrelevant to such processes. Although one can devise tasks in which schizophrenic patients are different from control patients, there is no guarantee that such tasks reveal factors which *make a difference* to any significant behavior or experience of the patients. Although the question of relevance is always an issue in laboratory tasks in psychology, it is particularly disturbing in the present case. It is possible that, in the very many studies of verbal responses in which information processing constructs are used, one can generalize neither to language use in ordinary situations nor to any specifiable information processes.

The interpretative problems raised by these studies seem to be a legacy from the 1950s' premises about verbal behavior studies. The investigators seem to assume that there is nothing unique about language, and also that biology is of little interest in the study of language (premises 2 and 3 above). The first assumption is suggested by the apparent lack of concern for the form of response. Language is treated as an epiphenomenon to information processing, and the emphasis seem to be on measuring behaviors that fit a model. If verbal behavior does not support the model being tested, one can always try other behaviors. For example, if experiments with verbal responses do not support a particular model, one can try size estimation measures, or depth perception, or auditory detection. And this strategy suggests the assumption that biology is unimportant. If this is assumed, then one need not be concerned with issues of hemispheric differences in processing different sorts of materials, or in processing the same materials with different biases. Again, measures of verbal responses should not be substantially different from measures of pattern perception or auditory discrimination.

Finally, there is an ironic footnote to the practice of studying "verbal behavior" but ignoring questions of language use. Neale and Cromwell (1970) suggest that a major methodological problem in some studies of information processing is the lack of clear instructions. Some of the findings may be artifacts, they explain, because the language use in those studies was ambiguous.

2. Psycholinguistic Experiments. It is possible to distinguish between experiments on "verbal behavior" and experiments on "psycholinguistics" in the study of schizophrenic subjects. Although both use verbal tasks, the former use them to study information processing, and the latter to study language processing. The different aims are reflected in different procedures: information processing is inferred from the subject's identification or discrimination of target words that are either isolated or presented in sentence frames; language processing is inferred from the subject's recognition, recall, and perhaps comprehension of full sentences.

If we abide by this distinction, then psycholinguistic experiments with schizophrenic patients begin with David Gerver's (1967) attempt to replicate Miller and Isard's (1963) work with normal subjects. Gerver presented chronic schizophrenic patients and control subjects with "normal" sentences (e.g., Trains carry passengers across the country), syntactically admissible but semantically anomalous sentences (e.g., Trains steal elephants around the highways) and random strings (e.g., On trains hive elephants simplify). Subjects listened to the sentences on earphones and then repeated them aloud. The results were surprising: although the schizophrenic subjects recalled fewer words than control subjects, as expected, they showed as much improvement as the control subjects as the word strings became more like normal sentences. For all groups—schizophrenic patients, psychiatric control patients, and normal subjects—normal sentences were recalled best, and semantically anomalous sentences were recalled better than random strings. And for all groups, the rate of improvement in recall over the three sentence types was about the same.

a. Earlier Studies. What was surprising about this result was the evidence that schizophrenic subjects were able to benefit, somehow, from the syntactic and semantic structure in the three sets of sentences. This seemed to contradict the findings of a persuasive clinical report and several experimental studies which suggested that schizophrenic listeners are unable to take advantage of "the organization inherent in language" (Lawson, McGhie, & Chapman, 1964).

The clinical study summarized subjective reports from 26 young schizophrenic patients and presented some absorbing accounts, such as the following:

> When people talk to me now it's like a different kind of language. It's too much to hold at once. My head is overloaded and I can't understand what they say. It makes you forget what you've just heard because you can't get hearing it long enough. It's all in different bits which you have to put together again in your head—just words in the air unless you can figure it out from their faces. (McGhie & Chapman, 1961, p. 375)

This description and others like it were convincing demonstrations for several workers that one must extend studies of "verbal behavior" beyond the isolated word and target word analyses to become "psycholinguistic" studies of sentences and discourse. As McGhie (1970) observed later, the subjective reports suggested that the patient's difficulties in understanding speech arose "not from an inability to perceive the individual words comprising a connected discourse, but from an inability to perceive the words in meaningful relationship to each other as part of an organized pattern" (p. 12).

The problem was to find a means of demonstrating that comprehension failures were due to an inability to organize language or to an inability to use the organization that was already part of language. Lewinsohn and Elwood (1961) were the first to study the effects of language structure on behavior. They borrowed Miller and Selfridge's (1950) paradigm in which, using words as units, various orders of approximation to English passages were constructed. At the lowest approximation, words were picked at random from a dictionary. At successively higher approximations, a game was played in which one person wrote, say, two words, and these were given to another person with a request to write two more words which would follow; and then another person was requested to do the same, and so on. At higher orders of approximation, each participant wrote longer series of words.

Miller and Selfridge found that normal subjects could remember more and more words as the order of approximation to English increased from 0 to about 5 (after 5 there was essentially no increase). The results showed that as the transitional probabilities of words increased (to some point), verbal strings were easier to retain. This suggested that the structure of language was important to its recall.

Lewinsohn and Elwood adopted the Miller and Selfridge procedure to test whether schizophrenic patients could "use structure" to recall verbal strings to the same extent as control subjects. They found no differences between acute schizophrenics and control subjects, but chronic schizophrenics recalled fewer words than other subjects in all passages. However, when the chronic patients were matched to general medical patients on verbal IQ, the differences disappeared.

In effect, the Lewinsohn and Elwood study gave no support to the notion that schizophrenic patients are impaired in their ability to "use" syntactic structure. However, the same study was repeated by three other sets of investigators. In the first and most influential of these, Lawson *et al.* (1964) compared young schizophrenics to normal subjects. Here, though verbal IQ had been equated, the schizophrenics recalled fewer words than normals for word strings with higher approximations to English. The authors conclude that the schizophrenics' failures were "related to an inability to perceive the organization inherent in normal speech" (p. 378).

This conclusion was not, in fact, supported by the remaining two studies. However, each of the subsequent replications gave some evidence that schizophrenic listeners could not recall textlike strings so well as control subjects. Levy and Maxwell (1968) found that acute schizophrenics were impaired relative to normal subjects, just as Lawson *et al.* had reported. But they also found that acutely depressed patients were even more impaired than schizophrenic patients, suggesting that the finding was nonspecific to schizophrenia. Raeburn and Tong (1968) found that almost half of their schizophrenic subjects failed to improve their recall as approximations became increasingly textlike. This result suggested that for some schizophrenics at least, there was evidence of impairment. Raeburn and Tong went on to explore this result in a series of experiments and concluded that it might be due to an inefficiency in the patients' recall, perhaps reflecting psychomotor retardation and lower vocabulary skills.

Thus, of the four attempts to study schizophrenics' recall with the Miller and Selfridge paradigm, one indicated impairment in acute schizophrenics and three suggested this impairment was either not specific to schizophrenia or was due to the operation of confounding variables. Nevertheless, the interpretation of impairment was the more compelling. It fit nicely with theorizing in the mainstream of psychology, and it seemed to account for some of the most disturbing experiences encountered by young schizophrenics. Consequently, in the subsequent decade, there were many attempts to test the schizophrenic listener's ability to "perceive the structure inherent in language."

b. The Criticisms. There have been many direct and indirect criticisms of these early studies. Pavy (1968) has pointed out that all the studies suffer from a major confounding: orders of approximation to English were always presented from random words to sentences so that subjects would be most fatigued and stressed at higher orders of approximation. This was likely to operate selectively against schizophrenic subjects. In addition, the use of order of approximation in itself has been subjected to both methodological (e.g., Coleman, 1963; Hörmann, 1971, Ch. 13) and formal (e.g., Miller, 1965) criticism. The essential problem here is that the nation of transitional probabilities between words is based on a view of the native speaker's verbal "habits." It is much too narrow to account for how speakers produce and listeners understand language. As we noted earlier, to vary the transitional probabilities in strings of words in some way captures a kind of quantitative measure of structure in language. But what is being measured is not clear.

Finally, in addition to the particular criticisms directed at these four studies, there have been at least three more demonstrations supporting Gerver's 1967 results in which "structure" seemed to be used to the same extent by schizophrenic and normal listeners. Truscott (1970) followed a procedure from Marks and Miller (1964) and her results showed, as Gerver's did, that schizophrenic subjects had the same pattern of improvement in recall as medical patient controls. Rochester, Harris, and Seeman (1973) used a version of the "click" experiments taken from Garrett, Bever, and Fodor (1966). In this study, some schizophrenic and normal patients were asked to recognize the location of "clicks" in a series of sentences and others were to recall the locations. In both cases, although the performance of the schizophrenic subjects was absolutely lower than that of the controls, the pattern of performance was the same. Both groups tended to displace the clicks into the nearest syntactic boundary, suggesting that they were perceiving and recalling sentences in terms of (at least) major syntactic units.

Carpenter (1976) replicated the Rochester *et al.* findings and presented an experiment based on Jarvella's (1971) work. In this latter study, listeners heard narrative passages that were interrupted at various intervals. During the interruptions they wrote down the last words they could recall. Schizophrenic listeners, like normal adults and 11-year-old children, recalled adjacent clauses better if the clauses belonged to the same sentence than if they belonged to different sentences. Carpenter concludes that: "The sensitivity to syntactic structure is left intact in schizophrenic subjects" (1976, p. 49), a conclusion that seems appropriate to the other three studies as well.

c. The Psycholinguistic Premises. In several respects, the studies discussed in Section *b* are new. Unlike studies of "verbal behavior," these studies of sentence recall have been based on assumptions about language use as a special function that is not necessarily identical or even similar to other systems of response. The experiments performed by Gerver, Truscott, Rochester *et al.*, and Carpenter—all of which were taken from the "new" psycholinguistics of the 1960s—can be characterized in terms of the assumptions that were generally accepted by psycholinguists in those years.

- *a'* Language use is a special behavior which must be studied in terms of its own, language-based variables.
- *b'* Biological considerations are of some interest.
- *c'* Speaking and listening are best thought of as a collection of mental operations.
- *d'* The best way to study language is to study the ways in which characteristics of input sentences are reflected in regularities of listener's (or reader's) responses.
- *e'* The most interesting input characteristics have to do with structural (syntactic) features of sentences.

Premise *e'* is too narrow to characterize psycholinguistic assumptions about normal speakers at the end of the 1970s and should be expanded to read approximately:

- *e"* Any features of the sentence—syntactic or propositional or lexical or phonological—are interesting, and structural features of discourse (e.g., in narratives) are interesting as well.

However, *a'* to *e'* are fair characterizations of the psycholinguistic study of schizophrenic language which, as we have seen, lags about 4–10 years behind studies of normal language.

The experiments that began with Lewinsohn and Elwood (1961), and extended to the work of Raeburn and Tong (1968), were all based on the Miller and Selfridge work in 1950. They reflect the new notion of language as a unique behavior which must be studied systematically; but they also reflect the older view that all responses can probably be explained in the same way. As a result, these studies represent an intermediary step between studies of "verbal behavior" and psycholinguistic experiments.

All these studies—the psycholinguistic experiments, the intermediary studies, and the studies of "verbal behavior"—have similarities that are as striking as their differences. However, before we examine these, let us review the particular limitations of the "psycholinguistic" experiments. Although none of these has been criticized directly (in the sense that a major confounding could be demonstrated) they nevertheless can be criticized indirectly.

   d. Indirect Criticisms. Several methodological and theoretical issues have been raised about the original studies from which the studies of schizophrenic listeners are derived. As with studies of verbal behavior, one can complain justly that these studies are designed for undergraduates in laboratories. Consequently, they yield data that are unrepresentative of ordinary language use (see especially Fillenbaum's 1970 paper). Moreover, they may require special skills from the subjects that are not part of normal language use. And finally, one must ask for more developed variables. In what sense does the listener use syntax—or the underlying semantic propositions—in any of the experiments? Should the interpretation of the "click" experiments be in terms of semantics or surface syntax or perceptual processes?

   There will undoubtedly be modifications in the form these studies take in the next few years. If the lag still persists between the development of a psycholinguistic method and its adoption in studies of schizophrenia, these modifications will be in the direction of a greater emphasis on sentences in extended texts (as in Carpenter's second study), on presuppositions and on efforts to make the listeners' situations more dialogic (e.g., Suchotliff, 1970). However, if these are the only changes, it will be a misfortune. If the study of schizophrenic language use continues to borrow its total methodology from mainstream psycholinguistics, it will mean that experimenters studying schizophrenic language have, once again, neglected their data, ignoring what their patients are doing and saying in order, once more, to make their awkward stepchild into a model one.

   e. Limitations. The most cogent criticisms that can be directed toward psycholinguistic studies of schizophrenic language are criticisms derived from the data themselves. And these are several. First, although it is true that schizophrenic listeners appear to use "structure" or surface syntax to the same extent that normal subjects do in psycholinguistic experiments, it is nevertheless puzzling that many schizophrenic listeners report that they have great difficulty understanding connected discourse. What accounts for these reports? We must consider the clinical data—and not simply to dismiss these reports because we have failed to demonstrate the comparable effect in a laboratory experiment.

Second, and very critically for the role of laboratory experiments in studying schizophrenic language use, it is not clear that the response of a *listener* to a sentence or a set of sentences tells us anything useful about the aberrant productions of schizophrenic *speakers*. Lenneberg (1967) observed that it is easier to study the capacity for understanding than the capacity for speaking, because there are fewer factors affecting the former than the latter. But this does not mean, as Lenneberg seemed to imply, that by studying the listener one knows the speaker. We do not yet have any clear notion of how the capacities of the listener and speaker overlap. This is serious because it is the schizophrenic *speaker* whose behavior is so clearly aberrant. Although one would not wish to neglect studies of the listener, one must note there have been no systematic psycholinguistic studies of the schizophrenic speaker to date. If the practice of borrowing from psycholinguistics without returning anything continues, it is difficult to imagine how such studies will ever be launched. For, as Olson and Clark (1976) observe, listeners are studied by experiment and speakers by naturalistic observations. If one is committed to experiment, then it would seem that one will not study the behavior of the schizophrenic speaker for some time.

Finally, still with a focus on the data, it seems critical to try to extend the social and situational contexts of psycholinguistic experiments to approximate the contexts in which patients normally find themselves (as Del Castillo, 1970; Seeman, 1975; and Seeman and Cole, 1977 have attempted). Language is a social act and it is doubtful that we can learn much about the behavior of language users from highly controlled laboratory settings. Also, language is used in several different contexts—in interviews, in conversations that are face-to-face and over the telephone, in storytelling, in group discussions. How can one understand the potentially profound effects of variations in contexts if one is intent on formalizing mental operations?

3. The Common Premises of Experimental Studies. The preceding discussion has been concerned with distinctions. The present one is concerned with similarities. The premises which experimental studies of schizophrenic language use seem to share are as follows:

1. The role of the language user is as a listener.
2. The processes of interest are the mental operations underlying perception, recall, and comprehension of words and sentences.
3. The best context for studying language is the laboratory because of the controlled conditions.

4. The best descriptions of language are functional relations like: Treatment X has Effect Y.
5. The best things to study are response variables with an interval or at least ordinal character.
6. The goal is ultimately to characterize the mental operations underlying schizophrenia.

In 1965, Fodor commented that most experimental psychologists were still behaviorists. Perhaps it is still true, so perhaps it is apt that so many of these common premises seem to be a legacy from behaviorism. The strength of the approach that results from these premises lies in the capability of testing precisely a particular hypothesis or set of hypotheses. This is a considerable advantage. It means that one can sort through the plethora of assertions about schizophrenic deficiencies and determine to what extent any one of them can be supported. But there is also a weakness in this framework of assumptions, for it constrains the ways in which behavior may be studied. The behavior of the listener is examined in a highly controlled setting and there are limitations in the explanations offered to account for that behavior. These limitations are discussed in more detail after the premises underlying naturalistic studies are presented.

D. Naturalistic Studies and Their Premises

To understand the schizophrenic listener, one experiments. To understand the schizophrenic speaker, one observes behavior in more or less natural settings. The goal in the latter case is ultimately to formulate the processes underlying the speaker's productions. The more immediate goal is to describe those productions. Once the speech is recorded and (perhaps) the accompanying extralinguistic context noted, the investigator must decide what to do with the utterances. With utterances from normal speakers, the immediate goal is to capture the distributional properties of the corpus—to summarize in some satisfactory way the whole collection of recorded utterances. One way to approach this problem is to formulate sets of rules that characterize the essential properties of the corpus.

The practice with schizophrenic speakers is different. Here, the aim has been to capture, not the distributional properties of the corpus, but its deviant features. That is, rather than describing the utterances as a whole, investigators of schizophrenic speech have attempted to characterize those features of the corpus that differ from normal. In effect, the effort has been to describe the failures rather than the overall performance of the schizophrenic speaker.

There have been a few exceptions to this practice. One has been the work of Laffal, discussed below. Another has been the experimental studies of Bertram Cohen and his colleagues (e.g., Cohen, 1967; Cohen, Nachmani, & Rosenberg, 1974; Rosenberg & Cohen, 1964, 1966), which is reviewed in Chapters 4 and 7. And a third exception has been the theoretical work of Harry Stack Sullivan (1925, 1944). Sullivan is outstanding for his early recognition of language and communication processes, rather than thought, as the interesting central phenomenon in schizophrenia. His informal observations of patients are pertinent today to many systematic efforts to study the schizophrenic speaker. For example, his conception of a normal speaker's process of pretesting utterances before producing them for actual listeners is one model used by Cohen and his colleagues in their study of reference processes in schizophrenia. And Sullivan's description of the changing course of the schizophrenic speaker's awareness of disturbed speech, from initial painful chagrin to a lack of concern, predates this issue in the experimental literature (see Maher's 1972 discussion). However, for the most part, naturalistic studies of schizophrenic speakers have aimed to describe deviant features. As a consequence, they have developed a peculiarly one-sided understanding of the schizophrenic speaker. Events or behaviors that seem somehow aberrant have been described in excellent detail, but there have been no broad descriptions of the schizophrenic speaker's corpus. Lacking this description, one only knows that in some schizophrenic speakers certain categories of deviant behavior occur on some occasions.

The narrow focus of naturalistic studies of the schizophrenic speaker is easy to understand. The studies were designed primarily by those who treat patients, rather than by those who conduct experiments. The clinicians needed to identify the problems of new patients and to trace their progress through treatment. The concern was therefore on distinctive features of the utterances. Experimentalists, as we have mentioned, were very rarely interested in schizophrenic listeners' use of language. They were probably even less interested in schizophrenic *speakers* since there was little hope of studying speakers through controlled experiments. Finally linguists, like experimentalists, were uninterested in nonnormal speakers in the early parts of this century and then for some time were concerned with idealized rather than actual speakers.

Two theoretical problems result from a focus on deviant features in a corpus. First, a workable theory about schizophrenic speakers cannot be developed because one knows only what speakers *cannot* do and not what they can do. And secondly, even the speakers' failures are difficult to formulate without a baseline of overall behavior. Thus, the construction of a general model of the speaker is precluded, and the notion of deviant features is left rather undefined.

These theoretical problems may not seem serious because naturalistic studies, after all, are primarily initial data collection procedures. They are largely pretheoretical. However, the theoretical problems affect the data collection in some very concrete ways. Essentially, the problem is a theoretical one. The only basis for choosing "distinctive" or "deviant" behaviors is some version of what normal behavior is. But if this normal version is not based on a principled analysis, there will be no systematic basis for categorizing behavior. As a result, one may expect to be plagued by overlapping categories; by categories that include many different kinds of events; by categories that differ markedly from each other, requiring diverse kinds of judgments from coders; and by categories that are difficult to justify theoretically.

The last point is especially troublesome. Most investigators have not derived their categories from general principles that are independent of their choice procedures. Instead, categories have been made up from sets of events that will potentially discriminate schizophrenics from control speakers. The categories are refined so that the sharpest possible discriminations can be made. But their development and refinement has been entirely with a practical aim: What will separate schizophrenic speakers from others? Then, on an *ad hoc* basis, the categories are vindicated (cf. Feigl, 1952) by showing that the procedures lead to accurate predictions about the speakers' identities. However, the categories are not justified in a theoretical sense from this demonstration, for it has not been shown that they can be derived from some principles or rules of language use. As a result, the constructs developed to account for the speaker's behavior are only weakly connected to that behavior.

These comments are made as an introduction to the resourceful studies which have been attempted since about 1960 in an effort to describe the distinctive features of the schizophrenic speaker's production. The studies are divided into content analyses and clinical studies.

1. Content Analyses. Content analysis is a method for making inferences from texts (not necessarily language-based) to the source of the texts. It is "the use of replicable and valid methods for making specific inferences from text to other states or properties of its source" (Krippendorff cited by Gerbner, 1969, p. xiv). In the present discussion, studies are considered content analyses if they use some methodological procedure to make inferences about schizophrenic speakers from their spoken or written productions. This means that the investigators must establish reliability and some validity for their categories. Clinical studies discussed in Section 2, omit these steps. In general, content analyses are refined procedures for categorizing schizophrenic language use; and clinical studies are initial descriptions of the schizophrenic speaker that can be developed into content analyses. Table 1 gives examples of the procedural differences between the two sorts of studies.

Since 1960, there have been about five or six efforts to analyze methodically the productions of the schizophrenic speaker. We will summarize these briefly since they are frequently neglected in reviews of the experimental studies.

a. Laffal's Work. Laffal (1960, 1965) analyzed the productions of schizophrenic speakers in an effort to understand "the subject's core conflicts and significant psychological configurations" (1965, p. 148). In one extensive study based on the autobiography of a famous psychiatric patient, Daniel Paul Schreber, Laffal transcribed contexts that contained certain key words. The context words were categorized, and the frequency of cooccurrence of context words and key words was computed. From the correlations, inferences were made about the psychological significance of the key words for the subject.

Laffal's work provides a valuable counterpoint to most studies of schizophrenic speakers. His primary interest has been to develop a lexicon to describe the experience of all native English speakers—a kind of psychological thesaurus. This makes his analyses among the few in the literature based on a conception of general language use. However, since they are directed toward the personal dynamics of the speaker, they do not provide a model of language use for the schizophrenic speaker.

b. Gottschalk and Gleser. Gottschalk and Gleser (e.g., 1964, 1969; Gottschalk, Winget, & Gleser, 1969) developed a series of scales to serve as "verbal behavior measures" that would discriminate between groups of speakers and within individual speakers over time. Their scale for schizophrenic patients is designed to describe the "relative severity of social alienation and personal disorganization of schizophrenic persons" (Gottschalk & Gleser, 1964, p. 400). Patients are asked to talk about some personal life experience for five minutes, and their tape-recorded speech is divided into clauses. The clauses are coded "whenever a theme or verbal act occurs which . . . can discriminate the severity of the schizo-

Chapter 1

Table 1. Procedures for Taking Speech Samples in a Range of Naturalistic Studies

	Content analyses	Clinical studies	
	(Wynne & Singer, 1963)	(Reilly *et al.*, 1975)	(Lecours & Vanier Clément, 1976)
1. Situation			
(a) Location	Testing room in hospital (?)	Testing room in hospital (?)	Clinic or ward
(b) Formality (status relationship)	Experimenter with parents of patients or volunteer parents	Doctor with patient	Doctor with patient
(c) Mode (channel)	Spoken; attention on Rorschach cards	Spoken; conversation ("free interview")	Spoken; conversation ("clinical interview")
(d) Role (purpose)	Description of Rorschach cards	Relate personal experience	Relate personal experience
(e) Field (topic)	Rorschach cards	Personal experience	Personal experience
2. Speakers			
(a) Groups	Parents of sz, borderline, neurotic and normals	Sz and non-sz patients	Aphasic and sz patients
(b) $n=$	10–20	25	?
(c) Similar on age	Yes	Yes	?
education	Yes	Yes	?
social class	Yes	?	?
hospitalization	N/A[a]	Yes	Yes
medication	N/A	No	No (?)
3. Analysis			
(a) Sample size	Full utterance for first card	Total utterance (4–7 min segments)	(?)
(b) Categories	Coding manual	Coding manual	*Post hoc*
(c) Reliability between raters	82% agreement	?	?
$n=$	2–6	1(?)	1(?)
(d) Blind scoring	Yes	No (?)	No
4. Results			
(a) Between groups	*t* tests	*t* tests	Estimates
(b) Within a subject	No	No	Estimates

Note. For register categories (i.e., "formality," "mode," "role," and "field") see Ellis and Ure (1969). Gregory (1967) and Benson and Greaves (1973) refer to "formality" as "personal tenor," and "role" as "functional tenor."
[a]N/A = not applicable.

phrenic syndrome" (1964, p. 40). The categories are weighted according to the discriminative power each has shown in validation experiments. Typical categories (from Gottschalk *et al.*, 1969) are as follows: Others avoiding self (e.g., "She didn't want to go hunting with me."); Disorientation (e.g., "I don't know what this place is—a police station?"); and Incomplete sentences, clauses, phrases and blocking (e.g., "I had good spectacles./ I just uh that fine print.").

These analyses demonstrate some of the difficulties of naturalistic studies discussed in the introduction to this section. Their purpose is to describe the deviant features in the productions of potentially schizophrenic speakers. In this case, the features are largely aspects of the content. The categories for describing content seem to overlap in some instances. They include a diversity of phenomena that seem to require very different kinds of judgment from coders. And they are difficult to justify theoretically.

The theoretical justification of the content analysis categories is difficult for two reasons. First, the categories are not independently derivable from principles. They have been developed on grounds that whatever discriminates the productions of schizophrenic speakers is a potential item for the scales. Since items chosen for their discriminability have no necessary relation to "social alienation and personal disorganization," the constructs and the categories also have no necessary relation. Second, this technique for performing the content analysis intuits content rather than analyzing it. In the late 1950s when these scales were developed, the accepted approach in content analysis required that "the judges' intuitions be constrained by explicit coding instructions while the critical process of semantic interpretation was left entirely implicit" (Krippendorff, 1969, p. 6).

The development of computer techniques for analyzing texts has made the distinction between the intuition of content and the analysis of content very clear. In the early 1960s, the only techniques available were dictionary look-ups in which words, precoded for form class (grammatical) membership, could be categorized. Gottschalk and Gleser and their colleagues rejected this approach for the greater sensitivity to be gained with human coders. But what was gained in sensitivity—in the judges' familiarity with the language, in their expertise with the subject matter, and in their pragmatic knowledge of speech acts—was lost in explanatory power. One simply cannot state how much of the application of categories depends on the human coder's knowledge of the world and language, and how much is due to the putative measurement of the categories.

Recently, Gottschalk and his colleagues have attempted to computerize their content analysis scales. They have not yet met with success, possibly because so much of the semantic and pragmatic decision process has been left up to human coders. As Gottschalk, Hausmann, and Brown (1975) observe in their report of efforts to computerize one of the simpler scales, "perhaps the most fascinating aspect of this research is the discovery of the amount of inferencing that a human scorer does—something that present-day computers are ill-equipped to handle" (p. 87).

c. *Singer and Wynne.* Singer and Wynne (e.g., Singer & Wynne, 1963, 1965; Wynne & Singer, 1963a,b) present a sensitive approach to language use in the parents of schizophrenic patients. Although their work is not addressed to the schizophrenic speaker *per se,* it provides a very interesting technique which we review briefly here.

Like Gottschalk and Gleser, Singer and Wynne developed a set of categories for discriminating deviant productions of, in this case, schizophrenics' parents from the parents of other groups of subjects. But unlike the content-based categories of Gottschalk and Gleser, the categories of Singer and Wynne have a strong language base. For example, among their most sensitive categories (cf. Singer, Wynne, & Toohey, 1978, Table 1) are the following: unintelligible remarks; ordinary words or phrases used oddly or out of context; uncorrected speech fragments; inconsistent and ambiguous references; and odd, tangential, and inappropriate remarks. Moreover, these language-based categories are relatively closely tied to an etiological hypothesis, as follows:

> Parental communication, if characterized by disruptions, vagueness, irrelevance, and lack of closure, can impair the child's ability to focus attention.

Singer and Wynne argue that the impairment that results from such communication forms a basis for schizophrenia in the child.

In their original studies, Singer and Wynne gave each parent to be tested a series of Rorschach cards, asked for the parent's first impression of the card, and later asked for an elaboration of that impression. Responses to the first card were analyzed in terms of "deviances." These are summarized in Table 2.

The accomplishments of this program of study have been summarized by Hirsch and Leff (1975). Ten years of research, they observe, have produced results "consistently in the same direction using increasingly more objective techniques." Singer and Wynne have been able to use their technique with such discrimination that "no pair of parents of

Table 2. Categories of Communication Defects and Deviances: Some
Examples[a]

I. Closure problems

Speech fragments
Unintelligible remarks
Unstable percepts
Gross indefiniteness and tentativeness
Responses in negative form
Subjunctive, "if," "might-response"
Disqualifications
   "Derogatory," disparaging, critical remarks, if "disqualifying"
   Nihilistic remarks
   Failures to verify own responses or perception

II. Disruptive behavior

Odd, tangential, inappropriate remarks or answers to questions
Nonverbal, disruptive behavior
Humor
Swearing
Hopping around among responses

III. Peculiar language and logic

A. Peculiar word usages, constructions and pronunciations
     Ordinary words or phrases used oddly or out of context
     Odd sentence construction
     Peculiar or quaint, private terms or phrases. Neologisms
     Euphemisms
     Slips of tongue
     Mispronounced words
     Clang associations, rhymed phrases, and word play
     Abstract or global terms
B. Peculiar logic
     Illogical combinations of percepts and categories. Failure to keep incompatible or
     alternative percepts, images, or concepts distinct

[a]From Hirsch and Leff, 1975; adapted from Singer, 1967.

schizophrenics has been found to score within the range of parents of
normals . . . , and taken individually, only 32.5 per cent of parents of
non-schizophrenics have scored above the lowest scoring schizophrenic
parent" (Hirsch & Leff, 1975, p. 113).

In a painstaking attempt to replicate this last finding, Hirsch and Leff
studied a sample of English parents of schizophrenic and neurotic hospitalized patients. Although they found reliable differences between
groups in the direction which reproduced the Singer and Wynne finding,
there was considerable overlap in the performance of the two groups.
Several thoughtful statistical techniques were tried in an effort to improve
the discrimination, but no strong differences could be found between the
parent groups.

Wynne (1977) and Singer (Singer *et al.*, 1978) have criticized Hirsch and Leff's procedures for administering and scoring the Rorschachs. They suggest that insensitive or hasty techniques during initial viewing and subsequent elaboration of the cards might have restricted or seriously biased the corpus. Although this may be so, one must also acknowledge that not only Hirsch and Leff but also Singer and Wynne appear to have gone to great lengths to ensure that every important procedural detail was followed, and that any coding difficulties were discussed before decisions were made (c f. Hirsch & Leff, 1975, Appendix i). The failure of the second pair of investigators to replicate the first pair's work would seem to say more about the complexity of the procedure itself than about the conduct of the inquiry.

One possible source of difficulty, though not necessarily the one that accounts for Hirsch and Leff's failure to replicate, is the status of the descriptive categories. As we mentioned, there are two major methodological problems with content analysis categories for schizophrenic speakers: (*a*) the categories are very weakly connected to the theoretical constructs, and (*b*) the categories are based on inferential procedures so that one does not know the extent to which different analyses are applied.

With regard to (*a*), there is some basis for believing Singer and Wynne's categories to be motivated independently by theory. Wynne (1977) reports that he and Singer "used a certain face validity" in selecting events that seemed to require the maintenance of a shared task set and a common focus of attention. And indeed some of the categories offer a strong face validity. One can imagine that, say, "unintelligible remarks" and "forgetting responses" and "nihilistic remarks" might well have an impact on how families share their experiences. However, it is difficult to imagine that certain other items could be chosen simply on the basis of their presumed negative impact on communication (e.g., slips of the tongue, mispronounced words, humor, and swearing). These categories seem better explained by the remark that, in constructing the coding manual, the authors "sought to identify features in Rorschach communication which we had found especially frequent in the Rorschach protocols of our initial samples of parents of schizophrenics (Singer *et al.*, 1978, p. 9).

With regard to (*b*), the inferential procedures on which category coding is based, the problems are evident. Even though the categories in this work seem less intuitive and more solidly based in language use than those used by Gottschalk and Gleser, one must still ask: "What is it in fact that they are scoring?" (Hirsch & Leff, 1975, p. 114). In particular, the following problems exist:

1. The categories seem to require various sorts of judgments from coders and presumably would require many different sorts of decision-making models to account for the coders' decisions.
2. Categories overlap (cf. Hirsch & Leff, 1975, p. 139) and it is difficult to score global categories. These problems are especially acute because the units of measurement are not divided into easily distinguishable sets like words or clauses but are "deviances" which can cooccur and overlap without restriction.
3. The categories call extensively on the intuitions of the coders, on their familiarity with the language, and on their pragmatic skills. Wynne (1977) acknowledges this: "Raters differ in the degree to which they are willing or able to give sustained, consistent attention to this quite arduous task," he observes, and he outlines some of the knowledge which the human coder must bring to bear: "Testers and raters should be very familiar with the range of ordinary and deviant behavior shown by subjects on Rorschach, including varieties of idiomatic language used by persons of a given social class, educational and cultural background" (p. 268).

   d. *Summary.* The content analyses proposed by Gottschalk and Gleser and by Singer and Wynne have shown great promise in discriminating between groups of schizophrenic patients or groups of schizophrenic parents and control groups. However, the dimensions on which these discriminations have been made are not well understood. The Singer and Wynne procedures have a more highly developed language base, and the results produced by these procedures provide valuable hints as to distinctive features of language use. Nevertheless, the coding procedures in both cases rely so strongly on human coders' decisions that it is not clear how one could use these procedures to construct a language-based model of the schizophrenic speaker.

   e. *The General Inquirer Studies.* Two groups of investigators, Maher, McKean, and McLaughlin (1966) and Tucker and Rosenberg (1975; Rosenberg & Tucker, 1976) have used content analyses based on the General Inquirer computer system developed by Stone, Bales, Namenworth, and Ogilvie (1962; and cf. Stone, Dunphy, Smith, & Ogilvie, 1966). The Gen-

eral Inquirer was one of the early attempts to develop formalized procedures for dealing with texts. It was designed as an "aid to the investigator" in organizing and making explicit text-analytic procedures, but was
not intended to "completely simulate or otherwise substitute for the in-
spections, analyses, and insights of the investigator" (Stone *et al.*, 1962,
p. 485). The system has a dictionary look-up which can categorize words
and an ability to examine sentences under various conditions. The major
unit of analysis is the "sentence" which "so far as possible . . . should be
self-contained and not depend upon a larger context for its meaning."
Any vagueness or ambiguity in the sentence would "cause confusion for
the reader and hinder further work with the retrieved data" (p. 490). In
addition, all words entered must be tagged for their individual form class
memberships.

In about 1965, the General Inquirer was the most sophisticated alternative to intuitive category systems like those offered by Gottschalk and
Gleser and Singer and Wynne. Its capacities were extremely modest,
compared to the capacities of the human coder, but it did have the advantage of objective techniques. One could be sure, as Krippendorff claimed,
that "no part of the procedure [would] be delegated to the inexplicable
process of intuition" (1969, p. 6). About all that the system would do was
categorize words in a text according to some predetermined catgories, so
a fruitful use of the system depended strongly on an investigator's re-
sourcefulness.

Maher's Work. Maher *et al.* present an outstanding series of studies
using this system. They used the General Inquirer to analyze written
texts from over 100 schizophrenic patients in hospitals. In one study, 50-
word samples were analyzed in terms of words falling into various form
class categories (e.g., subject, subject modifier, verb, verb modifier) and
thematic categories (e.g., natural-world, legal, political). In a replication,
similar sorting procedures were used with 100-word samples.

These studies are remarkable in many respects. First, Maher and his
colleagues recognized the critical problem which "thought disorder"
poses for the study of schizophrenic language. They pointed out that,
since many samples of schizophrenics' speech are not aberrant, it is necessary to find samples which are. But if judges are used to distinguish
thought disordered from normal samples, one may simply be studying
"the judging habits of raters rather than any independently consistent
attribute of psychotic pathology" (Maher *et al.*, 1966, p. 471). This is especially true where the judges are mental health professionals. Their

common training in descriptive diagnosis could lead them to agreement but might have little or nothing to do with the patient's state.

Next, having posed the problem of judges' evaluations of thought disorder, Maher et al. attempted to identify the cues that judges use in their assessments of thought disorder. The primary aim was "to discover explicitly the rules the judges use implicitly when diagnosing thought disorder from language samples" (p. 472). They determined assessments for various documents from the original hospital clinician, from three clinical judges unacquainted with the writers, and from two under-graduates.

Along with the original study, a replication is reported that uses longer (100-word) samples, new lay judges, and new samples of 60 documents. The results of the studies are presented not simply in terms of differences between groups, but in terms of likelihood-ratios, which indicate the proportion of individuals in a group who are described by that measure. For example, the authors found that writers who were judged thought-disordered tended to use more objects than subjects in their sentences. What is new and useful is that they report the likelihood that a given subject-to-object ratio will result in a writer being judged thought-disordered. For example, where writers used 3 objects per subject, 8 out of 8 documents were judged thought-disordered; and where writers used 2 objects per subject, 5 out of 6 cases were judged thought-disordered.

Maher et al. return to their data to try to account for their findings and to develop hypotheses to describe the possible language use of the schizophrenic speakers. The hypotheses they offer are speculations about information processing and attentional mechanisms, but they are based on observations that bear rather closely on the hypotheses. The authors note that high ratios of objects to subjects occur often at the ends of sentences: "Doctor, I have pains in my chest and hope and wonder if my box is broken and heart is beaten for my soul and salvation and heaven, Amen," (Maher, 1968, pp. 32–33). They speculate that "the attentional mechanisms that are necessary to the maintenance of coherent language are weaker at the end of the sentence than elsewhere" (Maher et al., 1966, p. 489).

Finally, it is noteworthy that these investigators present a failure of their own hypothesis in their third experiment. Records from 90 patients were examined, and they found no significant differences between schizophrenic and nonschizophrenic patients in the use of high object-to-subject ratios. Their conclusion is a model for other such studies where failures in predictions seem not to occur: "where high ratios exist [schizophrenic patients] are likely to be judged thought-disordered, but the absolute probability that [such ratios] will be found in a randomly selected document from a schizophrenic patient is not high" (Maher *et al.*, 1966, p. 497).

There are some limitations too. For one thing, as the authors themselves point out, their observations do not allow one to identify most documents which would be called thought-disordered. However, they are able to identify some events (e.g., more objects than subjects) which, when they occur, almost always signal evaluations of thought disorder. Next, no model is presented which might describe how much weight particular events have in judges' decision-making. For example, judges are likely to assess thought disorder where there are references to political themes and religion. How important are these? Do they depend on the object-to-subject ratio or other factors of language use? This is not specified. Finally, because the analyses are restricted to words, the authors are not in a position to offer a model of the schizophrenic speaker's production of discourse.

Tucker and Rosenberg. Tucker and Rosenberg (1975) also used the General Inquirer system. In a pilot study, they took 600-word samples from acute schizophrenic patients and from two control groups of patients and normal subjects. The patients' samples were taken from 15-min interviews collected during their first week in hospital; the normals' samples were taken after they had experienced 10 min of REM sleep and were awakened and asked to describe their dreams. An adaptation of the Harvard III Psychosocial Dictionary was used to sort words from the samples into 84 categories which had been "specifically selected for their psychological and sociological relevance" (Tucker & Rosenberg, 1975, p. 612). They found that 14 out of 84 categories differentiated schizophrenic from nonschizophrenic subjects.

In a replication (Rosenberg & Tucker, 1976), the authors studied larger samples (which included subjects from the original samples) and refined their procedures. The results of the replication, once gender differences were controlled, were that 3 out of 31 categories differentiated schizophrenic from nonschizophrenic patients. Thus, when the technique was refined and the sample size increased, the replication was no more promising as a discriminative procedure. The categories that discriminated the larger sample of schizophrenic patients were "Not" (schizophrenics used more words denoting negation), and two categories that schizophrenics underused relative to nonschizophrenic patients:

"Pleasure" (states of gratification) and "Ascend Theme" (words associated with rising, falling, fire and water, supposed to indicate concerns
relating to the Icarus complex).

These studies are developed from a series of clinical studies done in
conjunction with other workers (e.g., Reilly, Harrow, and Tucker, 1973;
Reilly, Harrow, Tucker, Quinlan, & Siegel, 1975; Siegel, Harrow, Reilly
& Tucker, 1976). In the clinical studies, the categories were essentially
based on Bleuler's observations and consequently relied very heavily on
the intuitions of judges. Tucker and Rosenberg's work is a welcome attempt to analyze the schizophrenic speaker's productions objectively,
and theirs is the first to use a computerized approach with *speaker's* productions.

There are, however, some limitations to these efforts. First, it is dis-
couraging to find no serious account taken of the similar but more developed analyses published by Maher and his colleagues some ten years
earlier. Several important points made in the earlier study seem to be lost
to the later workers: namely, the problems in defining and selecting
"schizophrenic" or "thought disordered" speech; the need to describe
results for individual subjects as well as for groups; and the significance
of syntactic considerations as well as themes in assessing texts. Second,
the authors' goal of providing "phenomenological" descriptions of
schizophrenic speakers has, in practice, been addressed by previous
workers, as we indicate above. It is not clear that the categories provided
by the Harvard III Dictionary adaptation are superior to the other categories, nor is it clear on which dimensions they differ from previous
work. Moreover, it is not the case that the Harvard III categories are the-
ory-free. Some, like the "Ascend Theme" mentioned above, have a powerful set of psychodynamic assumptions underlying them.

f. Summary of Content Analyses. The five sets of content analyses reviewed here offer an overview of the problem facing those who attempt
to understand the schizophrenic speaker. They demonstrate a stubborn
conundrum: analyses performed by human coders can produce remarkable discriminations, but the bases on which they operate are obscure,
whereas analyses performed by computers are based on well-defined
procedures, but the discriminations that they produce are rather weak.
To exaggerate the situation a bit, it seems that when our measures are
discriminating, we cannot tell what they are measuring; and when we
can tell what they are measuring, they are not very discriminating.

In the next few years, it is likely that the computer systems for analyzing discourse will be applied to schizophrenic speech. Gottschalk and

his colleagues (1975) have already begun this effort. But if their experience is a fair guide, even these techniques are rather far from human coders' decisions. Hirsch and Leff (1975) commented in their review of Singer and Wynne (1965): "The magnitude of Singer's accomplishment in these studies is truly remarkable" (p. 75). Those who study schizophrenic speakers are attempting to transform the clinician's truly remarkable skill into explicit criteria of judgment that describe the speaker's behavior. And this seems to be an inordinately difficult task.

2. Clinical Studies. Clinical studies, even more than content analyses, have been neglected in reviews of language in schizophrenia. The reason given is that the premises underlying these studies are so far from experimental studies that fruitful comparisons are not possible. This is probably true if one attempts a strict comparison, but it is too narrow a statement if one wants to understand the schizophrenic speaker. In fact, the last two decades have produced clinical studies that are at least as enlightening as experimental efforts on these problems.

The studies can be divided into (a) controlled observations by psychiatrists and (b) descriptive analyses by linguists and aphasiologists. Both categories provide insights into the schizophrenic speaker, and their separate perspectives give a valuable diversity.

a. Controlled Observations by Psychiatrists. Among the several studies of schizophrenic speakers, a few have provided welcome expansions of the Bleulerian descriptions. These expansions are important because it is primarily the Bleulerian accounts that are used in hospitals across North America for the diagnosis of thought disorder and schizophrenia.

Clinical studies are difficult to summarize because their value lies primarily in the detailed accounts they provide. However, we can mention some important observations that have been made in recent studies.

Reilly et al. In an interesting study entitled "Looseness of Associations in Acute Schizophrenia," Reilly and his colleagues (1975) interviewed acute schizophrenic patients and other psychiatric patients in 15 min "free verbalization" interviews (details of this study are given in Table 1). One rater coded 10 categories of "deviant verbalizations." The rater gave scores of 0 to 4 (maximum pathology) whenever he found one of the 10 categories appropriate. "Looseness of associations" was one category. It was defined as "a lack of connection between ideas so that the reason for a shift in thought is questionable or incomprehensible . . . where continuity of thought and the logical development of a concept is lacking to some degree" (p. 242). Six subcategories of looseness were defined as follows: L1—mild shift in thought within a sentence; L2—slight shift from one sentence to next, same topic; L3—drastic shift from one sentence to next, same topic; L4—mild shift from one sentence to next, different topic; L5—drastic shift from one sentence to next; different topic; L6—drastic shift within a sentence. The authors decided (on some unspecified basis) that L3, L5, and L6 should receive higher scores for deviance than the remaining subcategories.

Another category was "gaps in communication" in which "information essential for comprehension by the listener is missing, and the speaker behaves as if he presupposes information or knowledge on the part of the listener that he has no right to expect" (p. 242). What is interesting about these categories is (a) the recognition of the use of language as a social act in which the speaker must take some account of the listener's needs, (b) the notion that topic shifts can be "drastic" or "mild" and can occur within as well as between sentences, and (c) the idea that there is a gradient of topic shifts reflecting how well the speaker takes account of the listener's needs. By tying these categories to events within and between sentences, the authors suggest a way of rooting notions of the comprehensibility of the speaker to specific discourse events. Instead of talking only about ideas being "vague and wooly," they suggest some concrete ways in which this "wooliness" might be manifested.

There are problems in extrapolating from this study. Briefly, one must note that a single rater coded the texts (though the authors assert that interrater reliability was satisfactorily established, they give no details about this); the categories still rely to a considerable extent on the rater's intuition; and the parametric statistics used were probably not appropriate for the data. Nevertheless, what is impressive and valuable is the attempt to use categories that are rather more language-based than those used by earlier workers, and at the same time to use categories that are immediately relevant in clinical practice.

Andreasen. Andreasen (in press-a,b) has also attempted to refine Bleulerian descriptions of thought disorder. Her primary contribution has been to show the distribution of these categories in patients with various diagnoses. A summary of her preliminary findings is given in Table 3.

Her results provide evidence in support of several frequent clinical observations: (a) not all schizophrenic patients show signs of "formal thought disorder" in their productions; (b) some Bleulerian categories are more common than others in schizophrenic speakers ("poverty of speech content," and "tangentiality"); and (c) several Bleulerian categories de-

Table 3. Recent Clinical Descriptions of Thought Disorder

To characterize the features of "formal thought disorder" Andreasen (in press) designed 18 categories of language use and counted the occurence of these categories in the psychiatric interviews of manic, depressed, and schizophrenic speakers. She found that seven of the categories occured in at least 25% of the schizophrenic patients' ($n=32$) interviews. Only two of these (*), however, discriminated schizophrenics from other patients.

Measure	Brief description	Percentage of schizophrenia
(a) Poverty of speech content*	Speech conveys little information; is vague, overabstract or overconcrete, repetitive and stereotyped. Information is not adequate and replies may be incomprehensible.	41
(b) Tangentiality*	Refers only to replies to questions. Replies are oblique, tangential or somewhat irrelevant, though clearly related to the question in some way. E.g., when asked for today's date, speaker replies, "I was born November 11, 1935."	41
(c) Derailment	Spontaneous speech in which ideas are clearly but obliquely related. E.g., "Yesterday we played volleyball in the afternoon. Babe Ruth and Lou Gehrig both played for the Yankees. Too bad Gehrig got sick."	53
(d) Pressure of speech	Speech is rapid and difficult to interrupt; tends to be loud and emphatic; excessive amount.	25
(e) Loss of goal	Speech begins with a particular subject, wanders away and never returns to it; failure to follow a chain of thought through to a logical conclusion.	47
(f) Perseveration	Persistent repetition of words or ideas, though words are used appropriately.	25
(g) Poverty of speech	Restriction in amount of speech so replies are brief, concrete, and unelaborated; unprompted talk is rare.	34

Note. All the above measures have high positive intercorrelations (r typically yields $p < .001$) except for (g) poverty of speech, which is typically negatively, though not reliably, correlated with the other measures.

scribe behaviors that are as common in depression and mania as in schizophrenia (5 out of 7 categories given in Table 3).

The studies of Andreasen and Reilly *et al.* demonstrate the increasing sensitivity of studies of language use in schizophrenic speakers. In both studies, there are careful attempts to show how psychiatric designations are based on the speaker's behavior. These demonstrations are necessary to the development of a baseline from which to describe and perhaps model the speaker's performance and knowledge. However, they still rely very heavily on unspecified decisions by sophisticated coders, and they provide descriptions only of what schizophrenic speakers can *not* do—there is no baseline of general performance provided.

b. Descriptive Analyses by Linguists and Aphasiologists. Since 1975, there has been a remarkable development in the study of "schizophasia." Schizophasia is "a deviant linguistic behavior observed in certain—not in all, by far—people considered to be schizophrenics" (Lecours & Vanier-Clément, 1976, p. 524). The term, and the publication of several studies by linguists and aphasiologists, reflect recent efforts to describe as objectively as possible the phenomena that characterize the deviant use of language by schizophrenic speakers.

Chaika. Elaine Chaika's description of a single schizophrenic patient (1974a), and her discussions of this and other work (1974b, 1977), and Victoria Fromkin's (1975) discussions of Chaika's work, mark efforts by linguists to describe "schizophrenic language" in terms of a small number of definable features. Chaika (1974a) analyzed a tape-recorded interview from a 37-year-old patient "who had been repeatedly diagnosed as schizophrenic." The interview was virtually a monologue, Chaika reports, and "the patient's intonation was usually not amenable to intrusion." Indeed, the patient "often seemed to be speaking to herself" (1974a, p. 259).

Chaika examined the corpus using a variety of linguistic approaches. She identified six characteristics as follows: (*a*) disrupted ability to match semantic features with sound strings; (*b*) preoccupation with too many of the semantic features of a word in discourse; (*c*) inappropriate use of phonological features of words; (*d*) production of sentences according to phonological and semantic features of previously uttered words, rather than according to topic; (*e*) disrupted ability to apply rules of syntax and discourse; (*f*) failure to note speech errors when they occur. She concluded that these characteristics indicated a disruption in the ability to apply "linguistic rules which organize elements into meaningful structures," and suggested that "schizophrenic language" might be due to an intermittent aphasia over which the patient has no control.

Fromkin (1975) argued that all the behaviors described by Chaika could be found in normal productions, except for the disruption in discourse. She argues that the latter feature is nonlinguistic and that disconnected discourse is evidence of "schizophrenic thought" rather than "schizophrenic language:" "Any attempt to include constraints on logical sequencing or social relevance in a model of linguistic competence would seem to me to be too ambitious and bound to fail" (1975, p. 501). Fromkin, like Roger Brown (1973), argues that there are not disruptions of *language* in schizophrenics but disruptions of *thought*.

The Aphasiologists. The question of whether the aberrant productions of schizophrenic speakers reflect a true aphasia, that is, a failure of language production which is distinct from the patient's ability to conceptualize and to engage in social acts, has a long history. It has been of particular interest to clinicians who must decide whether a new patient has a temporary language disturbance or an imminent psychosis. Recently the question has also been raised in connection with the etiology of schizophrenia. Benson (1973), DiSimoni, Darley, and Aronson (1977), and Gerson, Benson, and Frazier (1977) present reviews of this literature among aphasiologists.

One example of this recent work is the Lecours and Vanier-Clément (1976) description of "schizophasia," in which they summarize four characteristics, as follows: (*a*) a normal or greater than normal speech flow; (*b*) a normal use of intonation and pronunciation; (*c*) a production in various amounts and combinations of *paraphasia* (deviant production of elements from known target), e.g., verbal paraphasia would be "a scent of cadaver" instead of a "scent of caviar"; a syntactic paraphasia would be a replacement of one word or phrase by another of the same syntactic function, e.g., "people's opium" for "taxpayer's money"; and/or *téléscopages* (several units are condensed into one), e.g., a verbal téléscopage would be a single word which results from borrowing phonemic or morphemic units from several conventional segments (e.g., "transformation" for "transmission of information"); and/or *neologisms* (deviant segments used as single words; these are reserved for items that cannot be identified by other categories); and (*d*) a *glossomania*, in which components of sentences are chosen mainly on the basis of phonological or semantic kinship to each other; *formal glossomania* would be sentences in which components are chosen mainly on the basis of phonological kinship; *semantic glossomania* would be sentences in which components are chosen mainly on the basis of conceptual associations that seem unrelated to the conversational topic.

The authors compare their conclusions to those of Chaika and note that her characteristics (a) to (e) correspond to deviations they have noted as well in schizophrenic speakers. However, they claim that all—with the possible exception of (b)—also define linguistic deviations observed in the jargonaphasias. In addition, they report that her observation (f), a failure to note speech errors, did not characterize their data for "archetypical schizophasic" patients. Chaika's (1977) response to this and to Fromkin's critique appears part of an ongoing discussion of these problems.

Summary of the Descriptive Analyses. A profound advantage of these studies is their power to describe individual patients very well. This is particularly apparent in studies such as the Lecours and Vanier-Clément report and in the work of James Chapman (1966). From these studies we can learn two very important facts: (a) not every schizophrenic patient is schizophasic; and (b) not every schizophasic patient is schizophasic all the time.

These facts have been responsible for great confusion in experimental investigations. Experimenters have behaved as if "schizophasia" could be sampled at random from unselected schizophrenic patients. It is no wonder that there have been so many failures to replicate even the simplest "verbal behavior" studies. If the phenomenon under study is episodic, then one must capture the episodes and describe them. To do otherwise by attempting unselected observations will necessarily lead to weak and often unreplicable outcomes. Although many investigators must have suspected this fact, very few have acknowledged and attempted to use it.

A profitable next step for these clinical descriptions would be to introduce some tabulations and patient characteristics of the sorts used by Andreasen (in press-a,b) and other clinical investigators. The lack of such procedures means that many essential features of the data are left unspecified (as indicated in Table 1). In particular, one knows neither the characteristics of the patients being described nor the frequency of the various behaviors. Without systematic observations, we cannot know whether some sorts of patients are more likely than others to, say, show discourse failures rather than "verbal paraphasias"; whether "phonemic téléscopages" can occur without other manifestations of schizophasia; whether phonemic aberrations always occur with aberrations at the verbal level and at the level of discourse; or whether chronic patients are more likely to show some of these behaviors and acute patients to show others.

3. The Common Premises of Naturalistic Studies. Although there is a very wide range of studies of schizophrenic speakers included under the general heading of "naturalistic" observations, the following premises seem common to most naturalistic studies:

1. The role of the language user is as a speaker.
2. The processes of interest are the mental and/or social and/or pathological processes underlying the production of words, sentences, and connected discourse.
3. The best context for studying language is the clinic or hospital in which interviews are given. This is best because of the diversity of conditions provided.
4. The best descriptions of language use are lists of (all) behaviors that are distinctive to schizophrenic speakers.
5. The best things to study are the distinctive characteristics of the speaker's productions.
6. The goal is to identify schizophrenic patients or their families, or to identify the features of productions which prompt listeners to diagnose schizophrenia.

These common premises are not a legacy from behaviorism. If they must be derived from one tradition, they are in the tradition of the clinic. The aim in these studies is essentially a practical one: How may we de-

Table 4. Premises of Experimental and Naturalistic Studies of Language Use in Schizophrenia

Premises	Planned experiments	Naturalistic studies
(a) Role of language user is as ...	listener	speaker
(b) Processes of interest are ...	information processing	production
(c) Best context for study is ... because of ...	laboratory controlled conditions	clinic diversity of conditions
(d) Best descriptions of language use are	functional relations like: "treatment X has effect Y"	lists of behaviors that are distinctive to schizophrenic speakers
(e) Best things to study are ...	response variables with interval or ordinal character	distinctive speech events and uses
(f) Goal is to identify ...	cognitive/perceptual processes underlying schizophrenia	schizophrenic patients or their families; (psychosocial processes underlying schizophrenia)

scribe the schizophrenic patient so that he or she can be treated? The remaining premises are predicated primarily on this aim. The patient is seen as a producer, one who produces symptoms that must be diagnosed. And the effort of study is devoted primarily to a careful description of these symptoms such that differential diagnoses are facilitated—with organic syndromes, if possible, with aphasias, and with other psychiatric disorders.

Table 4 summarizes the premises that underlie both naturalistic and experimental studies of language use in schizophrenia. The contrasting traditions underlying the two categories of studies provide investigators with a broad range of procedures from which to approach the study of schizophrenics' language use. In the next section, we discuss the problems and advantages of the individual approaches, and examine two problems that are common to both.

III. The Study of the Schizophrenic Speaker in Light of Prior Work

How is one to study the schizophrenic speaker? More precisely, how is one to study this speaker in a manner that is systematic and at the same time relevant to the everyday uses of language? The answer would seem to lie somewhere between the experimental and the naturalistic traditions. The experimental premises allow strong tests of particular hypotheses, but the tests are very narrow and are restricted primarily to listeners. The naturalistic premises allow broad descriptions of relevant behaviors, but the descriptions are generally unsystematic and intuitive. To find a middle way, let us examine some of the general issues associated with the two approaches. The issues we shall be discussing are summarized in Table 5.

A. Three Issues

Briefly, there are three issues that seem important in considering limitations in one or the other or both approaches to language use in schizophrenia.

1. Unrepresentative Data. The effect of the formal testing situation presents a general methodological problem in psychological studies and is particularly acute in studies of "deviant" language. The dangers of bias from the testing situation are revealed in a dramatic study that Labov

Table 5. Some Issues in the Study of Language Use in Schizophrenia

	Planned experiments	Naturalistic studies
A. 1. Settings provide unrepresentative data because of role and social class differences	Lab setting: experimenter-subject	Clinic setting:doctor–patient
2. Tasks require unrepresentative skills	Recall and recognition tasks do not measure comprehension	
3. Narrow hypotheses dictate narrow designs	Only know if subject responds more or less	
	Common problems	

B. 1. Theoretical constructs are adopted from other disciplines but not made relevant to language use
   2. Theoretical goals are directed toward models of *deviance* so descriptions and formulations are not general for language use

(1970) conducted in New York. He demonstrated the unrepresentativeness of verbal behavior elicited from black children by white investigators and even by unsympathetic black investigators. Black children, who were virtually silent with white experimenters going through the formal ritual of psycholinguistic tasks, displayed great linguistic sophistication with black experimenters who understood the dialect and ways of life of the black ghetto.

Table 5 indicates that there is a risk of unrepresentative data in both experimental and naturalistic studies. In both cases, there are role differences between subject and experimenter, or patient and doctor (or nurse, psychologist, etc.). And in both cases, there are likely to be marked social-class differences in which the schizophrenic subject is from a lower social class than the graduate student or Ph.D. experimenter or the doctor or nurse, etc.; (cf. Nuttall & Solomon, 1970; Seeman, 1970; Turner, Raymond, Zabor, & Diamond, 1969).

2. Special Tasks; Special Skills. Several aspects of the methodology of experimental studies limit the extent to which one can generalize from the individual studies. These are really further aspects of the problem of unrepresentative data discussed in Section I, but in this case they pertain to the task rather than the observational setting. Two problems are outstanding.

First, all the following—the verbatim recall of sentences or lists of words, the recognition of written texts, the recall and/or recognition of the exact location of a click in a sentence—all these are tasks which are unrepresentative of ordinary comprehension processes. This has been demonstrated in several experiments. For example, Jacqueline Sachs (1967, 1974) has shown that normal subjects are very good at recognizing changes that alter *meaning* of sentences but are very poor at recognizing changes that alter structural or lexical characteristics while preserving the meaning. And Bransford, Barclay, and Franks (1972) have demonstrated that subjects remember the situation a sentence describes much better than the linguistic deep structure of the sentence. In view of these studies, it seems that the psycholinguistic and information processing studies reviewed in Section II are demanding unrepresentative kinds of language use from the subjects, language use which may require special skills not necessarily relevant to ordinary comprehension processes.

Next, Clark (1973) has demonstrated the limitations of analyses of variance in psycholinguistic research. He shows that the usual approaches to sampling and statistical analysis prohibit the experimenter from generalizing beyond the data of the immediate experiment. Clark's critique is appropriate to very many of the experimental studies of schizophrenics' language use.

3. Narrow Hypotheses. In the experimental studies summarized in Section II, hypotheses about information processing or language comprehension are put forward. The hypotheses are frequently so narrowly conceived that the designs to test them do not permit the consideration of competing hypotheses.

B. The Common Problems

There are two theoretical issues that affect all studies of schizophrenics' language use. The first pertains to the development of theory and the second to the theoretical goals.

1. Development of Theory. In a discussion of the young discipline of psycholinguistics, Olson and Clark (1976) observe that there has been an adoption of theoretical constructs from other, older disciplines. The risk in this adoption, they warn, is that one may accept criteria from other theories that are irrelevant to one's own concern. For example, one could adopt the formal criteria of abstract automata, supposing that the grammars these produce are relevant to actual language production. But "to suppose that a distinction made on the basis of another metatheory will

ipso facto be of use in cognitive psychology is to make a serious error"
(p. 64).

This risk is especially profound in the study of schizophrenics' language use. This study, which perhaps may be considered a subdiscipline of psycholinguistics, has also adopted theories from other disciplines: from theories of perceptual processes (e.g., Shakow, 1962), from Shannon's mathematical theory of communications, from the transformational theories of Chomsky and other linguists, and in earlier years from the constructs of neurologists (e.g., Goldstein, Vygotsky), psychobiologists (e.g., Meyer), and psychiatrists (e.g., Freud).

The problem with these adoptions is that, although they permit easy initial approaches to schizophrenics' language use, they do not allow for development of alternative approaches when hypotheses fail. The adopted constructs have in effect been cut from already developed theories in other fields, but the roots of these constructs have been left behind. For example, Shakow's (1962) theory is developed from perceptual data, not from language use. To modify it for language use, one must tie the theory very carefully to the data—to the detailed behavior of speakers and listeners. This has not been done. Each of the adopted constructs has been grafted onto the language data, without troubling to ensure that the data and theory are matched.

As we mentioned in Section I, the failures of studies of schizophrenic language users reflect the failures of psycholinguistics in general. But in recent years, there has been a great increase in the level of sophistication about language within psycholinguistics. The notion that one could study language with little or no interest in the details of language has been largely abandoned. It now appears that an ignorance of linguistic function leads one to naive experimental designs in which obvious properties of language are confounded with the effects of interest. It seems, as well, that one is able to describe and formulate behavior more systematically and in greater detail than if one simply views language use as responses to internal and external stimuli.

Perhaps, as the study of schizophrenics' language use becomes a more self-conscious discipline, the difficulties of wholesale adoption of constructs from other fields will give way to a more considered use of those constructs. For, as Olson and Clark (1976) note, constructs from other theoretical approaches can be useful heuristics for guiding research—if they are redesigned to fit the data for which they are intended.

   2. Goals of the Theory. To conclude this review, let us again note a decision that seems to have had profound effects on the field. This is the decision to study *deviant* behavior. As we argued earlier, one cannot hope to provide an adequate account of behavior simply from an account of what is "deviant" about that behavior. It is worth stressing this point again because most recent studies of schizophrenic speakers have maintained the focus on deviance. We believe that this is an unproductive approach because it precludes the prediction of successes and it prevents the systematic description of failures.

IV. A Final Comment

A. Goals

As psycholinguistics has developed into a self-conscious discipline, it has had to confront the problem of borrowed ideas. So many of its central constructs have been borrowed from neighboring disciplines, it has had to ask: How do we build a model which fits language *use* and not formal structures or machine processes or philosophical theories about speech acts? This is an important problem now in psycholinguistics, but it has a direction. Investigators are asking how to formulate the processes that concern them.

Those who study language use in schizophrenic subjects (and perhaps also in psychopathology generally) have a more troublesome question to confront: Is it important to formulate a model of language use in schizophrenia? Is it necessary to formulate a model, or at least principles of language use, in order to understand how the language processes of schizophrenic patients bear on their being schizophrenic?

This is an uncomfortable question to ask because, once posed, it can be answered in the negative. It is possible that the language processes of the schizophrenic patient tell us little or nothing that is critical to an understanding of the patient's state or to its cure. And this possibility leads us to ask another discomfiting question: Why study schizophrenics' language use? There seems to be three answers to this question in the literature: (*a*) because it is there; (*b*) because it aids in the diagnosis of schizophrenia; and (*c*) because it offers significant clues to the origin of or cure for schizophrenia. We would argue that, as goals for a discipline, (*a*) is unacceptable and (*b*) is unrealistic. Answer (*a*) is unacceptable because, no matter how fascinating the productions of the schizophrenic speaker are, one cannot justify asking the patients' participation in a study which will be of no benefit to them. Answer (*b*), the promise of improved diagnostic performance, is illusory because forty years of research efforts appear to have had no effect on clinical practice. The verbal behavior scales or indicators that have been developed by researchers have simply not been adopted in the clinic (with the rare exceptions of a few teaching clinics). This may be because the procedures are too complex, or because they are troublesome to teach, or perhaps because they are too expensive to implement. Whatever the reasons, there is no evidence that clinicians have adopted such measures in the past, so one cannot be optimistic that they will do so in the future.

It seems that answer (*c*) is the only goal which can be justified. Only if the study of a patient's language use will teach us something critical about the patient's disorder can we justify our studies. But even supposing this assertion is valid, how do we proceed? Especially, how do we discover anything apart from what we already know from some six decades of research and observation?

Is it necessary to study language use so carefully that one can build a fair model of that performance? Or is it sufficient to extract pieces of that performance, or to list instances of that performance? The former is the approach that has been used in experimental studies; the latter, in most naturalistic studies. Perhaps it is the lack of an answer to these questions which, in the end, is responsible for the great discouragement of those reviewing this field. Not knowing if it is even necessary to formulate language processes, we have had no clear direction for our efforts.

At the present time, it seems worth aiming for a formulation of language use by schizophrenic speakers that is as broadly based as possible while being as relevant as possible to the clinical descriptions of "thought disordered" or "schizophasic" speech. In this book, we attempt to contribute to such a formulation by developing an account of how speakers form coherent "texts"—stretches of speech which form a more or less unified wholes for the listener. We begin by studying how speakers link the clauses of their discourse together through a variety of strategies that Halliday and Hasan (1976) term "cohesion devices." We soon discover that speakers can use very similar strategies of linking their texts together, while they in fact produce texts that are widely different in coherence. This leads us to examine one kind of cohesive strategy, referential cohesion, in detail. Chapter 2 gives an introduction to these efforts. Before proceeding, however, we should mention two limitations on our ability to generalize from the present study.

B. Two Caveats

1. Definition of Discourse. In the foregoing review, we have tried to show how a focus on single words has limited our understanding of how schizophrenic speakers actually use language, and we have been critical of attempts to study sentences outside the framework of a fuller text. However, we commented only briefly on the need to study dialogues as opposed to monologues, and on the more general issue of language as speech rooted in a social act. Many observers have pointed out the limitations of a study of the individual in schizophrenia (e.g., Haley, 1959; Laing, 1967) and it is clear that the transaction is of critical importance in understanding the communication process. In addition, students of language processes have argued cogently that a failure to study dialogues is a failure to understand the essential process in language use (e.g., Carswell & Rommetveit, 1971; Riegel, 1975, in press; Rommetveit, 1968, 1974; Sacks, 1972; Voloshinov, 1973). The argument is presented very clearly in Jaffe and Feldstein's (1970) study of conversational patterns. They cite Roman Jakobson's critique of studies of monologues, which argues that "to tell a story outside the frame of a dialogue, and without being interrupted, is for many natives an utterly artificial situation" (1964, p. 163). A monologue, Jaffe and Feldstein insist, is a special case of dialogue in which one participant is silent or absent. Consequently, dialogue is the essential unit of verbal interaction.

These arguments for the study of dialogic patterns are very persuasive, but we have not followed them. Our study of discourse has been a study of speakers who produce largely uninterrupted productions in the presence of a listener. The productions are considered "discourse" because they represent connected, ongoing texts, and because the texts are spoken, rather than written. The contexts of the discourse vary in the degree of spontaneity afforded the speaker, from a low degree in the retelling of a narrative, through moderate in the description and interpretation of cartoon pictures, to relatively high spontaneity in the course of an unstructured interview in which the speaker could determine the topics to be discussed. Even the interview, however, was not a conversation in the sense of two participants sharing the speaking part of the interaction. Instead, the person doing the interview made an effort not to interrupt the subject.

We would like to study conversational behavior in schizophrenic speaker–listeners, but we believe that the present effort is a necessary first step. We suspected that many of the incoherent stretches in schizophrenic discourse might reflect the speaker responding to him- or herself. For example, Salzinger, Portnoy, and Feldman (1964) have shown that as the time elapses since the schizophrenic speaker begins to talk, the utterances become increasingly more difficult to understand. Studies by Cohen, Nachmani, and Rosenberg (1974) confirm this, showing that references to objects in the situational contexts become more obscure as the schizophrenic speaker continues to speak in an uninterrupted stream. So it seemed that our best chance of finding samples of incoherent speech was to provide a nondialogic situation.

In addition, we were particularly interested in the phenomenon Bleuler terms "a loss of goal directedness," in which one cannot follow the development or at least sequence of topics presented by an individual speaker. We wanted to trace how an account comes to lack unity, even though the word and clause elements of the account are largely intact. And again it seemed better to study uninterrupted discourse than free conversation. Thus, we have viewed the present study as a necessary beginning to plotting some of the elements of discourse production in schizophrenic speakers. But even at the beginning we must recognize its limitation as a study of everyday language use.

2. Schizophrenia versus Psychosis. In our title, and throughout the following chapters, we attempt to characterize the language use of schizophrenic speakers who are and are not considered "thought-disordered" (a term we leave for definition until Chapter 2). To the extent that this practice describes the samples of speakers we studied, it is accurate; but to the extent that it suggests our findings are distinctive to *schizophrenia* as opposed to other forms of psychosis or organic syndromes, it is misleading. We cannot make any statement about language behaviors distinctive to schizophrenia because we did not attempt any cross-sectional comparisons with other groups which might show similar behaviors.

There is some clinical evidence that the phenomena of schizophrenic thought disorder are not distinctive to schizophrenia. Some investigators claim that there is evidence of "formal thought disorder" in acute depression (e.g., Ianzito, Cadoret, & Pugh, 1974) whereas others do not (e.g., Andreasen, 1976). Andreasen and Powers (1974) suggest that overinclusive thinking, often based on aberrant language use, occurs in mania as well as in schizophrenia. Harrow and Quinlan (1977), in a study of 200 patients which included schizophrenic, manic, and depressed patients as well as those with neurotic symptoms, conclude the signs of mild and moderate thought disorders are not unique to schizophrenia. It is very difficult to generalize from these studies, however, because they combine observations of aberrant language use with a variety of other observations including responses to test items and analyses of logic.

There are, however, two studies which indicate rather firmly that the language phenomena that characterize "thought disorder" in schizophrenia are present in mania as well. In a study of over 100 patients with diagnoses of mania, depression, and schizophrenia, Andreasen (in press-b) examined 20–45 min structured and unstructured interviews. She used a scale that contained definitions of 18 "linguistic and cognitive behaviors" (described in Table 3), and found that the language uses traditionally associated with schizophrenic thought disorder occurred about equally often in manic and schizophrenic patients. These included tangentiality, derailment ("the ideas slip off the track onto another one which is clearly but obliquely related, or onto one which is completely unrelated"), and incoherence. She concludes that her data "indicate quite clearly that the concept of thought disorder as pathognomic for schizophrenia is incorrect" (p. 10).

This conclusion seems to be supported by the results of a study of six manic patients by Durbin and Marshall (1977). In a series of analytic tests and in unstructured interviews, they assessed their subjects' ability to comprehend and generate grammatical sentences and to use complex linguistic transformations such as relativization and complementation as well as prepositional placement and pronominalization. They found that the patients were generally able to perform these operations according to the level of their education. In such tests, the subjects also had no difficulty in using anaphoric reference within a sentence (reference within a sentence to a participant in the same sentence) or ellipsis (the deletion of a lexical string and replacement by some syntactic marker). However, in extended discourse and in conversations, all the manic patients made frequent ellipsis errors which they did not attempt to correct. In addition, the patients made a great number of errors in "semantic or discourse anaphora," that is, in reference to participants across sentence boundaries. For example, the following text is presented:

My son, I have waited for 29 years. That's for damn sure I can wait 29 more but I don't want to.

This is followed by:

I never have let this hand know what this one is doing. Never.

And this is followed by:

You see, my husband doesn't even know his wife.

Each of the separate samples are said to show a failure to use "discourse anaphora," to bridge the sentence-to-sentence change in theme by some semantic marker.

Durbin and Marshall conclude that in manic speakers there is a preservation of basic linguistic competence with regard to phonology, lexical use, and the generation of complex and grammatical sentences, and a failure in the use of ellipsis and anaphora at the level of discourse that occurred even when speech was produced at a slow rate.

These results resemble our own conclusions about the competence of "thought-disordered" schizophrenic speakers to use language, as we discuss in Chapter 7. In view of these findings, and those of Andreasen, it seems possible that the results we shall be reporting here are general to some acute psychotic states and not unique to schizophrenia. In the absence of careful cross-sectional studies, we simply do not know. As techniques for describing language use become more precise, it is hoped that the tasks of such comparisons will grow easier.

2

Procedures

I. Introduction

This chapter and the following five chapters describe a psycholinguistic approach to the discourse of the schizophrenic speaker. At the heart of this work is a comparison of interview texts from schizophrenic speakers who are judged to show thought disorder and from schizophrenic speakers who are judged to show no signs of thought disorder. The first group of speakers is referred to as TD speakers; the second group, as NTD speakers. There is a third group of speakers who are not patients (N speakers). In addition to the interview texts, we also analyze narratives and cartoon descriptions and interpretations from the speakers.

The aim of the following chapters is to examine the intersentence relations of coherent and incoherent texts. The analysis proceeds in two stages. First, in Chapter 3, the cohesion analysis of Halliday and Hasan (1976) is used to examine linkages between independent clauses. These analyses indicate that cohesive ties are used differently across contexts and are used differently by schizophrenic and normal speakers. However, there are few reliable differences between the texts of TD and NTD speakers.

In Chapter 4, second level analyses are introduced in which we look in greater detail at discourse relationships that are based on nominal groups (or noun phrases). These analyses are process-oriented, in the sense that they ask what the speaker's utterances demand of the listener. In Chapter 5, we study nominal groups that present new information in the discourse. In Chapter 6, we reverse our perspective and examine all nominal groups which presume[1] old information in order to be under-

---

[1]As the term "presupposition" is widely used by linguists to refer to what remains true of

stood. In that chapter, we distinguish several different retrieval operations that are demanded of the listener: retrieval (*a*) from the explicit verbal text; (*b*) from the nonverbal situation; (*c*) from the implicit text; (*d*) from some unclear context. Both chapters 5 and 6 provide analyses that discriminate the productions of TD speakers from those of NTD speakers and, as well, distinguish productions of NTD speakers from those of normals.

Chapter 7 is a general discussion of the findings from the foregoing analyses. In this chapter, we find that the ability of the analyses to discriminate the three groups of speakers is quite good: using the most sensitive measures, 29 out of 30 speakers can be correctly identified. The bulk of the chapter is devoted to a discussion of the processes that seem to underlie the speakers' discourse production, and, in particular, those that seem implicated by the successes and failures of the thought-disordered speaker.

The assumptions that underlie these efforts are as follows:

1. To understand the productions of the schizophrenic speaker, one must examine productions. It is not adequate to study listener's responses in experimental situations. Hence the present efforts are essentially naturalistic descriptions of speakers' discourse productions.

2. Since not all schizophrenic speech is "schizophasic" or "thought-disordered," we intentionally select samples of speech that clinical judges find "thought-disordered" and compare those samples to speech that is judged not to show signs of thought disorder. In this sense, the critical texts are sampled selectively rather than at random.

3. A great deal of what speakers do in producing texts depends on their reaction to the context in which they are speaking. In order to examine context effects, we have varied the contexts in which the texts were produced. Three types of context were used and will be outlined in detail below: interviews, description and interpretation of cartoons, and retold narratives.

4. A full description of schizophrenic discourse would include discussion of semantic, lexicogrammatical, and phonological patterns since as speakers talk, they code their meanings in words and structures and recode these as sounds. Our approach here focuses on semantic patterns (including pragmatic and textual patterns in the systemic model assumed here). This is not expected to provide an exhaustive account of the schizophrenic speakers' productions. However, it is expected to dem-

---

an utterance when it is negated, we will use the term "presumption" when referring to what a speaker assumes the listener knows.

onstrate (*a*) the advantages of a systematic account of discourse over a nonsystematic portrayal of "deviances," and (*b*) the potential power of a discourse-based analysis over analyses restricted to sentences or words.

5. The descriptions presented are based on the use of linguistic entities, with most emphasis placed on the use of nominal groups. These descriptions are not intended as psycholinguistic accounts of the very sophisticated semantic processing that is required for natural language production. However, to the extent that the present descriptions distinguish coherent from incoherent productions, they can serve as clues to the necessary features of natural language producers and indicate which operations may be failing in the incoherent productions of thought-disordered speakers.

6. The present descriptions cannot provide any information as to whether or not "thought disorder" is peculiar to schizophrenic speakers, or is general to psychosis or high-anxiety states or other conditions. Such distinctions require further work with specially selected patient samples.

II. Describing the Sample

A. Speakers

Speakers were three groups of 10 subjects each. The groups were selected from larger samples of 20 each, described in Rochester, Martin, and Thurston (1977). The selection was nonsystematic with the restriction that subjects were speakers of Canadian English with about half females and half males in each group. Subgroups were used to make qualitative analyses of each subject feasible. The total data base over all contexts and speakers for cohesion analyses is about 1,000 independent clauses and about 3,000 cohesive ties; for second stage analyses the data base is about 8,000 nominal groups.

1. Patients. The patient subjects were 20 schizophrenic patients interviewed during their first month in hospital at the Clarke Institute of Psychiatry, University of Toronto. Patients were invited to participate when they received an admission diagnosis of schizophrenia uncomplicated by alcoholism or organic syndrome. Those who had received ECT within the previous four months were not approached. Although patients were invited to participate on the basis of initial diagnosis and were interviewed shortly thereafter, their performance was not analyzed until they had received a discharge diagnosis of schizophrenia arrived at by consensus of the senior psychiatrist and other members of the treatment team. All patients thus diagnosed also met the criteria for a schizophrenic diagnosis of the New Haven Schizophrenic Index (Astrachan, Harrow, Adler, Brauer, Schwartz, Schwartz, & Tucker, 1972).

2. Subdividing the Patients. The patients selected for the study were divided into two groups on the basis of clinical assessments of their videotaped interviews. Two senior psychiatrists (MS and AB) separately viewed unstructured interviews and indicated whether the patients showed clear signs of "thought-process disorder." Since the clinicians were not familiar with the cases, their assessments were based entirely on the videotapes.

They used Cancro's (1969) Index of Formal Signs of Thought Disorder to guide their ratings. This involves a four point scale, as follows:

0   No characteristic thought process disorder
1   Mild thought disorder (e.g., circumstantiality, literalness, concreteness)
2   Moderate thought disorder (e.g., loosening of associations, punning, autistic intrusions)
3   Severe thought disorder (e.g., perseverations, echolalia, extensive blocking, neologisms, incoherence)

A total of 71 videotaped interviews were examined. Of these, the clinical judges agreed that 20 showed no clear signs of thought disorder, and 20 showed clear signs. Summing the judges' ratings, we found that the median and modal values for the latter subjects were both 4, and no one judged thought-disordered received a rating of less than 3.

Cancro's Index and the judges' comments suggested that "thought-process disorder" represented an evaluation of the patients' use of language. The judges commented that they were evaluating the process and not the content of the discourse. And indeed, even speakers who talked extendedly about "somebody depressing me with ESP . . . [who] reads my thoughts . . . and makes me shake" or about "this rug [which is] . . . sort of vibrating now" received ratings of 0 on the thought disorder index from both judges. To be "thought-disordered," the judges said a speaker must show some aberration in the flow or coherence of the talk. An aberration in the content or topic was, in itself, insufficient basis for an assessment of thought disorder.

In these comments, our judges were supported by an extensive clinical literature, founded on the observations of Bleuler (1950) and extended by Cameron (1938a, b, 1944), Payne (e.g., 1962, 1968, 1971), and others. However, we were anxious to establish a less inferential designation than the term "thought-process disorder," since this label seemed to be answering the question of causality before it was properly asked. Toward this end, we turned the question around a bit and asked what task the *listener* faces when confronting a so-called thought-process-disordered patient. We (Rochester, Martin, & Thurston, 1977) gave 10 lay judges samples from the interviews of the original subject pool (from 20 normal subjects, from the 20 schizophrenic subjects who had been assessed as thought-disordered, and from the 20 who were nonthought-disordered according to our clinical judges).

The lay judges were grade school teachers and undergraduate students of English. They were told only that they were to serve as editors for transcripts from interviews. They were asked to read over the interviews twice and then check any segments that seemed to disrupt the flow of the talk. They were told not to be too concerned with word or phrase repetitions, with false starts or with occasional grammatical errors, since these events are natural in spontaneous speech. Instead, they were to mark only those segments in which they had difficulty in following the discourse, in which the flow of talk seemed disrupted. Our analyses indicate that the lay person's evaluation of incoherence corresponds to the clinician's assessment of "thought-process disorder." It was possible to make an optimal decision rule on the basis of lay judges' responses, as follows:

> Where 7% or more of speaker's sentence units[2] are considered disruptive by lay judges, the speaker will be diagnosed as thought-process-disordered. Where fewer units are disrupted, the speaker will not be so diagnosed.

This rule yielded a correct identification (hit) rate of 75% for subjects evaluated as thought-disordered and a false identification rate of 5% for other schizophrenic subjects and 0% for normal subjects. Thus, the lay person's assessment of incoherence in discourse seems to distinguish approximately the same sample of speakers as the clinician's diagnosis of thought-process disorder.

---

[2]These approximately correspond to independent clauses in the surface syntax. The boundaries of sentence units and independent clauses coincide in about 85% of independent clauses. In our later work on cohesion, these units were abandoned in favor of independent clauses (cf. Section B.2).

The first line of Table 6 summarizes the lay judges' evaluations for the groups of (n = 10) speakers used in the present analyses. Most TD speakers, as already mentioned, had at least 7% of their sentence units rated disruptive. The mean for the TD group used in the present analyses was 10.4% disrupted units, and two speakers received relatively low ratings of 6% and 2%. The latter speaker proved to be unlike the other subjects in this group and is described further in Chapter 6, footnote 9.

Nine of the ten NTD speakers studied here had no more than 5% of their sentence units rated disruptive; the tenth had 8% of her units judged disruptive. The mean for this group was 5.5%. None of the normal subjects had more than 5% of their units considered disruptive. The mean for this group was 0.4%.

3. Other Patient Characteristics. The patients in groups TD and NTD did not differ reliably on any of the measures of hospitalization, medication treatment, age, verbal IQ, or education reported in Table 6 (and given in detail in Appendices 1 and 2). All were relatively young schizophrenics with a mean age of about 25 years. Their average number

Table 6. Subject Characteristics (n = 10 per group)

		TD	NTD	N
Incoherence	$\bar{X}$	10.4	5.5	0.4
(percentage disrupted units) [a]	Range	2–17	0–8	0–5
Age	$\bar{X}$	23.3	25.8	31.0
	SD	(6.3)	(8.0)	(13.4)
Vocabulary score	$\bar{X}$	28.8	31.6	32.8
(Shipley-Hartford Scale)	SD	(5.0)	(6.3)	(3.0)
Education (in years)	$\bar{X}$	12.6	12.5	14.3
	SD	(2.7)	(2.8)	(2.5)
Number of prior	$\bar{X}$	1.6	1.3	
hospitalizations	SD	(0.6)	(1.3)	
Months hospitalized[b]	$\bar{X}$	2.7	1.8	
	SD	(1.2)	(1.1)	
Medication[c]	$\bar{X}$	864	778	
	SD	(957.5)	(537.8)	
Weeks on	$\bar{X}$	2.6	3.5	
medication[c]	SD	(2.4)	(2.5)	

[a] From interview samples.
[b] Including present stay.
[c] At the time of testing.

of previous hospitalizations was 1.4, and their mean length of stay (including the present hospitalization) was about 2.2 months. All but one were receiving phenothiazine medication, with a mean chlorpromazine equivalent (Hollister, 1970) of 821 mg/day. About 80% had been receiving medication for no more than three weeks.

4. All Subjects. All subjects, normal volunteers and patients, were either native speakers of Canadian English or had come to Canada by the age of 12. The normal volunteers were solicited through newspaper advertisement asking for persons to participate in interviews. Those selected for the study said that they had never been seen for regular psychological treatment and had never been hospitalized for such treatment. They also said that they were not taking hallucinogenic drugs. They were paid a small fee for their participation ($2.50 per hour), as were the patient subjects. Probably because the fee was small, only those who lived in the catchment area of the hospital applied. Consequently, both normal and patient volunteers came from the same downtown section of the large Canadian city where the study was conducted.

Over all subjects, the mean age was 26.7 years, ranging from 18 to 48 years, and the mean educational level was 13.3 years, ranging from 8 to 18 years. There were 4 females and 6 males in each group. Over half the subjects were single, and only three were engaged in full-time employment outside the home. This is probably what one would expect from so young a sample. There were no reliable differences using chi square analyses among the three groups on these measures.

Because our subjects were so young and so irregularly employed, we estimated their social class status according to the socioeconomic index values of their father's or mother's occupation, whichever was higher. Using a Canadian scale for "relative prestige rankings" (Blishen, Jones, Naegele, & Porter, 1968), we again found no reliable differences among the three subject groups. However, there was only one TD subject in the social class ranks above 50 (which include the professions and some skilled occupations), but three NTD and five normal subjects received the high rankings.

B. Speech Contexts

Each subject participated in three speech situations: (1) an unstructured interview of about a half-hour in duration; (2) a brief narrative, which was read to the subject at the end of the interview and retold in the subject's own words; and (3) a cartoon task adopted from Goldman-Eisler (1968) in which the subject described and interpreted ten cartoon pictures.

Discourse was recorded through Uher M822 low-impedance lavelier microphones input to a Uher Royal Delux Stereophonic tape recorder at 7.5 ips.

1. The Interview. In the interview, subject and interviewer (SR or ST) sat facing each other, and the subject was asked to choose the topics from anything he or she found interesting. If necessary, the interviewer suggested topics (e.g., what you've been doing in the past two years; a trip you'd like to take; things which made you happy or sad). In general, the interviewers tried not to speak for extended periods and not to interrupt the subjects. Rather, they attempted to facilitate the subjects' discourse by nodding and murmuring "mmhmm" and asking brief questions such as, "What was that like?" "Did you have fun?" "Were you scared?" or "I know what you mean." In the final 5 or 10 min of the interviews subjects were usually asked to explain a proverb that they found familiar. The interview was videotaped for patients but not for normal subjects. This is not ideal but funds were not available to tape everyone.

From the approximately half-hour interview, 3-min samples of uninterrupted speech were taken. For TD speakers, these samples were taken from the portions in which our clinical judges found evidence of thought-process disorder. Such selection was essential since only portions of the discourse were considered to provide such evidence. There was no comparable selection to be done in the interviews of the other speakers, so we took "informal" selections which involved slang, laughter, and/or increased tempo (see Labov, 1973).

The selection of speech samples in this context deserves comment, because it will affect our interpretation of the data in several respects. First, the sampling in interviews was not done at random, so one cannot assume that each speaker's interview data represent a fair estimate of his or her speech in interviews. This is a necessary restriction because the disruptive segments occur only infrequently in the texts. However, this restriction means that one cannot properly make inferences from an analysis of variance model under the assumption that each sample contributes to an unbiased population estimate. We therefore restrict our use of analysis of variance to simple descriptions of the data and do not intend them as bases for inference about full interview texts.

Second, since the samples of TD speech were particularly selected to include instances of clinical thought disorder, it would be surprising indeed if these samples do not differ from those of NTD and normal speakers. Our concern is not to demonstrate a difference, however, but to determine how such differences in language may be described. This is a very elementary goal, but we are at a very elementary stage in our study of schizophrenia.

Finally, our selection of thought-disordered samples in interviews makes the interview context rather special. In the narrative and cartoon contexts, there was no effort to make such selections. Therefore, of the three contexts, the interview should reveal TD speakers at their worst since interview samples were selected for this purpose. If the interview is *not* the most sensitive context for identifying TD speakers—and as we shall see, it is not—then we must conclude that the sensitivity of the other contexts is impressive indeed. With no selection at all, narrative and cartoon contexts prove more discriminating than the carefully chosen interview contexts.

2. The Cartoon Task and the Narrative. These contexts allow us to determine what is the best a speaker can do within the framework of a well-defined discourse task. They differ from the interview texts because here, if speakers completely left the frame of the task, the experimenter brought them back to the task, and the extraneous comments were not included in the analyses. In the cartoon task, this meant that four TD speakers had 5–20 clauses edited from their transcripts, and one normal speaker had a single clause deleted. In narratives, three TD speakers, one NTD speaker, and two normal speakers had 1–2 clauses deleted from their transcripts.

a. The Cartoon Task. All subjects were shown a set of 10 cartoons that had been chosen in three steps. First, 35 cartoons were selected. Each contained no more than one word, required only general knowledge for its interpretation, and contained no more than five panels. Then three judges (volunteers solicited through newspaper advertisements) indicated why the cartoon was supposed to be funny. Unanimous agreement occurred in 26 cartoons. Finally, each judge selected 15 of the remaining cartoons that were most clearly humorous. Ten of these were chosen by all judges and these became the experimental materials. They were redrawn to 7" × 7" size and mounted on a beaverboard.

In the experimental task, subjects were instructed that they would be shown a series of cartoons. For each one, they were to describe the picture(s) as fully as possible (cartoon descriptions) and then explain why the cartoon was supposed to be funny (cartoon interpretations). Two samples were shown. Then the ten test cartoons were presented in a systematically counterbalanced order so that no more than one subject per group received the same sequence of cartoons.

b. *Narrative.* The narrative was taken from Bleuler (1950, p. 84). It was read to each subject at the end of the interview, followed by the request: "Now, will you tell me that story back in your own words?" The original 108 word narrative follows:

> A donkey loaded with bags of salt had to wade across a river. He slipped and fell and remained lying comfortably in the cool water for a few moments. Standing up, he noticed how much lighter his load had become because the salt had dissolved in the water. The donkey noticed this advantage and decided to use it the following day when he was carrying a load of sponges across the same river. This time, he fell deliberately but was badly disappointed. The sponges had soaked up a great deal of water and were far heavier than before. Indeed, the load was so heavy that it drowned him.

The contexts are summarized in Table 7. Here we use the Ellis and Ure (1969) categories for the description of register. Field encompasses the topic or context of a text: what it is about (including the nonverbal action of the participants). Formality refers to social relations between speaker and addressee. Mode includes the channel (i.e., oral or written) as well as the orientation of the language to its immediate situation (i.e.,

Table 7. Summary of Contexts

	Interview	Narrative	Cartoons
Field	Relatively unrestricted (suggestions: sad times; happy times; threat of death)	Donkey fable	Various
Formality	Psychologist/patient and volunteer (+ video for patients)	Psychologist/patient and volunteer (+ video for patients)	Research asst./patient and volunteer (no video)
Mode	Oral: major orientation to nonimmediate situation	Oral: orientation to preceding spoken narrative	Oral: orientation to pictures
Role	Relate past and future experience	Retell story just heard	Describing cartoons and saying why funny

describing something present in the context, relating past experiences, or projecting future events). Role deals with the purpose of the language in question: what it is for as conceived by speaker and listener.

It should be noted that putting volunteers and patients in the same situations does not mean that the contexts in which they speak are identical. Clearly for patients, because they have been hospitalized, both the formality and role of the situation must be given a more general interpretation. The relation of interviewer and patient will be conceived as an instance of the more general relationship: those treating the patient and the patient who is being treated. And similarly the role or purpose will be construed more generally as having something to do with diagnosis and treatment. The same situation can evoke in different subjects different register responses. This must be kept in mind when interpreting our results.

In terms of mode and role, the cartoon task and the narrative have more in common with each other than with the interview. Both have a mode oriented to the immediate situation and a role that sets out a task to be completed. Because of this, we find it useful to refer to the cartoon and narrative contexts in discussion below as *task-based* and the interview context as *talk-based*. And as will be argued in Chapter 5, the task-based contexts, the cartoon and narrative, are more highly structured than the interview context in that the field is sharply delimited. The mode involves an orientation to the immediate or immediately preceding situation, and the role is more narrowly defined.

III. Preliminary Analyses

A. Statistical Procedures

In the analyses presented below and in the following chapters, the standard statistical test was a groups' × contexts' analysis of variance. The error term for groups was based on variations among the 30 subjects in the three groups; the error term across contexts and for the interaction of groups × contexts was the residual of subjects, contexts, and any higher group interaction terms. Values of F which yielded $p < .05$ were considered significant. When effects were significant, Scheffé tests (at $p < .05$) were performed to assess the significance of differences between individual groups and individual contexts. In addition, one-way analyses of variance were performed within contexts to determine whether overall differences between groups were reliable in individual contexts. Unless stated otherwise, all analyses of variance were treated in this manner.

Proportions were the most common measures used in the analyses. Where there was any question of nonnormal distributions, the data were submitted to arc sine transformations and reanalyzed. These procedures were necessary only with the small numbers of observations studied in the general reference analyses of Chapter 5 and the cultural reference analyses of Chapter 6. In no case were the results of the analyses of variance changed by the transformations, so they will not be mentioned again.

In the analysis of variance presented in this monograph, an important summary statistic is $\hat{\omega}^2$: this expresses the effect size—the proportion of the variance accounted for by the effect under study (Winer, 1971, pp. 429–430) and is reported in each of the ANOVA tables. The tables also contain the F values but as a rule these will not be reported in the text.

B. Description of the Samples

The number of words, independent clauses, and words per clause were computed for each of the three speech contexts. Because one of those contexts, the cartoon task, actually had two parts that were a bit different, we present that context in two parts below. Thus data are presented for four speech contexts: cartoon descriptions, cartoon interpretations, narratives, and interviews. Table 8 gives the means for each group in each context for words, for independent clauses and for words per clause, and presents the results of two-way analyses of variance on the three measures.

1. Words. The average speaker used about 391 words to describe the ten cartoons and 247 to interpret them. He or she used about 86 words to retell the original 108 word narrative and about 439 words for the 3-min interview samples. These frequencies did not vary reliably across groups. However, in each of the four contexts there is a trend for NTD speakers to use fewer words than normal speakers. This approaches significance ($p = .08$) for the four contexts and is reliable in the narrative in which NTD use about 61 words and normals use about 116 words, and in the interview in which NTD use 364 and normals use about 476 words.

2. Independent Clauses. The basic unit of analysis was the independent clause. This was defined as a unit which selects for MOOD, i.e.,

Table 8. Description of Texts

	Cartoon description			Cartoon interpretation			Narrative			Interview		
	TD	NTD	N	TD	NTD	N	TD	NTD	N	TD	NTD	N
Words	222	202	316	433	325	413	82.4	60.6	115.7[a]	444	364	476[a]
Independent clauses	26.5	20.6	25.9	47.4	35.4	36.1	9.4	7.2	11.5[a]	50.4	52.0	45.9
Words/independent clauses	8.4	8.7	11.6[b]	9.1	9.0	11.4[b]	9.1	8.2	10.5	8.1	7.8	9.2

ANOVA

	Groups	Contexts	Groups × contexts
df	2,27	3,54	6,54
Words: F	2.84	54.5[d]	<1
$\hat{\omega}^2$		.56	
Independent Clauses: F	3.32[c]	75.08[d]	<1
$\hat{\omega}^2$	.01	.64	
Words/Independent Clauses: F	5.99[c]	5.57[c]	1.21
$\hat{\omega}^2$	.07	.09	

[a] Scheffé tests show NTD < N (p < .05).
[b] Scheffé tests show NTD < N; TD < N (p < .05).
[c] p < .05.
[d] p < .001.

stands by itself as a declarative, interrogative, imperative, or exclamatory structure. Accordingly, relative clauses (e.g., the boy *I saw*), fact or report complements (e.g., John knows *Mary has arrived*), and adverbial clauses (e.g., John came *before Mary left*), were all treated as part of this basic unit. An exception was made for sentence modifiers (e.g., John came *which was nice*). Although these do not select for MOOD, they seem close to a coordinate construction. Thus 1 was analyzed as one basic unit, whereas two units were present in 2 and 3:

1. Sharon saw Harris while he was in Ottawa.
2. Snoopy is a human dog/which makes him a laughable character.
3. A dog arrives on the scene with the usual barrel of rum around its neck/
   but this time it has 25 cents written on it.

Again, there is a modest trend ($p < .05$) for NTD speakers to be less productive than normal speakers, and again this result is reliable in the narrative.

3. Words/Clause. In every context, normal speakers produced longer clauses than schizophrenic speakers. This is a reliable trend that accounts for 7% of the variance in the data and does not depend strongly on the context in which the clause is produced. In task-based contexts (i.e., cartoon descriptions and interpretations and narratives), schizophrenic speakers used about two less words per clause than normal speakers; and in interviews, they used about one less word per clause than normals.

C. Discussion

Preliminary analyses of the speech samples indicate that schizophrenic speakers produce shorter clauses than normal speakers in all four of the contexts examined. These results are interesting in light of some additional analyses of these data which suggest that decisions at clause boundaries distinguish schizophrenic speakers from normal speakers, and TD from NTD subjects.

The additional data come from a study of timing patterns reported by Rochester, Thurston, and Rupp (1977). Those data were taken from the original groups of 20 subjects each and were from only the cartoon contexts and the interview. We found that schizophrenic speakers paused longer than normal speakers at clause boundaries but tended not to differ in their pause durations within clauses. For example, boundary pauses occupied about 16% of TD speaker's cartoon interpretation times, about 12% for NTD, and about 6% for normals. In interviews, all subjects spent more of their total time in pausing. Here, TD used 30%, NTD used 26%, and normals used 14% of their speech time in boundary pauses.

Because the groups differed in their pausing at clause boundaries, but not within clauses, we speculated that the boundary pauses might be related to differences in the coherence of the speakers' productions. There has been some fair support for the notion that clauses serve some significant role as major organizational units in speech processing. In the comprehension of spoken sentences, there seem to be "lulls in processing" at clausal boundaries (e.g., Holmes & Forster, 1970, 1972), and when sentences are to be recalled, they tend to be segmented into clausal units (e.g., Aaronson, Lorinstein, & Shapiro, 1971; Jarvella, 1971; Lackner, 1974). In sentence production, silent pauses and voiced hesitations have been offered as evidence that clauses serve as one kind of organizational base in processing (Grosjean, Grosjean & Lane, 1978; Lindsley, 1975, MacKay, 1970).

If clauses do serve as major organizational units, then the significantly longer pauses produced by schizophrenic speakers at clause boundaries might indicate something of what is occurring in the planning process underlying their productions. We suggested that the particularly long boundary pauses of TD speakers might be evidence that the bonds between their clauses were weak. There was support for this supposition from the literature with normal speakers (e.g., Goldman-Eisler, 1972; Rochester & Gill, 1973). For example, Goldman-Eisler found that clauses with weak structural ties to a main clause are preceded by longer pauses than are clauses with strong ties. She suggests that the longer pauses indicate that the speaker is attempting to form a new "sentence-whole" or thought unit. She argues that fluent transitions occur only "where no new thought has entered the utterance" (p. 111).

Conceivably, the TD speaker's transitions that are signaled by long pauses are also attempts to articulate new ideas, but these new ideas might be difficult to integrate into the previous discourse. There was some support for this notion in the data. We found that, for longer boundary pauses, there was an inverse relation between coherence and boundary pause duration. Clauses were two to three times more likely to be judged low in coherence when they were preceded by long (>5 sec) rather than shorter (<5 sec) pauses. This suggested that the TD speakers' long boundary pauses often preceded clauses that were inadequately linked to the preceding text.

There are many possible accounts of why the TD speaker might be having some processing problems in producing coherent discourse. Maher (1972, p. 13) for example, proposes that language disturbances in schizophrenia are most likely to intrude at "terminal points in an utterance such as commas, full stop or period points." This prediction describes our findings rather well. Terminal points are probably vulnerable, Maher suggests, because they mark the boundaries of coherent attentional or thought units for the speaker. This interpretation seems feasible, but one must still determine the process or processes that are being disrupted. In Rochester, Thurston, and Rupp (1977), we discuss several possibilities, but all are rather speculative. Therefore, let us simply note that the TD speaker's discourse failures are conceivably a reflection of processing problems in linking new clauses to the existing text.

In our earlier paper we did not deal with the fact that NTD speakers also produce long pauses at clause boundaries—though they do not pause so long as TD speakers. Our problem there, and we face it again here, was to decide whether longer pausing by the two groups of schizophrenic subjects was a result of their phenothiazine medication or their condition, or some other factors related to their hospital stay. We could only state that both groups of schizophrenic speakers paused longer at clause boundaries than normal speakers.

A study by Feldstein and Jaffe (1963) suggests that it may be possible to eliminate phenothiozines as an explanation for the difference in boundary pauses between normal and schizophrenic speakers. In a replication of earlier research with medicated schizophrenic patients, Feldstein and Jaffe examined a new group of schizophrenic patients who were deprived of phenothiazines. The rates of voiced pauses ("ah", "er" and "uhm") and speech disturbances (e.g., word repetitions, stutters, false starts) did not differ in the two studies, and the authors concluded that speech fluency is not markedly affected by phenothiazines. This may be generalizable to silent pauses but should probably be tested directly since there may be some important differences underlying the production of voiced and silent pauses (cf., Rochester, 1973; Siegman, in press).

Although we cannot state with any certainty why NTD and TD speakers produce longer boundary pauses than normal speakers, the present results allow us to add one bit of information to the earlier finding: namely, both groups of schizophrenic speakers produce shorter clauses than normals in all contexts. So there is a coincidence of longer boundary pauses and shorter clauses in the discourse of schizophrenic speakers as compared to normal speakers.

It seems possible to rule out some possible explanations of this coincidence. First, it is unlikely that these results are due to a lesser verbal ability of the schizophrenic subjects. Table 6 indicates that the groups are not different on the vocabulary scale of the Shipley-Hartford, a test that appears to be insensitive to short-term changes in state and is supposed to reflect the more enduring competence of the speakers (cf., Chapman & Chapman, 1973, pp. 166–168).

A second possibility is that the schizophrenic subjects are somehow less able to "take advantage" of the organization afforded by the syntax of the language and therefore pause more and produce less adequate discourse than normal speakers. This notion does not actually explain how "syntax" could serve as a basis for organization, but it is conceivable that short-term memory for word strings could be reduced if the speaker's use of syntactic distinctions were reduced. This would contradict the findings by Gerver (1967), Truscott (1970), and others showing that schizophrenics are able to make syntactic distinctions to the same extent as normals. However, as we mentioned earlier, those studies were performed with listeners, and they may not be directly relevant to speakers.

A third possibility is that there is some problem with working memory in all the schizophrenic subjects. This need not be due to schizophrenia, of course, but may be a reflection of the early side effects of their phenothiazine medication. It may also be, as Koh (1978) proposes, that all schizophrenic subjects have difficulty in organizing materials they wish to remember. Koh has shown that although young schizophrenic subjects tend not to organize spontaneously, they are capable of verbal organization when the proper aids are provided. Problems in organizing verbal memory, as Koh proposes, or in attending to the task of production, as Maher (1972) suggests, could account for the schizophrenic speakers' use of short clauses and long boundary pauses.

Each of the three explanations considered above assumes that some sort of schizophrenic impairment exists in language-based processing. There is suggestive evidence for this but no direct support from the pause data. We do not know that it is only in language-based operations that the patients were slower to respond. It is possible that their motor responses were retarded and, hence, their reaction time to any stimulus was rather long. This could account for the NTD and TD subjects' equally long latencies in giving any response at all to the cartoon pictures (cf. Table 9 in Rochester, Thurston, & Rupp, 1977). In addition, there may have been a language-based factor that affected TD speakers significantly more strongly than NTD speakers, so that TD speakers produced reliably longer boundary pauses than NTD subjects.

Finally, we should note that the fact that schizophrenic speakers produce a combination of shorter clauses and longer silences than normal subjects[3] is consistent with the observation that there is a negative correlation between pause and vocalization duration (Anderson, 1975; Jaffe & Feldstein, 1970). As speakers talk for longer periods, they apparently pause less; and as they talk for shorter periods, they pause more. This within-subject phenomenon has led Jaffe (1977) to offer a "temporal compensation" explanation, suggesting that there are rhythmic cycles of communication events which may serve a biological purpose. Other writers have interpreted the negative correlations as evidence that longer pauses are prerequisites for more productive or coherent utterances (e.g., Butterworth, 1975; Henderson, 1974). However, we cannot state at this time whether the pause data *between* schizophrenic and normal subjects suggest a "temporal compensation" account. Moreover, as we mention above, it seems that for schizophrenic subjects the negative correlations between pause duration and coherence do not hold. Instead, long pauses are more likely to be followed by incoherent stretches than are short pauses, which again suggests that the production processes underlying discourse in schizophrenics may be somehow different from those of normal speakers.

[3]Since schizophrenic speakers seem to "balance" their vocalization plus silence periods— by speaking less and pausing more than normals—it seems that their speech rate should be markedly lower than that of normals. However, this is not uniformly the case. In the Rochester, Thurston, and Rupp cartoon descriptions and interpretations, all groups of speakers produced about the same number of words per min (about 173 and 202, respectively). However, in interviews, TD speakers have a significantly lower speaker rate than NTD speakers (132 versus 156 words per min, respectively), and the NTD speakers are significantly slower than normal subjects (174 words per min, with 3 groups, 20 subjects per group, the univariate F ratio is 5.39, $p<.01$). These results from our earlier study indicate that in structured contexts, schizophrenic speakers do not speak more slowly overall than normal speakers, but that in the unstructured context of the interview, they do.

3

Cohesion

In schizophrenia . . . thinking operates with ideas and concepts which have
no, or a completely insufficient connection with the main idea . . . sometimes,
all the associative threads fail and . . . ideas may emerge which have no recognizable connection with the preceding ones. (Bleuler, 1950, p. 22)

I. Introduction

ΓA failure to form "texts"—to produce stretches of language that seem
coherent to the listener—has long been regarded as an essential characteristic of the schizophrenic speaker.ĮAs we discussed in Chapter 1, these
discourse failures do not occur in all patients diagnosed as schizophrenic,
but they are an identifying feature in those who are considered "thought-
disordered." In such cases, as Bleuler observes in the above quote, "ideas
may emerge which have no recognizable connection with the preceding
ones."

In the present chapter, we begin the task of trying to describe these
discourse failures. But to describe failures, as we argued earlier, it is necessary to describe behavior generally and systematically. So it is necessary to use a principled description that captures at least some of the features of discourse that are responsible for its coherence. The description
adopted here is taken from the comprehensive linguistic framework provided by Michael Halliday and Ruqaiya Hasan (1976) for analyzing texts.
A text is a stretch of language that functions as a unity with respect to its
environment. Halliday and Hasan begin with this notion of a text as a
unified piece of discourse and develop an approach for understanding
how a text comes to cohere: to have texture. If every text were only one
sentence long, they argue, one would not need to go beyond the constit-
uent structure of the sentence to explain its internal cohesiveness. But

texts typically extend beyond the range of sentential structural relations. So cohesion within a text must depend on something other than the internal structure of clauses or sentences. It must depend on the properties of the text as such.

The concept of *cohesion* is used to refer to the semantic relations within a text that make it a unit. Cohesion is said to occur where the interpretation of some element in the discourse is dependent on another element. The one presumes the other, in the sense that the one cannot be effectively understood except by recourse to the other. For example, in

(1)   There was a donkey about to cross a river.
      It was loaded with bags of salt.[1]

it is clear that it in the second sentence refers back to a donkey in the first sentence. The referential relation between the two elements gives cohesion to the two sentences so that we interpret them as part of the same text.

Texture is provided not by the elements themselves but by the cohesive relations that exist between them. The cohesion would not be effected by the presence of the referring item, it, alone. To give a sense of unity to the two sentences, both the referring item and its referent must be present. As another example of a different sort of meaning relation which contributes to texture, consider:

(2)   Did I hurt your feelings?
      —I didn't mean to.*

Here, the second sentence coheres by virtue of the missing elements—I didn't mean to (hurt your feelings)—but, again, the *pair* of elements is needed to effect a bond.

To refer to a single instance of cohesion, which is the occurrence of a pair of cohesively related items, Halliday and Hasan use the term *tie*. Thus, the relation in (1) demonstrates one type of cohesive tie, and that in (2) demonstrates another. Any segment of a text can be characterized in terms of the number and kinds of ties it displays. The various kinds of ties are described below and are given in greater detail in Halliday and Hasan (1976, Chs. 2–5).

A. The Place of Cohesion in Halliday's Linguistic System

Halliday and Hasan define the concept of cohesion as a semantic relation, because it refers to meaning relations that exist within a text.

[1]This is a constructed example. Except where noted throughout by (*), all examples have been selected from the corpus.

The notion of semantic relation is much broader in Halliday's system than in standard transformational theory, so it may be useful to outline briefly how the language system is portrayed in Halliday's model (for a fuller account of the theory, see Halliday 1967a, b, 1970, 1973, 1977, 1978).

First, cohesion is seen as part of the system of a language. The potential for a stretch of spoken or written text to be cohesive is said to be built into the language itself. But its actualization in any given instance depends on two factors: selection of some option provided by the resources, and the presence of some other element that resolves a presupposition which this selection sets up. For example, as we shall see below, selection of the word *chair* or even *it* has no cohesive force (its potential is not actualized) unless there is some referent for the word available in the nearby context.

Next, since cohesion is part of the system of language, it is expressed through what Halliday sees as the strata organization of language. He describes language as a multiple system involving three levels of coding, or "strata": the semantic (meanings), the lexicogrammatical (forms), and the phonological and orthographic (expressions). Meanings are said to be coded ("realized") as forms, and forms are recoded as expressions. Or, in more popular terms, meanings are put into wording, and wording is put into sound or writing.

It is worth emphasizing that within the stratum of "wording" or lexicogrammatical form, there is no clear-cut distinction between vocabulary and grammar. More general meanings are expressed through the grammar, and more specific ones through the vocabulary. Cohesive ties can be fit into this pattern so that some are "grammatical" and some are "lexical." But this does not imply that there are only formal relations involved in such ties. Cohesion is seen as a semantic relation that is coded *through* forms, and the forms may be lexical or grammatical.

Finally, it is useful to locate cohesion in Halliday's linguistic system. The semantic level of language is said to have three major components: the ideational, the interpersonal, and the textual. The ideational component is concerned with the expression of "content," with the function that language has in being "about" something. The interpersonal component is concerned with expressing the speaker's role as an interactor with his addressee, questioning, commanding, etc. And the textual component comprises the resources that language has for creating text. In part, the textual component operates through hierarchical systems associated with particular ranks in the grammar (e.g., morpheme, word, group, clause). But it also incorporates patterns of meaning that are coded outside the hierarchical system. One way this is done is through cohesion. This leads us to a final definition for cohesion in terms of an overview of Halliday's model: Cohesion is part of the text-forming component in the linguistic system. It is "the means whereby elements that are structurally unrelated to one another are linked together" (Halliday & Hasan, 1976, p. 27). The linkage occurs through a semantic relation— through the dependence of one element on the other for its interpretation.

B. Categories of Cohesive Ties

The five types of cohesive ties are: reference, substitution, ellipsis, conjunction, and lexical cohesion, which are described below and examples are given in Table 9.

Reference is a semantic relation whereby information needed for the interpretation of some item is found elsewhere in the text. Only information given within the explicit verbal context (endophoric reference) is considered to be cohesive in this chapter. Pronominals, demonstratives and the definite article, and comparatives are the main exponents of this type of cohesion. In saying "John went down and later he returned home,"* "he" refers back to "John" in the previous clause. This relation between "he" and its presumed item constitutes one cohesive tie. In the data reported here, cohesion is analyzed between independent clauses. The clauses need not be adjacent. Cohesive relations *within* such clauses are not considered, since within a clause, structural as opposed to nonstructural unity is dominant.

Substitution consists in replacing a nominal, verbal, or clausal unit with substitutes (normally "one," "do," and "so," respectively). In saying, "John bought a new bicycle and I got a used one,"* "one" presumes "bicycle" and constitutes a cohesive tie. *Ellipsis* can be thought of as substitution by zero. In "I was born in New Brunswick. Were you?"* the second clause presumes "born in New Brunswick" from the first.

Conjunction expresses a logical relation between clauses. For example, in "John was tired so he went to bed,"* The conjunction "so" connects the two clauses as cause and effect.

Lexical cohesion involves the repetition of one item formed on the same root, relations between synonyms or near synonyms, and between hyponyms and their superordinate. For example, in "John loves dogs. He owns a collie,* "collie" and "dogs" are lexically tied as "collies" are a kind of dog. Because we were concerned with establishing coding reli-

Table 9. Categories of Cohesion[a]

Category	Subcategory	Examples[b]
Reference	1. Pronominal:	We met Joy Adamson and had dinner with her in Nairobi.
	2. Demonstrative:	We went to a hostel and oh that was a dreadful place.
	3. Comparative:	Six guys approach me. The last guy pulled a knife on me in the park.
Substition	1. Nominal:	The oldest girl is 25 and the next one's 22.
	2. Verbal:	Eastern people take it seriously, at least some of them do.
	3. Clausal:	I'm making it worse for myself. I would think so.
Ellipsis	1. Nominal:	He's got energy too. He's got a lot more ∅ than I do.
	2. Verbal:	I could go to university all my life, ∅ keep going to school.
	3. Clausal:	Have you ever been to Israel?—No, my brother has ∅.*
Conjunction	1. Additive:	I read a book in the past few days and I like it.
	2. Adversative:	They started out to England but got captured on the way.
	3. Causal:	It was a beautiful tree so I left it alone.
	4. Temporal:	My mother was in Ireland. Then she came over here.
	5. Continuative:	What kind of degree?—Well, in one of the professions.
Lexical	1. Same root:	Mother needed independence. She was always dependent on my father.
	2. Synonym	I got angry at M. but I don't often get mad.*
	3. Superordinate:	I love catching fish. I caught a bass last time.
	4. General item:	The plane hit some air pockets and the bloody thing went up and down.

[a]Adapted from Halliday and Hasan (1976).
[b]Presuming item has solid underline; the referent has broken underlines.
*Constructed example.

ability, Halliday and Hasan's lexical category of collocation was not examined here.

C. The Advantages of Cohesion Analysis

The concept of a cohesive tie makes it possible to use cohesion analysis for many different sorts of texts. In particular, in the present study, we are able to analyze interviews and narratives. The texts produced from these two situations can be analyzed in terms of their cohesive properties, and the results of the analyses compared across groups and contexts.

The flexibility of cohesion analysis across contexts is one of its most attractive features. It means that one is able to consider a broad range of behaviors for schizophrenic speakers and to give a systematic account of these behaviors in terms of the patterns of texture which the speakers create. It is unusual to find an approach with such scope. At present, there are very few analytic procedures for studying discourse production. Most (e.g., Collins, Brown, & Larkin, 1978; Thorndyke, 1976; Frederiksen, 1975) study comprehension and/or recall of texts by readers or listeners, so that one needs only measure deviations from a carefully defined text. Of the few procedures available for the study of speakers, virtually all rely on the narrative (e.g., Labov & Waletsky, 1967; Poulsen, Kintsch, Kintsch, & Premack, 1978) or on highly defined event sequences (e.g., Charniak, 1975, Minsky, 1975).

It is important to be able to describe the discourse characteristics of schizophrenic speakers across a variety of situations. There are two reasons for this. One is because this is an exploratory study. Very little systematic information is available about the schizophrenic speaker's discourse, so it is useful to sample from some range of behaviors in the initial stages of description. The second, more compelling reason is theoretical. The speaker's construction of texts happens in a context, and for the text to be coherent, it must be situationally relevant as well as internally cohesive. The situation (the extratextual features associated with discourse production) is a part of the production itself. It specifies the options that are available to the speaker at a particular time. As Halliday (1977) observes, one must ask what meanings the hearer will expect to be offered in a particular class of social contexts. The meanings in any given text "do not present themselves out of the blue," but the hearer has "a very good idea of what is coming." And "what is coming" is normally determined by the features of the situation in which the text is produced (cf. Firth, 1951).

Several workers have recently emphasized the importance of the use of language in context. For example, Bates (1977, p. 11) argues that every act involved in the construction of meaning is governed by the use of language in context: "The act of reference, the selection of lexical items to stand for referents, . . . and the combination of acts of reference into

. . . the proposition—all are contextually based uses of language." And several studies of language development indicate that children's early meanings are not entities which the child "acquires," but rather are developed from actions carried out in a particular context (e.g., Antinucci & Parisi, 1973; Greenfield & Smith, 1976; Halliday, 1977, 1978; Ingram, 1971).

In the particular situations we have presented, one might expect a variety of textual patterns. For example, narratives are usually "self-contextualizing," ideally providing within themselves most of the information needed for the listener's understanding (Halliday, 1977). Consequently, one would expect to find extensive cohesive ties in narratives. In the interview, one would expect much less within-text cohesion and a greater dependence on the situational context. There are several reasons for this. In the interview, the topic may shift more rapidly than in the narrative where the topic is fixed. Also, people tend to talk about themselves, so the main character in their interviews will probably be themselves. This will mean more exophoric references (as "I" and "we") and fewer endophoric references (as "he" or "they"). Furthermore, in interviews, the listener often has a part to play and would be referred to—again noncohesively—as "you."

How will schizophrenic speakers diverge from these patterns, and how should these differences be revealed by cohesion analyses? We must be conservative in our predictions because we can only guess at the patterns we would expect to see in normal speakers. Thus far, although there have been studies of literary texts (Gutwinski, 1976; Halliday, 1977) and of groups of children (e.g., Fine, 1977; Francis, 1975; Hawkins, 1973; Martin, 1978), there have been no studies of groups of adult speakers. Therefore, our predictions of schizophrenic patients cannot be put into formal hypotheses but only into hunches.

1. **Variation within a Context.** (a) Schizophrenic speakers seem often to refer to the immediate situation rather than to abstract aspects of the situation (e.g., Goldstein, 1939, 1944; Vigotsky, 1934, 1962). So we may expect them to depend less on cohesive ties within the text and more on ties to the situation. This should result in fewer ties for schizophrenic than for normal speakers.

(b) Thought-disordered speakers have been described as "vague, wooly, and tangential" in their discourse. This could reflect TD speakers' failure to link their clauses to their prior discourse. If so, then TD speakers should use fewer cohesive ties over all categories than other speakers.

(c) In addition, TD speakers may depend very strongly on some forms of cohesion and less strongly on others. If these patterns are regular and differ reliably from the patterns used by other speakers, this could be a clue to patterns that are problematic for the listener.

(d) In particular, we may expect that TD speakers, and perhaps also NTD speakers, will depend extensively on lexical cohesion. This would be indicated by the numerous reports that schizophrenic speakers are repetitive, using less variety in their productions than normal subjects (Fairbanks, 1944; Mann, 1944; Whitehorn & Zipf, 1943). TD speakers might depend more strongly on lexical cohesion than NTD subjects, since there is evidence that in written productions "thought-disordered" patients use fewer different words than other schizophrenic patients (Maher *et al.*, 1966). Morever, there is some evidence to suggest that lexical ties are less useful to the listener than referential ties (Lesgold, 1972). If some or all schizophrenic speakers rely on lexical cohesion more than other speakers, we may be able to infer that this pattern is disadvantageous to the listener.

We shall have to be cautious in these inferences. It is possible for writers to use different patterns of cohesion resulting in very different styles of discourse (cf. Gutwinski's 1976 analysis of Hemingway and Henry James), and yet still be perfectly intelligible to their readers. So it is too with schizophrenic and normal speakers, or with TD versus NTD speakers. Simply to find a difference between groups of speakers will not tell us that the difference is of any consequence to the listener.

This is true when the groups of speakers are TD and NTD schizophrenic patients, and it is true when they are working class and middle class adults, or younger and older children (cf. Rochester, 1978a). Where patterns of cohesive ties differ across groups, we must examine the texts to see what details the patterns are indicating. Then, if the differences seem important, we can estimate their effects on listeners by statistical techniques for predicting listeners' responses from measures of the speakers' behavior (e.g., Maher *et al.*, 1966; Rochester, Martin, & Thurston, 1977). At best, these will provide us with suggestive evidence of the relation between cohesive ties of the speaker and the listener's or reader's evaluations of coherence. To establish the relation between cohesion and coherence, we shall need experimental studies of listeners.

2. Variation across Contexts. The situational context, we have argued, presents important options to the speaker at each point in time. But these situational features are not divorced from the broader context of the culture and the social system in which the participants are acting. The culture does not dictate what will be said in a particular situation, but as Frake (1977) observes, it provides principles for framing experiences.

Within the cultural principles and the frames provided by social situations, there is an acceptable kind of talk. This is described by the generic framework that exists in different contexts. The use of an appropriate generic framework seems to be a social accomplishment. For example, in more structured contexts in which there is a task to do, one expects from the speaker more planning, more explicit signals of beginning and ending, and more elaborate procedures such as speaking in a more elevated style. In informal contexts, in which the talk itself is the "task," one does not expect elaborate planning and explicit presentation.

If variation across genres is a normal social accomplishment, then we would expect that normal speakers' cohesion might vary across contexts. We have indicated some of our expectations above. There are two interesting questions with regard to schizophrenic speakers in this connection. First, will schizophrenic subjects be able to recognize the social constraints of the different situations and use different patterns of cohesion as normal speakers do? And second, will both TD and NTD schizophrenic speakers differ in their sensitivity to social constraints?

Bleuler (1950) suggests that schizophrenic patients have great difficulty adhering to a frame of reference. He notes that the individual schizophrenic symptoms of peculiar associations and incomplete concepts are considerably less important than the relation of those symptoms to the psychological setting. His comments indicate that schizophrenic patients, or at least TD utterances, should be relatively insensitive to the social contexts. Therefore, we may expect to find the normal pattern of cohesion across contexts in some way changed in schizophrenic, or at least in TD, utterances. In detail, we expect that the total number of cohesive ties used by normal speakers will vary across contexts. The difference in amount of cohesion between contexts may not be seen in schizophrenic speakers. Also, for each of the five categories of cohesive ties, we expect some variation across contexts, though it is not clear what this will be. However, assuming that there are some reliable differences in normal speakers' dependence on each cohesive category, we may again expect little variation in the schizophrenic speaker's behavior.

On the other hand, if schizophrenic speakers show the same patterns of response across contexts as normal speakers do, we shall have no basis for inferring that they are insensitive to the social context. Indeed, there will be some persuasive evidence that in these young patients the ability to capture certain essential demands of the social context is intact.

D. The Disadvantages of Cohesion Analysis

Cohesion analyses are not entirely suitable for the purposes intended here. First, they are developed to analyze individual texts, and it is not clear which variables will be most significant in differentiating groups of speakers or the contexts in which they speak. Second, since no groups of adults have been studied, we do not know whether some kinds of cohesive ties are more useful to the listener, or are more likely to prompt evaluations of unity in a discourse, than are others. This is an interesting question, but the lack of research thus far means that we will be on rather weak grounds in attempting to infer what consequences speaker differences will have for listeners' experiences of the texts. Third, it has been assumed that cohesive ties account for coherence in texts. For example, Halliday and Hasan state that cohesion is responsible for establishing continuity in a text, and that continuity is a primary factor in the "intelligibility" of discourse. We do not know the extent to which this assumption is correct. However, the application of cohesion analyses to texts that are coherent *and* incoherent presents a test of the assumption. And finally, although the cohesion analysis is based on a comprehensive sociolinguistic framework, it offers no model of the psychological processes underlying the speaker's production.[2] This also is a disadvantage for us.

For each of these limitations, we have tried to develop a response. For the lack of summary procedures, we have developed various measures of cohesion in order to find those that are most sensitive to differences across contexts and groups of speakers. Because cohesion analyses have not been studied in adults before, we examine the results in some detail, looking at data for individual speakers as well as for groups. Next, we discuss the assumptions underlying cohesion analyses and coherence, at the end of this chapter, and present some different analyses in Chapters 4 to 6 that are based on our conclusions. And finally, in Chapter 7, we offer some proposals for a psychological model of the speaker, based on inferences from cohesion analyses and the later studies.

II. Cohesion Procedure

A. Data Base

Two contexts provided samples for cohesion analyses. From interviews, two sections of about 15 independent clauses each were coded for

---

[2]However, see Winograd (1972) who uses systemic grammar in his work on artificial intelligence, and also Fawcett (1972a,b) for discussion of the place of systemic grammar in a cognitive model of communication.

every speaker. This constituted about 900 clauses for the 30 speakers. From narratives, the full texts were coded, constituting a total of about 300 clauses. Thus, there were about 1,200 clauses coded from the two contexts. The average clause contained about 2.6 cohesive links to other clauses, giving an overall data base for the present analyses of about 3,100 observations.

B. Coding Cohesion

For each speaker in each context, every independent clause was scanned for possible links to items in previous clauses. Where a link was found, the item was coded in one of the five cohesion categories (reference, conjunction, lexical cohesion, ellipsis, and substitution). For all categories but conjunction, the presumed item[3] was noted. For example, in

(3)   (a) the best part is hopping these freight trains.
        (b) you come running up on the side of them and all that

coders would note them as the single cohesive element in (b), code it as *referential cohesion,* and record these freight trains as the linking presumed item.

C. Reliability of Coding Cohesion

Texts coded for cohesion require three kinds of decisions. The coders must (a) select items that presume other items in the text; (b) specify precisely which textual item is being presumed; and (c) identify the relationship that exists between the items in terms of one of the five cohesion categories.

One coder, JM, analyzed typescripts of the speech samples while listening to the samples on a taperecorder (described in Chapter 2). A second coder, HP, separately analyzed typescripts while listening to samples selected at random from 9 subjects, 3 per group. This was done in narratives and interviews for the three kinds of decisions described above.

In selecting cohesive items, coders agreed on a mean 96% of the items in both contexts; the range for interviews was 95–100% and for narratives was 87–100%. To correct for chance agreement in these measures, we calculated kappa values (cf. Cohen, 1960; Winer, 1971). Kappa

[3]Strictly speaking, conjunction and lexical cohesion do not involve "presumption." See Martin (1978) for discussion. Also note that since conjunction relates pairs of clauses, it is a moot point to argue which clause is presumed.

is negative where agreement is poorer than chance, zero if agreement is at chance level, positive if agreement is better than chance, and is 1 if there is perfect agreement between coders. Kappa values for selecting cohesive items were high in both contexts, with a mean value of .91 and a range of .80 to 1.0 in interviews and .73 to 1.0 in narratives. Significance tests (cf. Bartko & Carpenter, 1976) of kappa different from zero (chance) indicate that in both contexts the hypothesis of chance agreement between coders can be rejected at the two-tailed .001 level.

In specifying which item is presumed by a potentially cohesive element, the mean agreement in interviews was 96% and the range was 94–100%. The mean kappa value in interviews was .92. The values range from .87 to 1.0 and again were highly significant. In narratives, there were fewer items to be scored because of the shorter texts, and, hence, there were fewer opportunities for disagreement between coders. In eight of the nine comparisons, the two coders agreed perfectly. In the single case in which there was disagreement, the coders disagreed on one of 138 judgments.

Finally, in coding agreed-upon items into one of the five cohesion categories, there was almost no disagreement between the coders. In both contexts, there was complete agreement between coders for eight of the nine comparisons.

It is evident from these data that the cohesion analyses can be used consistently across coders. It remains to be seen, however, whether the analyses will permit us to discriminate among groups of speakers with different diagnoses or with different coherence ratings. This question is addressed in the next section.

III. Results

A. Total Cohesive Ties

For each speaker, the number of cohesive ties was computed. From this total, the percentage of ties in each of the five cohesion categories was determined. Percentages across two speech contexts (narratives and interviews) and across three groups of speakers (TD, NTD, and Normals) were compared using two-way analyses of variance. Table 10 summarizes the data across groups and presents the analysis of variance results. Data are not given for the substitution category since no more than 1% of the observations fell into that category.

Table 10. Amount of Cohesion

Group (n = 10)	Total ties per speaker		Total ties per clause	
	Narrative	Interview	Narrative	Interview
TD	24.7 [a]	46.9	2.61[a]	2.04
NTD	22.5	39.9	2.95	1.97
N	44.3	52.1	3.86	2.27
Mean	30.5	46.3	3.15	2.10

		Groups	Contexts	Groups × Contexts
		ANOVA		
	df	2,27	2,54	4,57
Total ties	F	7.57 [c]	26.7 [d]	1.92
	$\hat{\omega}^2$	.13	.26	
Ties per clause	F	7.32 [c]	52.3 [d]	4.33 [b]
	$\hat{\omega}^2$	.10	.41	.08

"One-way ANOVA F (2,27) = 7.2; $p < .005$; Scheffé tests show TD, NTD < N.
[b] $p < .05$.
[c] $p < .01$.
[d] $p < .001$.

The total cohesive ties per speaker is the base of the cohesion measurements reported below. It is a count of all cohesive ties in all categories for each speaker. Using this total as a base, we can determine the proportion of ties falling into each category, and comparing these across speakers and contexts we can study patterns of cohesion.

Table 10 indicates that normal speakers use more total cohesive ties than schizophrenic speakers. In narratives, normals use about double the ties that schizophrenic subjects do (about 44 ties compared to 23–25 ties for schizophrenics). This difference is reliable. In interviews, there is a similar trend: normal speakers use 52 ties compared to 40–47 ties for schizophrenic subjects.

B. Amount of Cohesion

Because there are differences among groups in the number of clauses produced in some contexts, and because the sample sizes differ across contexts, it is useful to divide total ties by the number of clauses each speaker produces. Amount of cohesion in terms of ties per clause can be compared across contexts and groups. Table 10 indicates that there are substantial differences across contexts for all subjects, with this factor accounting for 41% of the variance in the data. Again, there are reliable differences between groups, and now there is a significant interaction between groups and contexts. All groups depend on cohesion more in narratives than in interviews, with the mean number of ties being 3.2 and 2.1, respectively. However, the level of dependence varies according to the speaker's group. Schizophrenic speakers in narratives use about 2.6 to 3 ties per clause and normals use about 4. This difference is reliable. In interviews, schizophrenic speakers use about 2 ties per clause and normals use about 2.3. This difference is not reliable. Thus, for all subjects, there is a greater dependence on cohesion in narratives than in interviews, but normal subjects tend to rely on cohesion more than schizophrenic subjects.

   1. Effect of Clause Length. In Chapter 2, we saw that normal speakers produce more words per clause than schizophrenic speakers. Conceivably, this difference in productivity could account for some of or all the differences between groups in amount of cohesion. Schizophrenic speakers may appear less cohesive with our measures because there are fewer opportunities for scoring cohesive links. The schizophrenics' shorter clauses mean that there are fewer words which can connect one clause with another, so that there are fewer opportunities for scoring cohesive links in all categories except conjunction.

   A simple solution to this problem would be to partial out clause length from amount of cohesion to determine the extent to which the two measures covary. However, Woodward and Goldstein (1977) point out that this strategy is inappropriate in the present case. In this study, as in most studies of possible deficit groups, samples were not created through random assignment of subjects from the larger population. Instead, schizophrenic subjects were selected on the basis of their diagnoses, and TD and NTD subjects were selected on the basis of clinicians' judgments of interview behavior. Moreover, the latter were intentionally directed toward the subject's use of language. In cases in which the groups are not selected at random, Woodward and Goldstein show that observed differences may arise from very complex selection factors. In fact, they demonstrate that the differences can be due to the very same factors that are responsible for the effect under scrutiny.

   Thus, in the present case, several possibilities exist which preclude the use of covariance analyses. It is possible, as we initially observed, that schizophrenic speakers appear to rely less on cohesion in our analyses because they produce fewer words than normal subjects. It is also possible, however, that schizophrenics produce fewer words because they are less concerned with the construction of a cohesive text. Suppose, for example, that schizophrenic speakers do not attempt to provide referents in their discourse for elements that require referents: e.g., they might use "it" or "the other hat" without providing the necessary referents for those items. Or suppose that they do not attempt to mark explicitly conjunctive links between a present clause and the prior text; or that they introduce a participant like "an old woman who is knitting a sweater" and never again mention "the woman" or "the old lady." In such cases, there will be fewer referential ties, fewer conjunctive ties, or fewer lexical ties, respectively, than one would expect in a normal speaker's discourse. And in all cases the schizophrenic speaker will have produced fewer words because of a lack of concern for cohesion. In addition, it is possible that selection factors for schizophrenia such as low motivation or impaired information processing could affect both the speakers' productivity and their concern with or ability to form cohesive links. That is, there could be a mediating factor accounting for the results.

Although one may not wish to appeal to an analysis of covariance, it is nevertheless possible to estimate the strength of the connection between clause length and measures of cohesion and to rule out some explanations. Such analyses suggest, as we show below, that productivity is a factor in the cohesion scores of NTD subjects but is not a factor for TD speakers.

The analyses are relevant in narratives, in which schizophrenic subjects use fewer ties per clause than normal speakers. In the narrative, there is a strong positive correlation between clause length and ties per clause for normal speakers and for NTD subjects: Pearson's r values are $+.66$ and $+.80$, respectively, and p values are at least .05. For TD speakers, however, there is no significant correlation between amount of cohesion and clause length ($r = -.16$).

If we pursue these correlations and assume a standard based on normal speakers, it appears that NTD subjects' reduced dependence on cohesion can be predicted from their reduced productivity. The NTD speakers use about 2.7 words per tie in narratives, and this is one less tie per clause than normal speakers use. If NTD and normal speakers actually use the same number of cohesive ties per clause, we would expect that NTD subjects would use about 2.7 fewer words per clause than normals. They just about do: Table 7 in Chapter 2 shows that NTD speakers use 2.3 fewer words per clause than normal speakers. Thus, it appears that NTD subjects' relatively low dependence on cohesion is intimately related to their production of shorter clauses. It is conceivable that these speakers *appear* to rely less on cohesion primarily because they present us with fewer opportunities for scoring their cohesive ties.

The TD speakers do not fit this description. They use about 3.5 words per cohesive tie in narratives, and this is 1.3 fewer ties per clause than normal speakers use. So on the average they should use about (3.5 × 1.3=) 4.6 fewer words per clause than normal speakers. But this is not the case. They use only 1.4 fewer words — many less than could account for their low cohesion rates. Consequently, one must go beyond clause length and factors related to productivity to account for the TD speaker's relatively low dependence on cohesion. In the analyses that follow and in Chapters 5 to 7, we discuss an alternate explanation for these effects.

C. Distribution of Cohesive Ties

For each speaker, cohesive ties in a given category were computed as a percentage of total ties for that speaker in a particular context. The distribution of ties in four categories is shown in Table 11.

The most outstanding results are the powerful context effects that exist for all groups. Referential ties are most sensitive to context differences, lexical ties are next most sensitive, elliptical ties show a modest discriminative power, and conjunction is not sensitive to differences in context. These variations are shown in the bottom of Table 11: context effects account for 47%, 20%, 6%, and less than 1% of the variance in analyses of reference, lexis, ellipsis, and conjunction, respectively.

There is only one category in which the groups differ: lexical cohesion. In interviews, TD speakers use about 46% of their cohesive ties in lexical linkages, NTD use only 31% lexical cohesion, and normals use 36%. The 15% difference between the two schizophrenic groups is reliable, but neither group differs reliably from normals. In narratives, there is a trend for normal subjects to depend more on lexical cohesion than schizophrenics, but the differences among groups are not reliable.

D. Summary

The two measures of cohesion were highly sensitive to context differences and only modestly sensitive to differences among groups. With regard to context, speakers tended to rely more on cohesive ties in narratives than in interviews, and the distribution of cohesive ties in each category tended to differ in the two contexts. With regard to group differences, two were noteworthy. First, schizophrenic speakers relied less

Table 11.   Distribution of Cohesive Ties

	Narrative			
	Percentage of ties per category			
Group	Reference	Conjunction	Lexis	Ellipsis
TD	52.0	21.7	24.9	0.7
NTD	49.9	24.1	22.8	3.2
N	46.5	21.1	30.3	2.0
Mean	49.5	22.3	26.0	2.0
	Interview			
TD	28.6	20.2	45.8 [a]	4.0
NTD	33.8	25.9	31.3	8.1
N	29.9	28.1	36.0	5.8
Mean	30.8	24.8	37.8	6.0

		ANOVA		
		Groups	Contexts	Groups × Contexts
	df	2,27	2,54	4,57
Reference	F	1	60 [c]	<1
	$\hat{\omega}^2$	0	.47	0
Conjunction	F	<1	<1	<1
Lexis	F	3.79 [b]	17.5 [c]	2.8
	$\hat{\omega}^2$	.07	.20	0
Ellipsis	F	1.98	5.3	<1
	$\hat{\omega}^2$	0	.06	0

[a]One-way ANOVA yields $F\ (2,27) = 3.83$; $p < .05$; Scheffé tests indicate NTD < TD.
[b]$p < .05$.
[c]$p < .001$.

on cohesion (ties/clause) than normals in narratives. For NTD speakers, this difference could be largely due to their lower productivity; for TD speakers, productivity and amount of cohesion did not covary, and their reduced reliance on cohesion was unexplained. Next, in interviews, TD subjects relied more on lexical cohesion than NTD subjects.

IV. Discussion

Three aspects of the present findings are pertinent to an understanding of the schizophrenic speaker: (a) the variations in cohesion across contexts; (b) the variations across the two schizophrenic groups in particular contexts; and (c) the significance of measures of high lexical cohesion in the texts of TD speakers.

A. Context Effects

Both measures of cohesion, amount of ties and pattern of ties, reveal powerful context effects for all groups of speakers. This is an interesting and perhaps surprising result. It indicates that both groups of schizophrenic speakers, NTD and TD, are probably sensitive to variations of the amount and kinds of cohesion required by different contexts. It is interesting that schizophrenic speakers, like normal speakers, decrease their reliance on cohesive ties in interviews, and that this decrease is done in about the same manner for both schizophrenic and normal speakers. The schizophrenic subjects, like the normal speakers, use considerably smaller proportions of referential ties and greater proportions of lexical and elliptical ties in interviews than in narratives. This apparent sensitivity to generic structure suggests that both groups of schizophrenic speakers were relatively aware of the social demands of the different contexts, at least to the extent that they modified the ways in which they provided linkages within their texts.

B. Group Effects

The important differences in these data are those between NTD and TD speakers. As we mentioned earlier, we are in a difficult interpretative position when we find differences between normal and schizophrenic speakers because we do not know to which factors one may attribute the differences. However, variations between TD and NTD subjects are more susceptible to explanation.

1. Narrative. At this point, it is not clear how we may account for the narrative findings. As we suggested, it appears that NTD speakers rely on cohesion to the same extent as normals, once productivity is taken into account, but the same explanation does not fit for TD speakers. Instead, it seems that TD speakers rely less on cohesion for other reasons. There are two possibilities, and these are not mutually exclusive: (a) TD speakers may not be attempting cohesion as frequently as other subjects; that is, they may not be producing nominal groups that require referents, nor forming explicit conjunctive ties, nor repeating lexical items, and so forth; and/or (b) they may be attempting to form cohesive links and routinely failing in their attempts; that is, they may fail to provide needed referents, or repeatedly mention a participant but use lexical items that create lexical but not referential ties (e.g., a donkey . . . the mastodon; the bags of salt . . . the salty water).

A difference in amount of cohesion, in itself, tells us very little about the textual differences. What is revealing is the pattern of cohesion. But in narratives there are no reliable differences in pattern among the three groups. This is probably because the categories themselves are very broad and are not sufficiently sensitive to reveal differences between speakers. In Chapters 4 to 7, more developed analyses are presented, revealing differences between TD and NTD speakers.

2. Interview. In interviews, TD speakers rely on lexical ties to a much greater extent than do NTD speakers. This could be because TD speakers use more lexical ties absolutely than NTD speakers, or because they use about the same number of lexical ties but fewer ties in other categories than NTD speakers. The data show that TD speakers use absolutely more lexical ties: they use about 21 ties in the interviews and NTD speakers use about 12 (one-way ANOVA yields $F(2,27) = 4.08$; $p < .05$; and with independent clauses partialled out, the F value is slightly higher).

C. Lexical Factors in the Interviews of TD and NTD Speakers

Why do TD speakers rely more on lexical cohesion than NTD speakers? This question requires a more detailed examination of the texts in which high lexical cohesion is observed. First, however, let us consider what might be expected from the literature.

1. Previous Observations of Lexical Factors in Schizophrenic Language Use. Lexical factors have been widely cited in the clinical literature and have been important as well in experimental studies with schizophrenic listeners and readers. Taken most generally, the clinical and experimental evidence suggests that schizophrenic patients attend more strongly to lexical items than to the contexts in which those items are used. This means, roughly, that schizophrenic speakers are more likely to focus on lexical meanings in their discourse than on the meaning of whole clauses or the way in which clauses are related. And it indicates that schizophrenic listeners are more likely to be biased by the "strong" or "preferred" meaning of a word than the meaning of a word in its sentence or discourse context. In addition, there is a suggestion that schizophrenic speakers and listeners are more likely than normals to attend to the sound character of an individual word. These findings are summarized briefly below.

a. Lexical Meanings. In discourse, schizophrenic speakers are said to follow lexical rather than conversational (Chaika, 1974; Lecours & Vanier-

Clément, 1976) or logical (e.g., Arieti, 1974) meanings. This can result in topics dictated by lexical rather than conversational themes ("semantic glossomania") or in the use of generalized themes dictated by "predilection words." For example, Arieti (1974, p. 254) cites a patient who says, "Since they've attacked Pearl Harbor, now they will attack Diamond Harbor or Gold Harbor." Here lexical cohesion between the two clauses is strong. The item "harbor" is repeated twice and "pearl," "diamond," and "gold" are all types of jewelry. But the causal relation which "since" encodes has no obvious interpretation. The conjunction, in fact, misleads the listener.

Additional descriptions in a similar vein state that schizophrenic speakers and listeners will respond more to the denotative than the connotative meanings of words (e.g., Goldstein & Scheerer, 1941); that schizophrenic speakers are controlled more by recently produced words than by distant words in their discourse (Salzinger, Portnoy, Pisoni, & Feldman, 1970); and that schizophrenic readers use the preferred meanings of words regardless of the biasing context in which the words are presented (cf. Chapman & Chapman, 1973, Ch. 6). For example, in a study by Chapman, Chapman, and Miller (1964), chronic schizophrenics given a multiple-choice test were more likely to choose the more common meaning, A, in the following example, than the correct meaning, C:

> Robert said he likes rare meat. This means
>   A. He likes meat that is exceedingly uncommon.
>   B. He likes meat with bones in it.
>   C. He likes partially cooked meat.

These results suggest that discourse structure in schizophrenic speakers is dictated by limited lexical meanings rather than by propositional meanings in sentences or readily interpretable conjunctive relations between sentences. They also suggest that the schizophrenic speaker's sentence-to-sentence or clause-to-clause relationships are based on "concrete" or literal word meanings that are independent of the extended semantic relationships of the discourse text.

b. Sound Features of Words. Schizophrenic speakers sometimes attend to the sound features of words rather than to the lexical meaning or the broader meaning of words in context. There is said to be a focus on the word as phonetic entity: "verbalization" according to Arieti (1974) can become "the identifying link in identifications" of elements, so that "ideas are associated because of the phonetic quality of the words they represent." Similar arguments are made by Chaika (1974a, 1977), Lecours and Vanier-Clément (1976), Bleuler (1950), Nöth (1978), and others. It is frequently mentioned that the importance of sound rather than meaning features is seen in rhyming, punning, and the extensive use of homonyms by schizophrenic speakers.

2. Present Data. In the present data, we can expect that a strong dependence on lexical ties would be associated with emphasis on lexical meanings but not with sound features of words. Lexical cohesion is scored between two clauses if both clauses contain the same lexical item, or items formed on the same root, or synonyms or words in a superordinate-subordinate relation to each other. It is not scored in the present analyses for collocations such as antonyms, or other words that are related as parts to wholes (e.g., family–mother; house–door). Moreover, measures of lexical cohesion will not be affected strongly by phonological kinship of words because a relation on the basis of sound is not scored. However, some items that rhyme can serve as cohesive ties where their meanings are synonymous (e.g., bonkers . . . crackers) or where they are formed on the same root (e.g., dependent . . . independent).

Not all TD speakers depend strongly on lexical cohesion. In fact 4 out of 10 subjects use about the same proportions of lexical ties as most NTD speakers do. But 6 out of 10 TD speakers depend on very high proportions of lexical cohesion: lexical ties constitute more than 50% of their cohesive ties in the interview. This exceeds the proportions used by any NTD speaker and by 8/10 normal speakers.

a. High Proportions of Lexical Cohesion. Let us begin by characterizing the lexical ties of speakers who use high proportions of lexical cohesion: i.e., the 6 TD and 2 normal subjects. It appears that 5 out of 6 TD subjects and none of the normal subjects fit the description of "semantic glossomania" given by Lecours and Vanier-Clément (1976). The verbal components of these subjects' sentences appear to be chosen mainly on the basis of conceptual associations apparently unrelated to the conversational topic. For example:

(4)   (S#TD7–51% lexical cohesion)
       (*a*) . . . I like to help people (1 sec)[4]
       (*b*) it's not a sad thing
       (*c*) it's not a funny thing (1.6 sec)
       (*d*) I'm bonkers
       (*e*) I'm crackers (4.1 sec)
       (*f*) I'm half way (2.2 sec) insane (4.8 sec)
       (*g*) but not all the time (3.7 sec) just when I let my old panties show

---

[4]Numbers in parentheses are pause times >1 sec.

(51% of cohesive ties are lexical for this speaker) (S#TD7)

1. (I: What sorts of things make you angry?) (4.4 sec)
   when people try to tell you what to do (1.4 sec)
   when you know what to do to keep yourself healthy and happy (1.6 sec)
2. who cares about money? (1.6 sec)
3. I sure as hell don't (2.8 sec)
4. you see a wino on the street corner (2.4 sec)
5. and you think (1 sec) he needs it to keep himself warm in the winter
6. maybe there's something else I can do to help him (1.8 sec)
7. I like to help people (1 sec)
8. it's not a sad thing
9. it's not a funny thing (1.6 sec)
10. I'm bonkers
11. I'm crackers (4.1 sec)
12. I'm half-way (2.2 sec) insane (4.8 sec)
13. but not all the time (3.7 sec) just when I let my old panties show

Lexical cohesion

Segment number	Cohesive element	Presumed element	Segment number
6	do	do	1
7	help	help	8
7	people	people	1
8	thing	I like to help . . .	7 (L4)*
9	thing	thing	8
11	crackers	bonkers	10 (L2)
12	insane	crackers	11 (L2)

*Items in parentheses refer to lexical subcategories described in Table 9. Where not otherwise noted, all lexical items fall into subcategory L1 (cohesive elements formed on the same root). L2 are synonyms and L4 are general items.

Figure 2. Lexical cohesion in a TD interview (S#TD7).

This speaker would be scored for lexical ties (a)–(b), (b)–(c), (d)–(e), and (e)–(f). She would not be scored for ties between (c) and (d) or between any clause and (g). The fuller text and its lexical scoring is presented in Figure 2. Again, it appears to be lexical cohesion that determines the organization of the text.

In another speaker, there also appears to be a choice of topics dictated somewhat by the lexical meanings of words rather than propositional meanings, but here the influence of lexical cohesion is less obvious:

(5)   (S#TD10–59% lexical cohesion)
       (Interviewer: A stitch in time saves nine. What does that mean?)
       (a) Oh! that's because all women have a little bit of magic to them
       (b) I found that out

(c) and it's called, it's sort of good magic (1.2 sec)
(d) and nine is sort of a magic number (1.1 sec)
(e) like I've got nine colors here you will notice
(f) I've got yellow, green, blue, gray, orange, blue, and navy
(g) and I've got black
(h) and I've got a sort of clear white
(i) the nine colors to me they are the whole universe
(j) and they symbolize every man, woman and child in the world

Like the previous speaker, this speaker uses a diversity of lexical cohesion. Clauses (a), (c) and (d) are tied together by the repetition of "magic"; and clauses (d), (e) and (i) are tied together by the repetition of "nine"; and clauses (e) and (f), (e) and (g), (e) and (h) are tied together by the superordinate-subordinate relationship between "colors" and the instances "yellow," "black," etc. The speaker appears to be answering the interviewer's question; "that" in (a) and (b) refer to the question, whereas "nine" in (d), (e) and (i) repeat part of it. Within the speaker's own text each clause seems to follow from the previous clause: in every successive clause, there is at least one lexical tie to the clause that precedes it. This gives the reader or listener an impression of coherence or at least flow in the text. However, (a)–(j) do not explain the meaning of the proverb, nor do they restate its meaning, nor do the ties that are present relate (a)–(j) to the conversational topic, i.e., the interviewer's question.

Another apparent example of semantic glossomania which coincides with high lexical cohesion can be found in the following example:

(6)   (S#TD5–58% lexical cohesion)
(a) . . . that's what I think hippyism is you know realizing you don't have to own the land to be part of this earth
(b) and I, and I would rather own a piece of land
(c) we own a farm
(d) and I would rather own the land than to be able to pick flowers off somebody else's land (2.8 sec)
(e) which isn't lawful taking flowers off other people's land
(f) and we don't want to break laws
(g) do we? (Interviewer: Do we?)
(h) no (1.1 sec) no
(i) I find, I find it's a lot easier swimming down stream than trying to swim against the stream
(j) and I find it's a lot easier to blow in the wind than to fight the wind . . .

The example above shows some lexical cohesion through repetition of the same items: "land" in (a) and (b), and (b) and (d); "own" in (a) and (b), (b)–(c) and (c)–(d); "law" in (e)–(f); and through hyponyms: "land" in (b) and "farm" in (c). There are also several instances which seem to demonstrate lexical tying of clauses that would fall under the category of "collocation" and hence are not counted here: e.g., "land" in (b) and "flowers" in (d); "own" in (b) and (c) and "lawful" in (e); "land" in (d) and "swimming" and "stream" in (i). In addition, there seems to be evidence of what Lecours and Vanier-Clément (1976) term "formal glossomania" in which verbal components of sentences are chosen mainly on the basis of phonological kinship to each other. The kinship seems to hold in the prosodic structure of clauses rather than in the phonological kinship of lexical items. In (i) and (j) there is a parallel structure to the clauses[5] which seems to serve as a basis for linkage. There is also a similarity of meaning in the two clauses and perhaps a collocational tie between "wind" and "stream."

The parallel structure and prosody in the last two clauses of (6) indicate a phenomenon that Lecours and Vanier-Clément describe as a combination of formal and semantic glossomania. This combination of focus on the lexical and phonological features of text can also be seen in Fig. 3.

In Fig. 3, lexical cohesion is very simple since all the lexical ties are repetitions of items. In addition, there is a repetition of syntactic forms in (1) and (2); in (3) and (4); in (5) and (6) and a repetition of tone in (1) and (2); in (3), (4), and (5); and in (6) and (7)–(8). Thus, the examples in (6) and Fig. 3 demonstrate the coincidence of lexical tying in combination with an occasional focus on the sound characteristics of the clause. This coincidence of lexical cohesion with parallel phonological and grammatical structures can also be seen in Fig. 2.

b. "Predilection Words and Themes." From the foregoing examples, it appears that high proportions of lexical cohesion in TD speakers frequently (a) reflect a discourse in which topics follow lexical patterning at the expense of interpretable relationships between clauses, and (b) coincide with a focus on phonological characteristics of words or clauses. However, not all subjects who rely on high proportions of lexical cohesion give evidence of (a) or (b). The two normal speakers and the one TD speaker who did not seem to show semantic glossomania could be said to show what Lecours and Vanier-Clément (1976) term "thematic production." That is, they produce segments that are uttered over and over again in conversation contexts. There are examples of this in Fig. 3. [e.g., (1)–(2)] and more generally in many of the other subjects who used "predilection words" which were conceptually related. One example is in the collocation discussed in example (6). Another example is in the following text from a TD speaker:

[5]That is, parallel rhythmic and tone structure.

(66% of cohesive ties are lexical for this speaker) (S#TD4)

1. they haven't enough to eat
2. they haven't enough to eat (7.9 sec)
3. why don't they help?
4. why don't the rich help the poor?
5. why don't we help the rich help the poor? (3.4 sec)
6. if we tell the rich they might help the poor (3 sec)
7. if we're good to the rich and
8. help the rich, be good to the poor (2 sec)
9. if we do something good for them
10. we did something for a rich person
11. they'd like it very much and they might do something else for someone else.

Lexical cohesion

Segment number	Cohesive element	Presumed element	Segment number
2	have	(In 15/15 lexical ties,	1
2	enough	the presumed	1
2	eat	element is identical	1
4	help	to the cohesive	3
5	help(×2)	element)	4
5	rich		4
5	poor		4
6	rich		5
6	help		5
6	poor		5
7	rich		6
8	poor		6
8	help		6
8	something		7
8	rich		7
9	good		7
10	something		9
10	rich		8
12	something		10

Figure 3. Lexical cohesion in a TD interview.

(7)   (S#TD3–52% lexical cohesion)
  (a) . . . each life you know you can't always remember your past lives
  (b) very f-few pe-people can remember their past lives (8.5 sec)
  (c) in India there's a lot of emp-emphasis on reincarnation in India and
      Buddhism and Hinduism and that kind of thing (1.3 sec)
  (d) but in western culture which we see variety and so forth
  (e) there isn't very very much emphasis there placed on reincarnation (1.1
      sec)
  (f) because I think that Plato (uhm)

(g) when was he in Greece?
(h) it was around the 6th century that Plato was in Greece
(i) I'm not too sure about that time . . .

Another example is in the text of one of the two normal subjects who depended strongly on lexical cohesion:

(8)   (S#N6–52% lexical cohesion)
(a) There is a great to do in the press these days about religion
(b) I'm sensitive because I said earlier I am an R.C.
(c) but it's true of all the churches and all the sects with exception I think of the Hebrew people (1.3 sec) who are confident of their age old fashions
(d) and they are going to go ahead on an orthodox (1.3 sec) basis or the New Dispensation Menonites or whatever
(e) the lines of communication to each and every Hebrew person of my acquaintance are very clear and satisfactory
(f) getting back to this hodge podge of Christianity and the related ah (1.4 sec) sects and so on . . .

These two examples, one from a TD speaker and one from a normal speaker, indicate that high lexical cohesion in itself does not necessarily imply an incoherent text. Rather, what is critical is the pattern of lexical cohesion. When lexical ties are based on limited word meanings and/or reflect phonological ties, the pattern seems to be unique to TD speakers. When lexical ties reflect concerns with a single conceptual issue, however, as in the two examples given above, the occurrence of high proportions of such ties is not a uniquely TD phenomenon and can occur in normal speakers as well.

c. *Summary of High Lexical Cohesion Data.* There seems to be a range of behavior that is reflected in high proportions of lexical cohesion. It is possible for the speaker simply to be speaking in great detail on one topic. However, this rarely occurred in normal speakers and in one instance in which lexical cohesion was very high, the speaker added an explanation for his extended discussion of one topic by saying: "as you can see, it's gotten under my skin." More commonly, proportions of high lexical ties reflect an aberrant discourse process in which components of clauses and sentences seem to be chosen mainly on the basis of limited lexical meanings. Frequently, such lexically tied clauses also contain phonological and syntactic parallels.

d. *Low Proportions of Lexical Cohesion.* There are 22 subjects in this study who used proportions of lexical cohesion lower than 50%. Of these, two showed some evidence of semantic glossomania. The two were TD speakers. No speakers who were not TD seemed to link their clauses on the basis of lexical ties unrelated to the apparent conversational topic. This was true even for the two normal speakers who relied on high levels of lexical cohesion.

3. Discussion of Lexical Data in Light of Literature Reports. In the literature review above, schizophrenic speakers and listeners were reported to focus on lexical meanings rather than on broader meanings in context. A few observers, notably Chaika and Lecours and Vanier-Clément, have emphasized that their observations pertain to patients who are "schizophasic," i.e., who show deviant linguistic behavior, and not to all schizophrenic patients. In addition, these observers have emphasized that "schizophasia" appears to be episodic so that one cannot expect to find evidence of deviant linguistic behavior routinely in a schizophasic patient.

The view that only some patients are schizophasic is supported by the present findings. It is remarkable that no NTD schizophrenic patients used high proportions of lexical cohesion, and that none gave evidence of semantic or formal glossomania. In none of the NTD interview texts did it appear that topics were dictated solely by the forms or meanings of words. This does not mean, however, that the NTD interviews were always comparable to normal interviews. In the following example, the themes would probably not be considered normal:

(9) (S#NTD8–27% lexical cohesion)
    (a) When I was small my mother never kissed me
    (b) which made me sad (10.9 sec)
    (c) and now somebody's depressing me with ESP
    (d) which makes me sad (1.2 sec)[6]
      (Interviewer: Why?)
    (e) he's tuned into me (3.7 sec)
    (f) he reads by thoughts and depresses me and makes me shake
    (g) he makes me stare

It is worthwhile reemphasizing at this point that thought disorder must not be equated with strange subject matter. It is possible to talk coherently about outlandish ideas, and incoherently about common ones. Although the text in (9) presents what might be termed "bizarre ideation," it does not exhibit any strong dependence on lexical cohesion. Indeed, the texts of the NTD speakers showed remarkably little dependence on lexical cohesion. They looked less like the texts of TD speakers in this regard than did the texts of normal speakers.

[6]Note that (f) is one unit because there is an elliptical subject in a branched structure.

D. High Lexical Cohesion as Evidence of Dysfunction

Why might the TD speaker depend so strongly on the limited lexical meanings of words to effect cohesion between clauses and sentences? Why would a speaker use this strategy in unstructured interviews but not in narratives?

Let us deal with the last question first. It is possible that the narrative task demands relatively little from the speaker in the way of creative productions. No new participants are to be introduced, and no new events are to be developed. The speaker has simply to rephrase what has just been given. The event line of the story gives direction to the speaker's text, and what cohesion is present reflects the development of the actions of the story's main participant (see Gleason, 1968 for the concept of an event line).

Returning to the first question, several hypotheses have been offered to explain language dysfunctions in schizophrenia. We shall consider these in some detail in Chapter 7. At this point, however, it may be helpful to examine the hypotheses briefly in order to see which are consistent with the present observations.

Two hypotheses are relevant to the questioning of TD dependence on lexical cohesion. One hypothesis states that schizophrenic speakers are schizophasic because of an episodic language dysfunction reflecting an intermittent aphasia, i.e., some focal disturbance (at least) in the language centers of the brain concerned with production (e.g., Chaika, 1974a, 1977; Chapman, 1976; Kleist, 1960; Werner, Lewis-Matichek, Evans, & Litowitz, 1975). This hypothesis is similar to a suggestion put forward by neuropsychologists to the effect that there is a neuropsychological dysfunction in schizophrenia which is lateralized to the hemisphere dominant for speech (e.g., Flor-Henry, 1969, 1976; Gruzelier & Hammond, 1976; Gur, 1977, 1978).

An alternate, popular hypothesis is the proposal that the schizophrenic's abnormal rhyming and use of lexical items "is just like the interest which underlies the genius of a Lewis Carroll" and does not represent a language disruption but "rather reveals the intactness of language competence" (Fromkin, 1975). Observers proposing this alternative point out that schizophasic discourse is rule-governed at the phonemic, phonetic, and morphemic levels and generally at the syntactic level as well. Lecours and Vanier-Clément (1976) make this argument most forcefully. They propose that schizophasic discourse is rule-deviant primarily in terms of "reality-bound syntagms." That is, the deviant segments consist of phrases, clauses, or sentences that contain (1) words that do not belong to the community's verbal inventory, or (2) concepts that would not be readily acceptable to most members of the community.

Both proposals recognize that there is deviance. The first associates the deviance with a brain dysfunction, and hence with a lack of competence in the speaker. The second associates it with an increased creativity on the part of the speaker which is, in some respects, equal to or greater than the creativity of normal speakers. Indeed, according to the second proposal, the combining of deviant segments containing legitimate morphemes (e.g., as in the combinations *hiver–été* or *j'ouvre–ferme*) to any great extent testifies to the "integrity of the neurological mechanisms that are seldom spared in aphasia" (Lecours & Vanier-Clément, 1976, p. 526).

The dispute seems to center on what constitutes evidence of a neurological dysfunction in the central nervous system. The cohesion data from the present chapter give partial support to the observation of competence in TD schizophrenic patients. These speakers seem able to some extent to take account of the different demands of the narrative and interview genres. The TD speakers, however, also gave evidence of two kinds of behavior that are not accounted for readily by either of the proposed explanations of schizophrenic speech. In interviews, they relied on lexical cohesion more than most other subjects, and they often seemed to depend on lexical items as a topical focus for their discourse—something no other subject did to any extent; and they sometimes seemed to rely on the prosodic features of clauses and words to link their clauses to the prior context. There is rather firm evidence of lexical focus, through the measures of lexical cohesion, and weak support for prosodic tying through *post hoc* observations of the texts.

These two exceptional behaviors are not accounted for well by the proposals in the literature. The proposal of an episodic aphasia falters on the competence of TD subjects in matching the cohesive patterns of normal speakers between clauses, and on their apparent competence in using syntax within clauses, to be discussed in more detail in Chapter 4. The proposed aphasia would seem to predict too much impairment to fit the data observed here. And the proposal that schizophrenic patients are just as competent or more competent than normal speakers in their use of words does not account for the unique features of TD discourse, nor does it explain why lexical items and the sound features of words and clauses might be focal for TD subjects.

E. Summary

In the present chapter, narrative and interview texts from TD, NTD, and normal subjects were analyzed in terms of the cohesion categories of Halliday and Hasan (1976). Two measures of cohesion were employed; amount of cohesion (cohesive ties per clause) and pattern of cohesion (percentage of ties in a particular category/total cohesive ties). The results pointed to an extensive competence of schizophrenic speakers in recognizing differences in context.

There were two ways in which schizophrenic speakers were distinctive: (*a*) they relied less on cohesion in narratives than normal speakers; and (*b*) TD speakers relied more strongly on lexical cohesion in interviews than NTD speakers. The first difference could be attributed at least in part to the lower productivity of NTD speakers compared to normal speakers; but productivity could not account for TD results. The second effect reflected the TD speaker's dependence on lexical items as foci for discourse topics. This did not occur in all TD speakers, but its occurrence was peculiar to TD speakers. In addition, *post hoc* examinations of the texts suggested that TD speakers sometimes depended on the rhythm and intonation of clauses with parallel grammatical structures as bases for linking clauses to the prior text.

Reference as a Speech Art

In the next three chapters, we shall be concerned with reference as a speech "art" — as an indication of the speaker's facility in guiding listeners through discourse texts. This kind of reference is not the referring of symbols to physical things in the environment characteristic of all language. It is rather a particular referring which occurs within language, within a text, marking out some items as requiring more information from elsewhere in the text or context, and other items as needing no further information. This particular referring is termed "phoricity."

I. Reference and Phoricity

A. Introduction

The phoricity systems (Martin, 1978) are those systems in English which structure utterances on the basis of what speakers assume their listeners know. There are several such systems.[1] The one we shall be studying here is the REFERENCE system. It applies to nominal groups and is used for telling about participants.

The REFERENCE system provides an interesting and potentially valuable approach to the use of language by schizophrenic speakers. It can be described in terms of a theoretical map, the REFERENCE network, which shows some ways in which English allows a speaker to mark out directions for listeners. The directions are accomplished through the use of different sorts of nominal groups, some of which are marked as requiring

---

[1]These include SUBSTITUTION and ELLIPSIS, TONICITY (or contrastive stress) and CLEFTING (including PSEUDOCLEFTING).

more information in order to be understood, whereas others are marked as requiring no further information. The marking can be seen as a kind of guidance that directs the listener to identify participants referred to in the discourse. In particular in the present study, the ways in which the schizophrenic or at least TD speakers use the REFERENCE system may be misleading. For example, if the speaker mentions *that old woman,* the listener will expect to recover the identity of *that* woman from the context of the utterance. The information may be in the immediate nonverbal situation, or in the recent verbal context. If the identity is recoverable, then the guidance will be a help; if not, the guidance will be a hindrance to comprehension. Helpful guidance would seem to be an "art" normally available to all adult speakers of a language. However, it may be that schizophrenic speakers, or at least schizophrenic speakers who are considered thought-disordered, do not provide helpful guidance. By studying the ways in which different groups of speakers use the REFERENCE system, we can determine whether the system is used differently by the various groups and estimate the consequences of different uses for listeners.

In the present chapter, we outline the REFERENCE network and describe the general procedures for its use. Then some preliminary analyses are reported, showing how TD, NTD, and normal speakers use nominal groups in various contexts. In Chapter 5, we examine how the speakers present new participants in text, and in Chapter 6, we study how the speakers presume participants which have already been given. In these analyses, we are able to see an impressive competence of TD speakers in producing complex nominal groups and some unexpected sensitivity to variations in context. However, there is also detailed evidence that TD speakers frequently mislead their listeners, in effect, by promising information that is not readily available and by introducing participants that are already known.

B. Some Key Distinctions

The REFERENCE network, as we have mentioned, applies to nominal groups.[2] Table 12 outlines the key distinctions in the way that nominal groups can be used to code reference.

Nominal groups in English can be divided into phoric and nonphoric groups. *Phoric* groups presume information. They contain a clear instruc-

[2]This is Halliday's term which roughly corresponds to noun phrases in phrase-structure grammar.

Table 12. Reference Categories and Their Instructions to the Listener

Category	Instruction	Examples
Nonphoric nominal groups		
General reference	"You don't need to know my particular identity"	(a) *You* say a prayer and *you* cut the egg-bread.
		(b) There's a lot of information about *drugs* in the school.
Specific reference	"My identity is important."	
PRESENTING nominal groups	"To understand me, stay here."	(a) The lift consisted of *a cable* coming down.
		(b) *Some of my friends* stopped in for tea.
Phoric nominal groups		
PRESUMING nominal groups	"To understand me, search elsewhere."	
Cultural context		(a) *The full moon* always makes me romantic.*
		(b) *Pierre Elliot Trudeau* wants to stay out of Canadian bedrooms.
Situational context		(a) Mary slapped Sam. I hope *she* doesn't hit *him* again.*
		(b) *This*[a] is simply outragaeous!

[a]This example assumes that "this" is exophoric to the situation.
*Constructed example.

tion to the listener which says, in effect, "To understand me, search elsewhere." The reference ties studied in Chapter 3 were based on ties from
phoric groups to referents in the text. They relied on an instruction to the
listener to retrieve information from phoric nominal groups such as: *that
old snail, him, the stronger bond.* However, as Table 12 indicates, many
other sorts of nominal groups carry the phoric instruction. The location
of "elsewhere" *may* be in the verbal situation, as it was in the analyses of
Chapter 3. But it may also be in the nonverbal situation, as in, *"This is
simply outrageous!";* or in the cultural context as in *"The full moon* always
makes me romantic,* or in *"Pierre Elliot Trudeau* wants to stay out of
Canadian bedrooms."

Nonphoric nominal groups, on the other hand, do not presume information. They simply introduce a person, place, thing, or concept and
require no retrieval operations of the listener. The instruction they seem
to carry is, "To understand me, stay here." Some nonphoric groups indicate a specific participant or participants, as in "An old man entered the
room."* Others do not require that a particular participant be identified,

as in the use of the generalized terms "one" or "you," or in the use of generic terms like "the tiger" or "tigers" in which no particular tiger is intended. In all cases, phoric nominal groups instruct the listener to search elsewhere, and nonphoric nominal groups do not.

The instructions, "Search elsewhere" or "Stay here" help us to characterize one important aspect of the creation of texts by speakers. As speaker and listener exchange meanings, not everything a given speaker says will be new. In part, a speaker reminds the listener of shared information. For example, in "//she *flew* home//,"* with contrastive stress on "flew," the speaker reminds the listener of two things. First, the pronoun "she" signals to listeners that they already know the identity of the flier; and second, the tonic on "flew" reminds listeners that they already know the flier got home. Of course "//she *flew* home//" conveys new information as well, namely, that the flier got home by air, she flew, rather than took a train, or drove, etc. We can abstract a general principle from the fact that most utterances include new and old information:

(1)   Speakers tell listeners new things on the basis of what they assume are old
       things for the listener.

What makes this principle interesting to us is its potential for revealing some of the ways in which TD speakers, or perhaps schizophrenic speakers generally, may disappoint their listeners. In normal discourse, what the listener is assumed to know is not generally taken for granted. Rather, speakers constantly remind their listeners about the shared knowledge between them at the same time as they are introducing new information. For example, once a participant has been introduced in a text, the speaker subsequently reminds the listener of this knowledge by using a definite article or pronoun, as in

(2)   a donkey was carrying salt/ and he went through a river/

However, TD and perhaps other schizophrenic speakers may "remind" their listeners incorrectly, indicating that a nominal group referent has already been given when in fact it has not. For example:

(3)   . . . (1) and he decided to go for a swim/ (2) and his salt started dissolving off of
       him into the water/ (3) and it did/ (4) it left him hanging there/ (5) so he crawled
       out on the other side and became a mastodon/ (6) it gets unfrozen/ (7) it's up in
       the Arctic right now/ (8) it's a block of ice/ (9) and a block of ice gets planted in/
       (10) it's forced into a square right? (11) ever studied that sort of a formation,
       block of ice in the ground?/ (12) well, it fights the perma frost/ (13) it pushes it
       away/ (14) and lets things go up around it/ (15) you can see they're like, they're
       almost like a pattern with a flower/ (16) they start from the middle/ (17) and it's
       like a submerged ice cube/ (18) that got frozen into the soil afterwards/ . . . .

In this example, a TD speaker has been asked to retell the Donkey Story in his own words. By using the phoric element they in (15) and (16), the speaker is "reminding" his listener that the referent of they is already known and is therefore retrievable from some context. But a search through the prior verbal text and the nonverbal situation reveals no unambiguous candidate. In fact, there seem to be a number of other phoric elements for which the referents are not readily and unambiguously accessible [e.g., it in (6); it in (14)].

If TD speakers falsely "remind" their listeners of referents that are unclear or missing, then the listener might conclude that TD speakers' discourse is "wooly and vague," perhaps with "an inconsequential following of side issues." That is, it is possible that come clinical descriptions of TD speakers are listeners' responses to the speakers' misleading use of phoric nominal groups. There are several other possible connections between phoricity and the use of language by TD and other schizophrenic speakers. These are presented in more detail in the chapters that follow. For the remainder of this chapter, we describe the REFERENCE Network in a more systematic way, and provide an overview of the data base for nominal groups.

II. Procedures

A. Basic Unit of Analysis

The nominal group is used as the basic unit in the reference analyses that follow. We have followed Halliday and Hasan's (1976, Chs. 2 and 4) description. This description, and indeed Halliday's whole approach to language, is based on an analysis of the way in which language is structured for use in a social world. Halliday's functional approach to language is reflected in the way in which he and Hasan analyze nominal groups. One way of depicting the structure of a nominal group is given in (4):

(4)

(a) Experiential structure	the Deictic	two Numerative	little Epithet	stone Classifier	cottages Thing	Susan owned Qualifier
(b) Typical word class	deter-miner	numeral	adjective	noun	noun	[relative clause]

Line (a) gives the "experiential structure" of the example. This is the way in which the nominal group is structured to express the speaker's experience of the real world. The elements of this structure are Deictic, Numerative, Epithet, Classifier, Qualifier, and what Halliday & Hasan term "Thing." The functional categories can be approximately represented in terms of the typical word classes which realize these functions, as indicated in line (b). So for example, the Deictic is normally a determiner, the Epithet an adjective, the Classifier and Thing a noun, and the Qualifier a relative clause or prepositional group. However, class and function do not correspond in a one-to-one manner, as comparison of lines (a) and (b) indicates. Nouns, for example, regularly function as both Classifier and Thing, and adjectives function both as Qualifier and as Epithet. The essential discriminations are therefore those in terms of functional roles (here given only as experiential structures, but see Ch. 2 of Halliday & Hasan). The Deictic, for example, is said to specify classes of things by identity, both specific and nonspecific (which cottage? a cottage, all cottages) and by identity based on reference (this cottage); the Numerative by quantity (two cottages); the Classifier by reference to a subclass (summer cottages); the Epithet by reference to a property (small cottages); and the Qualifier by reference to some characterizing relation or process (cottages in the lake region). Nominal groups consist of at least a Thing, typically realized by common nouns but also by pronouns and proper names. The Thing is open to premodification and postmodification, as indicated in (4).

B. Reliabilities

Among the several decisions which a coder must make in performing the reference analyses described in Chapters 4 to 6, three were selected for reliability checks. These were (a) identifying nominal groups in texts, (b) discriminating those nominal groups that make definite reference to the situation from those which do not, and (c) categorizing definite nominal groups into one of four retrieval categories. Again, one coder, JM, analyzed typescripts while listening to the samples on a tape recorder, and a second coder, ST, separately analyzed typescripts while listening to samples selected at random from nine subjects, three per group.

Coders agreed on about 91% of their nominal group identifications; the range was 81–100% agreement. It is difficult to estimate what chance agreement would be in this case. If we adopt total words in the sample as a baseline for the possible number of nominal groups, we will certainly overestimate the likely number of choices. However, this will give an approximation to the number of choices available to the coders. Using total words, therefore, we obtain a mean kappa value of .91 for interview and cartoon contexts. This result is different from chance ($\kappa = 0$) at the two-tailed .001 level. The kappa values for each of the 9 comparison subjects in two contexts are similarly reliable. In narrative contexts, the coders showed complete agreement in their nominal group selections in four of the nine comparison subjects. For the remaining subjects, kappa values were again reliably different from chance beyond the .001 level.

For all agreed-upon nominal groups, we asked how many were considered definite and how many were not. Those in the former category presume situational referents; those in the latter included both groups that presume information from the general culture and groups that present information for the first time. Coders agreed in about 96% of their divisions in both interview and cartoon contexts; the range was 88–98%. This result was reliably different from chance as indicated by a mean kappa value for the two contexts of .89 and by individual kappa values for each comparison subject that were reliably different from zero at the .001 level. Again, in narratives we find several instances of perfect agreement. Coders agreed in six of the nine comparison subjects. For one of the remaining subjects, however, agreement was only at chance level.

For all nominal groups that made definite reference to the situation, we asked to what extent the coders agreed in placing these groups into one of four retrieval categories: reference to the verbal situation, to the nonverbal situation, to the implied verbal context, and to some unclear or ambiguous context. In narratives, cartoon tasks, and interviews, the coders agreed on about 91% of their categorizations. The range of agreement was quite wide, extending from 52–100% ($SD = 15\%$). The mean kappa value over all contexts indicated that the coders' agreement was well beyond chance levels ($M\kappa = .81$). There was again one instance in which the kappa value was not reliably different from chance at the .01 level.

Overall, the reliability for these reference analyses is high, indicating that the analyses can be used consistently across coders. Presumably, this also means that the analyses can be used consistently by workers in other centers, although this remains to be established. In detail, there is one result that deserves further comment. In the retrieval analyses, we saw that there was about 91% agreement between coders. In fact, this measure is a composite of the coders' agreement on four categories of retrieval, and it obscures what seems to be a gradient of agreement between coders reflecting the accessibility of referents. When a nominal group's referent is present in the explicit context, coders show almost perfect agreement in their judgments. They agree on about 95% of their decisions for the verbal context, and about 98% for the nonverbal context. When the referent must be retrieved through a simple inference process, bridging from one nominal group to another, the coders' agreement drops to about 70%. And when the referent for a nominal group is ambiguous or obscure, the agreement drops to 50%.

With each drop in agreement, the decision required of the coders seems to be more complex. In the case of explicit reference, the coders must scan the verbal and nonverbal contexts and find some item or event that clearly provides a referent for the nominal group in question. This reference task is one which children appear to master at a very young age (cf. Garvey, Caramazza, & Yates, 1974/75; Maratsos, 1976). In the case of implicit reference, the task is more complex. It may require several levels of testing (cf. Garrod & Sanford, 1978; Hobbs, 1976), and we discuss these in more detail in Chapter 6. At the least, however, it requires that the coders exhaust every possible explicit referent, a task that requires more testing than does the search for any single explicit referent. And finally, in the case of unclear reference, the coders must establish that the needed referent is accessible neither from the explicit context nor from the readily inferrable verbal context. Again, at the least, more testing is required here than in any of the other categories.

C. The REFERENCE Network

The REFERENCE Network has been developed to describe the ways in which English is structured to introduce participants into text. Participants are persons, places, things, or concepts. They are typically "realized" (coded from meanings into lexicogrammatical forms) in nominal groups, and the network is based on distinctions in various sorts of nominal groups. The network is presented in Figure 4. Its systems are numbered from 1 to 7 for convenient reference.[3]

System 1 distinguishes GENERAL and SPECIFIC reference. GENERAL groups do not pick out individual participants in a context but rather refer to no participant in particular or the whole of a class. SPECIFIC groups, on the other hand, do pick out individuals. For example, "the tiger" is GENERAL in "*The tiger* is a carnivore" but SPECIFIC in "*The tiger* attacked at dawn."

System 2 sets up two subsets of GENERAL groups: GENERALIZED and GENERIC. GENERALIZED groups refer impersonally to no specific partici-

---

[3]Systemic notation is used here. See Berry (1975, 1977).

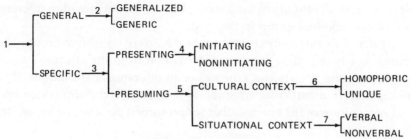

Figure 4. Reference network.

pant in a text. *One* and in less formal registers, *you,* are the typical realizations of GENERALIZED reference. For example, *you* is GENERALIZED in:

(5)   There's a big dinner and dance/ and *you* say a prayer/ and *you* cut the egg bread/
       and then there's a ceremony/

GENERIC groups refer to a set whose membership includes all participants characterized by the Thing and its modifiers. For example, *drugs* is GENERIC in:

(6)   there's a lot of information about *drugs* in the school you know[4]

System 3 introduces the subsets of specific groups: PRESENTING and PRESUMING nominal groups. These two groups are central to the analyses discussed in Chapters 5 and 6 and will be discussed only briefly here. PRESENTING groups refer only to a set of participants directly indicated; PRESUMING groups refer to participants whose identities are assumed to be be known.

System 4 distinguishes subsets of PRESENTING groups—groups that need not presume information—as INITIATING and NONINITIATING. INITIATING groups present a participant as if for the first time and are later used to provide referents for other nominal groups. For example:

(7)   well I see a telephone booth/ it's in the ground covered with snow an' all that/

a telephone booth both introduces a participant and serves as a referent for the nominal group it. Consequently, a telephone booth initiates a chain of specific reference. NONINITIATING groups introduce specific participants but do not provide referents for other groups. They do not initiate referential chains. In

(8)   the donkey was carrying salt/ he went through a river / the river got full of salty
       water/

---

[4]Actually "information" and "the school" are GENERIC here as well, although not enough of
 the context has been provided to make this clear.

salt is tied lexically to *salty* in salty water, but it does not provide a referent for a phoric nominal group in this text.

System 5 distinguishes two important kinds of PRESUMING groups according to whether they presume information from the CULTURAL CONTEXT or from the SITUATIONAL CONTEXT of an utterance. For example, it is participation in a particular community (i.e., Jewish culture) which enables recognition of the one member set presumed by "the egg bread" in (9):

(9)   Interviewer: What happens (in a bar mitzvah)—Well there's a big dinner and dance/ and you say a prayer/ and you cut the egg bread/

Thus, *the egg bread* realizes the feature CULTURAL CONTEXT. It need not be be present in the immediate verbal or nonverbal context for a listener to identify it. But in the cartoon description in (10), retrieval of the referents for *this* depends on the immediate nonverbal context of situation:

(10)   I presume *this* is a dog/ and I presume *this* is a dog/ and *this* is something else/

System 6 subdivides reference to the CULTURAL CONTEXT into HOMOPHORIC and UNIQUE reference. UNIQUE reference is typically realized through proper names and involves assigning a name to concepts, individuals, or things. Members of a social community must learn and share these names. Names are phoric and listeners will query them when they do not know whom the name intends, just as they will query pronouns, definite articles, and demonstratives whose reference they cannot resolve. HOMOPHORIC reference, on the other hand, involves shared reference. Through the definite article, it marks out some object whose referent is accessible because of shared knowledge deriving from membership in a community. This may involve communities consisting of just a few people or including all speakers of a language. So for example:

(11)   Where's *the dog*?*

is homophoric in a one-dog family, but not in a kennel; "the premier" is homophoric in Ontario except when an interprovincial premiers' conference is held; and "the moon" is homophoric on the planet Earth but not on Jupiter.

III. Analyses of Nominal Group Structure

A. The Complexity of Nominal Groups

Nominal group complexity is an interesting feature of our subjects' use of language because it bears on the question of the language competence of schizophrenic and especially TD speakers. As we mentioned in Chapter 1, there have been several studies in the last decade indicating that the recall of word strings by schizophrenic listeners is sensitive to manipulations of syntactic structure (e.g., Gerver, 1967; Truscott, 1970). Rochester *et al.*, 1973; However, there are several problems in extrapolating from those studies of listeners to studies of speakers. (1) The manipulation of structural features of sentences was very approximate, presenting in some cases strings that were supposed to vary in semantic but not syntactic dimensions and vice-versa, and in other cases sentences in which the surface syntax differed. (2) The observations were made for "schizophrenic" listeners, with no indications whether the patients were "thought-disordered" (or "schizophasic") at the time of testing. (3) The observations were made only for single word strings, except in Carpenter's (1976) study of paragraphs.

Thus, the best evidence available at present suggests that schizophrenic patients do not differ from normal subjects in their ability to use syntactic features. At least this seems to be true for relatively young patients who have not been chronically hospitalized or medicated. But this observation is based on limited examinations of schizophrenic *listeners*, unselected for signs of incoherent speech. It is not known whether the apparent syntactic competence of the schizophrenic subject will be supported by studies of discourse productions, especially by studies with patients judged by clinicians and lay persons to be relatively incoherent.

Our primary analyses have been in terms of the semantic-pragmatic categories of cohesion and reference discussed above. But in the course of these analyses, we did collect data that shed some light on the question of syntactic competence of TD and NTD schizophrenic speakers. These data are presented next.

B. Rank-Shifting over All Nominal Groups

Three small analyses were performed to study the complexity of nominal groups used by our subjects.

The first analysis is based on the notion of a rank-shifted group. A rank-shifted nominal group is one which is part of the structure of another nominal group. For example, in

(12)   a person I saw in the house on the hill

there are four nominal groups. Two are simple, containing only one thing: *I*, and *the hill*; and two are complex, containing more than one Thing: *a person I saw in the house on the hill, the house on the hill*. Three of the four nominal groups in (12) are "rank-shifted" in the sense that each one is part of the structure of another nominal group: *I* and *the house on the hill* are part of the qualifier element modifying "a person"; and *the hill* is itself part of a qualifier element and so is rank-shifted into the structure of *the house on the hill*. The fourth nominal group does not depend on the structure of any other group and so is considered not to be rank-shifted: *a person I saw in the house on the hill*.

In

(13)   a blond man

there is only a single nonrank-shifted group. One way of estimating the complexity of nominal groups is to compute the proportion of rank-shifted to nonrank-shifted in a text. Higher proportions indicate that speakers are constructing more complex nominal groups.

Table 13 presents the total nominal groups (NGs) used by the average speaker in each of the three contexts and shows the proportion of items that are rank-shifted into other nominal groups.

The results show that about 6 to 15% of all NGs were rank-shifted into other NGs, the exact proportion varying according to context and group. There are small variations according to context. This factor accounted for about 13% of the total variance. Speakers produced more dependent NGs in contexts based on pictures than in contexts based on words: about 15.9% of cartoon NGs were rank-shifted compared to about 9 to 11% of interview and narrative NGs. This variation in context was about the same for all three groups of speakers, there being no significant interaction between contexts and speakers.

Table 13.   Percentage of Rank-Shifted NGs per Speaker

| | Context | | | | | | | | |
| | Cartoon | | | Narrative | | | Interview | | |
Category	TD	NTD	N	TD	NTD	N	TD	NTD	N
Total NGs	186	144	195	25	18	30	65	52	72
Rank-shifted NGs (percentage)	11.9	14.3	21.4	10.5	9.0	13.0	10.2	6.3	10.6

ANOVA: Rank-shifted NGs (percentage)

	Groups	Contexts	Groups × contexts
df	2,27	2,54	4,54
F	4.12 [a]	8.15 [b]	1.26
$\hat{\omega}^2$	.06	.13	

[a] $p < .05$.
[b] $p < .001$.

There was a modest variation according to speaker. This factor accounted for about 6% of the total variance in the data. There are no reliable differences between groups of speakers in any one context, but there is a tendency for normal speakers to use more rank-shifted NGs in cartoon tasks. About 21% of normals' NGs are rank-shifted compared to about 12 to 14% of schizophrenics'. There is, then, some indication that schizophrenic speakers may produce less complex items than normal speakers.

C. Cartoon Contexts

Since all speakers tended to produce more complex NGs in cartoon contexts than in the narrative or interview, we analyzed the cartoon responses in greater detail. We divided the complex NGs produced in cartoon contexts into those which included two NGs and those which included three or more NGs. The last category reliably distinguishes schizophrenic speakers from normal speakers: 3 to 4% of the schizophrenic speakers' NGs are highly complex, compared to 8% for normal speakers (a z test of independent proportions yields p. < 001 for N versus TD and NTD subjects).

This difference seems to be a result of normal speakers' tendency to pack long strings of simple NGs into one NG in their initial descriptions of cartoons. Example (14) is fairly typical:

(14)   a low-roofed house with reindeers in the background with a rather large broad
chimney on top through which Santa Claus has come

This example contains four rank-shifted groups: *reindeers, the background, a rather large broad chimney,* and *Santa Claus*, which are dominated by the group: *a low-roofed house with reindeers in the background with a rather large broad chimney on top through which Santa Claus has come.* This contrasts with a typical response from a TD subject, given in (15):

(15)   *it* looks like *Santa Claus* is coming up behind

D. Rank-Shifting in the Presentation of Information

There is one further analysis which sheds some light on these data. As we mentioned above, normal speakers seem to produce highly compact NGs primarily in the *initial* sentences of their cartoon descriptions. They tend not to produce such NGs later on in the description, nor do they use compact NGs in interpretaions of cartoons. This suggests that it is primarily in the initial presentation of information that normal speakers use complex NGs.

We speculated that if we were to look particularly at NGs which introduce new participants into discourse, we might observe a stronger effect than could be seen by using all the NGs. This seemed especially likely since PRESENTING NGs constitute no more than about 11% of all NGs. With so small a proportion, it was possible that variations might be masked.

Table 14 shows the proportion of rank-shifted NGs in nominal groups which present information. It is similar to Table 13, but the data are restricted to PRESENTING NGs.

There is a strong difference between groups of speakers and an interaction of speakers with contexts. Variations among groups of speakers account for 14% of the total variance in these data. That is a substantial effect in itself, and noteworthy in the present analyses because it exceeds a context effect of 9%.

In both cartoon contexts and the narrative, normal speakers produce more rank-shifted groups than schizophrenic speakers. This trend is significant in comparisons with TD speakers. In cartoon contexts, about 10.8% of normal speakers' NGs are dependent, compared to 3.7% for TD speakers; and in narratives, the proportions are 8.2% for normals, and 0.8% for TD speakers. In interviews, all groups rank-shift about the same 4% of their NGs.

Table 14. Percentage of Rank-Shifted NGs in NGs Which Present Information

	Groups		
Contexts	TD	NTD	N
Cartoons [a]	3.7	6.3	10.8
Narrative [a]	0.8	2.8	8.2
Interview	5.2	2.3	4.5

ANOVA			
	Groups	Contexts	Groups × contexts
df	2,27	2,54	4,54
F	9.65 [c]	5.44 [b]	3.59 [b]
$\hat{\omega}^2$	.14	.09	.10

[a] One-way ANOVA yields $F(2,27) = 4.4$; Scheffé yields $p < .05$ for N versus TD subjects.
[b] $p < .05$.
[c] $p < .001$

IV. Discussion of Complexity in Nominal Groups

There are some marked similarities in the use of NGs across speakers. (1) All speakers use about the same proportions of rank-shifted NGs in the two verbally based contexts. (2) All speakers produce more complex NGs in cartoon contexts than in contexts with a verbal base. (3) And all groups of speakers produce at least some highly complex NGs in each of the three contexts. It is not the case, for example, that normal speakers produce NGs with more than two simple groups but NTD or TD never do. Each group of subjects produced some complex NGs in every context studied here.

However, there were also some interesting differences. In themselves these results are not conclusive, but they do suggest the need for careful analyses of syntactic factors in future studies.

Across contexts. Normal speakers double their proportions of dependent NGs as they go from a verbally based context to an image-based context. Their proportions change from about 11 to 13% in interviews and narratives to about 21% in cartoon tasks. Aproximately the same pattern holds for NTD speakers: they increase their proportions from 6 to 94 in verbally based contexts to about 14% in cartoon tasks. But this pattern does not hold for TD speakers: they produce about 10 to 11% rank-shifted NGs in interviews and narratives, and about 12% in cartoon tasks. Thus, the pattern of NG complexity does not change substantially across contexts for TD speakers, but it does for other subjects.

Presenting NGs. In introducing new participants into interviews, normal speakers rarely use complex NGs: only about 4.5% of their NGs are rank-shifted into other NGs. However, when participants are provided by the task-based contexts of narratives and cartoons, then normal proportions of dependent NGs increase. When provision is from the prior narrative text, the increase is almost doubled (to 8.2%). And when the provision is from the immediate nonverbal situation in the form of cartoon pictures, the increase is more than double (10.8%).

The pattern is similar for NTD subjects. There is a slight increase in the proportion of rank-shifted NGs from interviews to narratives and almost a tripling from interviews to cartoons. Again, the speakers seem to take advantage of the provisions made by the context and use these in their presentation.

Again, for TD speakers, there is a unique pattern. These speakers use about the same proportion of rank-shifted NGs in the interview as other subjects. But unlike the others, they do not increase their rank-shifting as the provisons of the context increase. If anything, there is a drop: from 5.2% in interviews, TD speakers use about 0.8% rank-shifted NGs in narratives and 3.7% in cartoon tasks. This suggests that TD speakers are not so responsive to variations in context as other speakers, at least when variations are studied in detail. It seems to indicate that TD speakers are uniquely failing to take advantage of some of the aids to production which the narrative and especially the cartoon contexts offer.

In fact, this conclusion about TD speakers is biased in the direction of verbal presentation. As we shall see in Chapter 6, TD speakers do indeed "take advantage" of the contextual provision of participants in narratives and in cartoons. But they do not use the contextual configuration as a basis for *verbal* encoding. Instead, they rely even more fully than other subjects on the nonverbal context: they refer to items presented in the nonverbal situation and do not introduce the participants in their own verbal productions. We discuss this result at length in Chapter 6.

Presenting Information in Texts

I. Introduction

As speakers use their language to exchange meanings with listeners, they both introduce participants and refer to participants already present in the situation. In the present chapter, we study how speakers tell listeners about new persons, places, things, and concepts.

A. Nonphoric Reference

To introduce a new participant into discourse, speakers often use nonphoric nominal groups. As we indicated in Chapter 4, nonphoric groups do not depend on any prior identification of their participants. They are self-sufficient. Fig. 5 indicates two ways in which nonphoric groups introduce participants into discourse: through GENERAL nominal groups (NGs) and through SPECIFIC NGs.

GENERAL NGs, as we mentioned, refer impersonally or generically to whole sets of participants so that no particular participant need be identified, whereas SPECIFIC NGs refer to some particular participant or participants.

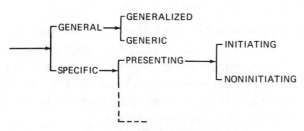

Figure 5. Nonphoric reference.

1. GENERAL Reference. GENERAL NGs rely either on GENERALIZED reference (e.g., *"One* never can tell about April days."*) or on GENERIC reference (e.g., *"Linguists* are always picky."*). Since GENERAL NGs pick out no particular member of a set, no particular member can be presumed and these groups are always nonphoric. They do not presume information from elsewhere but instruct the listener in effect, "To understand me, stay here." Another way to describe these groups is to say that to understand them, one need only know English, but to understand a SPECIFIC PRESUMING group, one must know English and the context in which the group is used.

GENERAL reference is interesting to us in two ways. First, it can show us the extent to which speakers rely on nonspecific referents to carry the action in various contexts. This may vary with speakers. Next, GENERIC NGs, in particular, are interesting because they include many of the lexical items which White (1949) and Maher and his colleagues (1966) term "universal concepts." Such items (e.g., "religion," "the Chinese," "mankind") are said to be used very extensively by thought-disordered schizophrenic patients. Since they refer to no specific participant, they can be used again and again without initiating any chain of reference in the text. Consequently, they may account for rather high proportions of lexical cohesion but contribute nothing to the referential cohesion within a text.[1] As lexical items, they may be used more frequently by schizophrenic and perhaps especially by TD speakers than by normal speakers. And since they contribute to lexical but not to referential cohesion, their extensive use in texts by TD speakers could tell us something of the consequences of depending on lexical versus referential cohesion for the creation of discourse.

2. SPECIFIC Reference. SPECIFIC NGs can either present or presume the identity of participants in text. When nominal groups introduce SPECIFIC participants into the text, they are termed PRESENTING groups. For example, in

(1)   there was *a big fight* the next day

a big fight is a PRESENTING NG that introduces a new participant into the text. The listener is not obliged to ask "What fight?" in order to interpret the nominal group, for the group does not trigger an expectation that some needed piece of information lies elsewhere. PRESENTING NGs need not be very specific in themselves but they must *not* hint to the listener that prior specification is available elsewhere.

---

[1]Of course, these groups can be referred to through pronouns and thus initiate identity chains.

PRESENTING groups are interesting primarily for their potential in providing referents for other nominal groups. For example, in

(2)   well first he tried to carry salt/ and the salt melted in the water/ the next time
        he tried sponges/ and the sponges absorbed all the water/

the PRESENTING NGs salt and sponges provide referents for the subsequent groups the salt and the sponges. PRESENTING groups that provide referents are called INITIATING NGs here, for they initiate chains of reference.

Not all PRESENTING NGs provide referents. Some introduce participants into the discourse which are never referred to directly again. For example, in the cartoon description in

(3)   it's like he's caught in an avalanche/ or else he's been talking for so long that
        snow just keeps falling on the telephone booth/ it builds up in drifts/

the PRESENTING NG an avalanche presents a new participant but does not provide a referent for later nominal groups. The participant appears not to be mentioned again in the text. Hence the PRESENTING NG is termed a "NONINITIATING" NG because it does not initiate a chain of reference in the text.

Nominal groups that do and do not initiate chains of reference allow us to trace one way in which speakers can create coherent stretches of discourse for their listeners. INITIATING NGs are often used to introduce participants that play major roles in the discourse.[2] The actions of these participants can be carried in part through the chain of reference begun by an INITIATING NG. NONINITIATING groups, on the other hand, frequently introduce participants that play minor roles in the discourse. The actions of these latter participants are limited and primarily provide background to the activities of the major role participants.

In Section II below, an overview of speakers' use of nonphoric reference is given for TD, NTD, and normal speakers in cartoon, narrative, and interview contexts. In Section III, there is a detailed examination and discussion of how speakers introduce participants through GENERAL reference. And in Section IV there are analyses and a discussion of how speakers present information through INITIATING and NON-INITIATING groups. Section V summarizes the findings of prior sections and presents our tentative conclusions about how speakers introduce new information into their discourse, and how these introductions are distinctive for TD and NTD schizophrenic speakers.

---

[2]For the significance of major and minor participants in text, see the work of the Hartford stratificationalists: Gleason (1968), Gutwinski (1976), and Taber (1966).

B. Procedures

For each subject, the total number of nominal groups was computed. From this total, the proportion of nominal groups that were phoric and nonphoric were determined and were classified as GENERALIZED, GENERIC, INITIATING, and so on. Table 15 presents the proportions of nominal groups that were nonphoric and gives the mean numbers of GENERAL and PRESENTING NGs.

Nonphoric NGs constituted about 22% of nominal groups in narratives, 32% of those in cartoons, and 36% of those in interviews. This means that for the average speaker about 5 NGs were sampled in narratives, 56 in cartoons, and 23 in interviews. For 30 speakers, this constitutes a data base of about 2500 observations.

II. GENERAL Reference

A. Analyses

Table 16 shows the proportion of GENERALIZED and GENERIC NGs used by each of the three groups in each context. The bottom of the table gives the results of 3×3 ANOVA for each category.

Of the two forms of GENERAL reference distinguished here, GENERIC reference is highly sensitive to speaker differences and GENERALIZED reference is not. GENERIC NGs are sensitive to differences among speakers, and these differences depend on the context. About 9% of the total variance in the GENERIC NG data depends on speakers, 10% on contexts, and 7% on an interaction of speakers and contexts. In contexts with a verbal base, NTD speakers use relatively low proportions of GENERIC NGs compared to other subjects: in narratives, NTD speakers use about 2.8% of their nominal groups in GENERICS, and normal speakers use about 7.3%;

Table 15. Nonphoric Nominal Groups: Mean Frequencies, over All Subjects
(n = 30)

Contexts	GENERAL NGs	PRESENTING NGs	Sum = nonphoric NGs	Percentage total NGs
Cartoons	37.6	18.8	56.4	32.2
Narratives	3.7	1.7	5.4	21.6
Interviews	10.7	11.8	22.5	35.7

Table 16. Percentage of GENERALIZED and GENERIC Nominal Groups in Total Groups

	Cartoon			Narrative			Interview		
	TD	NTD	N	TD	NTD	N	TD	NTD	N
GENERALIZED	6.1	6.0	6.2	3.5	0.9	1.0	11.2	9.2	8.5
(e.g., *One* never knows*)									
GENERIC	4.6	4.2	5.4	3.2	2.8	7.3[a]	13.1	4.2[a]	8.2
(e.g., *Tigers* are fierce*)									

		ANOVA		
		Groups	Contexts	Groups × contexts
	df	2,27	2,54	4,54
GENERALIZED:	F	1.09	17.9[c]	1
	$\hat{\omega}^2$	—	.27	—
GENERIC:	F	6.7[c]	7.14[c]	3.08[b]
	$\hat{\omega}^2$	.09	.10	.07

[a] $p < .05$ for one-way ANOVA, $F(2,27) = 4.42$ (narrative) and 4.57 (interview) Scheffé tests ($p < .05$) show NTD < N in narrative; and NTD < TD, in interview.
[b] $p < .05$.
[c] $p < .005$.

and in interviews, NTD use about 4.2%, and TD speakers use about 13.1% GENERIC items. These contrasts are reliable in each case.

GENERALIZED reference, on the other hand, is used to about the same extent by all speakers. All speakers use high proportions of GENERALIZED NGs in interviews. About 9.6% of all nominal groups were GENERALIZED items as in

(4)   oh another thing that *you* see on acid

Speakers use less GENERALIZED reference in cartoon contexts (about 6.1%) and narratives (about 1.9%).

The GENERIC data for individual speakers support the trends for groups. In narratives, normal speakers use relatively high proportions of GENERICS and can be identified with a hit rate of .90, yielding false-alarm rates for NTD and TD subjects of .30 and .50, respectively. In interviews, TD and normal speakers are almost indistinguishable from each other, yielding hit rates of .70 and .80 for high proportions of GENERIC items. Both groups are separable from NTD subjects who show a false alarm rate of .30.

B. Discussion of GENERIC Reference

In order to explore further how speakers use GENERIC items, we distinguish *partitive* GENERICS from *simple* GENERICS. The distinction is useful because there is a general problem with partitives in determining whether the group contains one or two Things, i.e., for "a block of ice," is the structure in Figs. 6(a) or 6(b) correct? If there are two Things contained in a partitive construction, then one should code twice for REFERENCE. If one Thing, then only one coding is required. We always coded partitives twice, and if no Deictic was present, we always coded an embedded Thing as GENERIC. Both kinds of reference are GENERIC in the sense that they mark out a class of participants as a whole, but *partitive* GENERICS refer to some particular instance of the class by virtue of premodifiers (such as "a block of" *ice* or "some bags of" *sponges*) while *simple* GENERICS refer only to the class as a whole (such as *women* or *vegetables*).

Table 17 reveals that all speakers use partitive constructions in about the same way, but they differ in their use of simple GENERICS in the interview. In the interview, TD speakers use simple GENERICS in about 9% of their nominal groups, and NTD speakers almost never use them (0.8%). These proportions are significantly different. Comparable differences are not seen in cartoon contexts or in narratives (the latter data are sparse and are not given in the table but are summarized below). In the next section we consider why these differences occur, and why they occur in interviews and not in other contexts.

1. The Function of Simple GENERICS in Interviews. Is there a relationship between the use of simple GENERICS and the occasional bizarre language of the schizophrenic speaker? There are two interesting possibilities, both of which seem tenable. First, frequent use of simple GENERICS may simply reflect the experience of schizophrenia and the interests and concerns which develop from that experience. Second, extensive use of

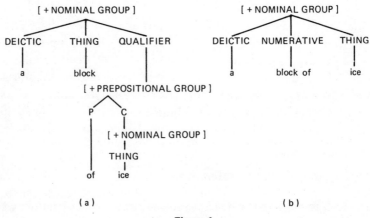

(a)   (b)

Figure 6

Table 17. Mean Percentages of G ENERIC NGs in Total NGS

		Context = interview		
	Partitives	Simple GENERICS	Sum = GENERIC NGs	Total NGs (n = 10 Subjects)
TD	4.0	9.1[a]	13.1[a]	650
NTD	3.5	0.8[a]	4.2[a]	520
N	4.2	4.0	8.2	720
		Context = cartoons		
TD	1.9	2.7	4.6	1860
NTD	3.1	1.9	5.0	1440
N	2.8	2.3	5.1	1950

[a] Tests of independent proportions between groups show highly reliable differences ($Z > 3.00; p < .001$).

simple GENERICS may result from severe problems in verbal encoding that occasionally confront the schizophrenic speaker.

Hypothesis 1: The Schizophrenic Life Experience. Let us consider some fairly typical examples from the interviews of TD speakers (*simple* GENERICS are underlined):

(5)   and it's like animals only mate some seasons/ you know I think man is the same way/ and I think if a woman has a, conceives a child/ . . .

(6)   mostly it's the Eastern people, the Chinese and the Indians and so forth/ that they take this sort of thing, reincarnation very serious/[3]

The use of simple GENERICS in (5) and (6) seems to reflect the interests of the speakers. Schizophrenic speakers, in general, seem more concerned with universal issues than normal speakers. This may be due to the nature of the acute schizophrenic experience and the particular life view which that confers (cf. Grof, 1976; Perry, 1976; Silverman, 1975). Any other speaker with similar concerns or experiences can be expected to use simple GENERICS in about the same way. The concerned Catholic speaker in the following example demonstrates that normal speakers can use similar proportions of simple GENERICS in discussing issues of religious significance:

(7)   there seems to be one unifying issue in all the literature you'll read/ and that is, that ah discontent ones former priests, former bishops, former husbands,

[3]With certain abstract nouns, the distinction between GENERIC and UNIQUE reference is less clear than with concrete nouns. "Heaven" and "hell" are clearly UNIQUE as Quirk, Greenbaum, Leech, and Svartvik (1972) show. Groups like "reincarnation" and "religion" are more borderline cases. We have to take them as GENERIC here since the surrounding GENERICS support the GENERIC interpretation and since one can imagine different religions and instances of reincarnation more easily than different heavens or hells.

<u>former wives, former everybody</u> is crying/ that religion is no longer relevant/ well now this has to be either the greatest incisive intellectual remark of all time of the most trivial expression/ . . .

To state this hypothesis succinctly:

> Hypothesis 1: Where simple generics are used in moderately high proportions (about 10% of interview NGs), they reflect the particular life experience and/ or concerns of the speaker.

That is, there is nothing special in the use of language underlying the TD speaker's moderate use of simple GENERICS.

Hypothesis 2: Encoding Difficulties. Hypothesis 1 is not adequate to account for some very interesting samples of TD speech. For example, consider examples (8) to (10) (*simple* GENERICS are underlined):

(8)   I like listening to <u>good music</u>/ I like playing <u>good music</u>/ I like to be <u>good music</u>/ I like to understand <u>music</u> all the time/ that is <u>music</u> which doesn't stop/ . . .

(9)   . . . /why don't <u>the rich</u> help <u>the poor</u>/ if we tell <u>the rich</u>/ they might help <u>the poor</u>/ if we're good to <u>the rich</u> and too quick to be, help <u>the rich</u> be good to <u>the poor</u>/ . . .

(10)   okay what else do you want me to talk about?/ I like <u>peaches</u>/ I like <u>pears</u>/ I like <u>plums</u>/ I like <u>apples</u>/ I like <u>vegetables</u>/ but I like I like <u>things</u> that are sweet/ I like <u>steak</u>/ and I like <u>stuff</u> like that/ but I like <u>sweet things</u> sort of sweet tasting/ I like <u>beaver</u>/ I like <u>bear</u>/ I like I never tried <u>muskrat</u>/ I like I like <u>milk</u>/ and I like I like <u>fruit</u>/

These are expanded versions of texts in which we found strong dependencies on lexical cohesion. As we noted in Chapter 3, there are some obvious characteristics of the speech in these samples. The sentences are mostly short with simple and parallel syntactic frames; the words are common ones; and the individual propositions are readily understood (though one could query "I like to be good music"). Moreover, although this might not be evident to the reader, there is a striking rhythm to the repetition of GENERIC items. The rhythm appears in the parallel intonation and stress patterns of the actual speech. The repeated presentation of the same or similar GENERIC items instead of balanced use of phoric and nonphoric groups also lends a distinctive continuity to the texts.

The use of the same or similar sentence frames and the use of parallel prosodic strings suggest that the speaker is playing with words rather than forming them into vehicles for communication. The speaker is somehow failing to create an adequate sequence of propositions, though the propositions considered individually are understandable. Perhaps we may characterize the speech as lacking in discourse structure. The speakers seem not to be processing their utterances at an overall text level but rather to be proceeding at a more superficial phonological and lexical level. It appears that the speakers are biased away from developing their texts through conjunction and biased toward grammatical, lexical, and phonological continuity. This characterization is somewhat speculative. Let us therefore state it in terms of an hypothesis:

> Hypothesis 2: Where simple GENERICS are used in high proportions (greater than about 20% of interview nominal groups) and accompanied by parallel grammatical and phonological structures, they reflect the speaker's difficulties in developing text at a semantic level.

This is to suggest that there is a problem in discourse production underlying the TD speaker's strong dependence on simple GENERIC items that is a language-based or language-implicated problem and not a matter of the speaker's world view.

2. The NTD Speaker and Simple GENERICS. Hypothesis 1 and 2 adcount for the moderate and extended use of simple GENERICS in interviews and are intended to describe the behavior of TD speakers. But they cannot account for the puzzling fact that schizophrenic speakers who are not diagnosed as thought disordered very rarely use simple GENERICS. At the very least, one might expect this latter group to conform to Hypothesis 1, and use simple GENERICS moderately often. They clearly do not. In fact, their use of GENERIC items is limited in several ways. First, they almost never use simple GENERICS. They use these items in only 1% of their total nominal groups, compared to 4% for normal speakers and 9% for TD speakers. Second, when they do use simple GENERICS, they do not use them in the universal sense that we saw in examples (5) to (10) above, but in idiomatic (cf. Quirk *et al.*, 1972, pp. 4–38) expressions:

(11)   I've already tried the R.N. course/ since I have a little bit of experience from the R.N. course/ otherwise I don't know what I'm going to be doing/ I could go to university all my life/ keep going to school/

And finally, their predominant use of GENERIC items is in the form of partitive constructions—constructions that are inherently limited by their premodifiers. For example:

(12)   /cause I just got a lot of bad memories there you know/

(13)   /and my mother needed a sort of independence/

It seems possible that these speakers are going out of their way to avoid using GENERIC items that have broad meanings. If they have had the same or similar life experiences as TD speakers, they should share a view or concerns about humanitarian or spiritual issues. But they very rarely express this in the texts collected here and this suggests either that they have not had those same experiences or that they have had that experience and are avoiding topics which are problematic.

The possibility that NTD speakers are somehow avoiding using simple GENERICS is interesting in light of the similar notion which we shall entertain for PRESENTING NGs in Section III. We shall see there that NTD speakers seem to avoid or at least very rarely use one kind of PRESENTING group. So there are two kinds of reference which seem to be used rarely by NTD speakers. Common to both is the fact that TD speakers rely strongly on these categories and perhaps "misuse" them. At least, TD speakers use both categories in the production of inappropriate stretches of discourse. Perhaps there is some connection between the errors of TD speakers and the apparent reticence of their companion group. Such an account is premature here but will be considered again in the general discussion of REFERENCE analyses in Chapter 7.

3. Why Do Some Contexts Reveal Differences between Speakers?
Why are we able to detect differences between speakers in some contexts and not in others? There appear to be two answers to this question. One has to do with the instructions given the interviewer in the cartoon task. The second has to do with the register variables outlined in Chapter 2.

The narrative and interview contexts can perhaps be opposed as respectively the most and least "structured" of our contexts. With the narrative context, the mode involves an orientation to the preceding story; the role demands that the story be retold; and the field is thus limited to the topic of that story. These variables normally circumscribe the subject's task. In the interview context, on the other hand, the mode does not necessarily involve an orientation to the immediate or immediately preceding situation; the role is simply that of conversing; and the field is more or less open, although some topics were suggested by the interviewer. The cartoon task falls somewhere in between in terms of structuring the subject's discourse. The first part of the task, describing the pictures, is perhaps as structured as the narrative context. The field is fixed by the pictures; the mode involves orientation to the immediate nonverbal context; and the role is to describe the cartoons. But the second part involves explaining the humor. Here the field is relaxed as different explanations of the humor were possible and the mode no longer tied the text wholly to the immediate context. The cartoon task is thus a kind of cross section of the interview and narrative contexts. However, the fact that the interviewer cut off talk irrelevant to the task probably lends this context more structure than a true compromise would afford. In a sense, we are arguing here that our task-based contexts are more highly "structured" than our talk-based context.

Narrative retelling then was the highly structured context in the present studies. It allows us to see deviation from normal use because every one of the normal speakers used almost exactly the same GENERIC items—they simply repeated at least one of the GENERIC nominal groups used in the original version of the narrative. Deviations from that norm occurred in what will be a standard mode for the two schizophrenic groups: NTD speakers did what the normal speakers did, only less frequently (in 6 out of 10 cases); TD speakers followed normal speaker's usage still less often (in 3 out of 10 cases), and more importantly, occasionally introduced GENERIC items which were new to the narrative. As one of our colleagues observed, "It's not always that what the thought-disordered speakers do is so bizarre—it's simply that no one else does it." So in the narrative, where the structure is very well defined, schizophrenic speakers are distinctive simply because normal speakers are so consistently alike.

Interviews were the least structured context studied. They allow us to see deviations from normal use because individual speakers are provided with so little definition of appropriate procedures for producing text. In this situation, some—but not all—TD speakers produce inappropriate strings of GENERIC items. Six of the TD group use GENERICS more frequently than normal speakers, and use them "inappropriately"— though we cannot define the inappropriateness very well. What is more systematic, however, is that NTD speakers again do what normal speakers do, only less often. This group of schizophrenic subjects uses GENERIC items only very rarely but when they do use the items, they use them in the same manner as normal speakers.

Finally, cartoon contexts were the situations that provided moderate structure to the speakers and a pictorial rather than a verbal base of reference. The content of the *description* was almost completely prescribed nonverbally, whereas the *interpretation* allowed the speaker rather wide opportunities for introducing an individual perspective. However, in this latter context, the experimenter cut the speaker off when the interpretation appeared completed. Reviewing the texts of the cartoon interpretations, one has the impression that TD speakers might have again relied strongly on GENERIC items or presented strings of GENERICS in parallel phonological and grammatical structures if only the experimenter had allowed more time for spontaneity. The following examples demonstrate how the experimenter sometimes cut off the speaker (GENERICS underlined):

(14) (Experimenter: Ok, why is it supposed to be funny?) Because who talks to
      mountain statues?/ who pays attention to stuff like that? You see I don't see any
      humor in it, maybe today/ I never did see much humor in comics/ the only humor
      I ever saw was in the, in the actual situations that people become involved in/
      (Next cartoon presented)

(15) (Experimenter: Why is that supposed to be funny?) I don't think they can
      drive right up a mountain/ that's all/ I don't see any funny thing/ a funny thing
      has, has to to be the, the sign itself/ cause it's not asking for peace/ it's asking
      for hope/
      (Experimenter: okay)

C. Summary of GENERAL Reference Analyses

1. All speakers used GENERALIZED nominal groups in about the same proportions, but GENERIC groups were used distinctively. These items (which deal with whole classes of events or things) were distinctive in two contexts:
    a. In interviews, TD speakers rely extensively and NTD speakers rely rarely, if at all, on simple GENERIC items.
    b. In narratives, normal speakers use only those GENERIC items that appeared in the original narrative. Many NTD speakers follow this practice, but only a few TD speakers do. Moreover, TD speakers are the only ones who introduce new GENERICS into the retelling.

2. It is hypothesized that speakers use simple GENERICS in interviews for two reasons:
    a. Moderate use reflects the speaker's life experiences and concerns for universal topics.
    b. High use, typically accompanied by a rhythmic stress pattern and parallel grammatical and phonological structures, reflects the speaker's difficulty in developing the text at a semantic level.

3. The hypotheses in 2 are supposed to fit the behavior of different groups of speakers:
    a. Normal speakers should rarely use GENERICS. If they do, it should be due to a particular preoccupation with universal topics (e.g., in theology students).

    b. Thought-disordered speakers should use GENERICS in moderate and high proportions, reflecting their concerns and their occasional encoding difficulties, respectively.

    c. Schizophrenic speakers who are not diagnosed as thought–disordered should at least use GENERICS in moderate proportions since they share the schizophrenic experience with their companion group. However, this group uses very small proportions of simple GENERICS. We speculate that this may be due to a restraint with items which are problematic for the TD speaker.

III. Presenting Participants in the Text

A. Analyses

Every nominal group which could be said to present participants in the text was classified as either initiating chains of reference in the text (INITIATING NGs) or as not initiating referential chains (NONINITIATING). Table 18 gives the mean percentages of INITIATING and NONINITIATING items. We are interested in three questions. First, do the groups of speakers differ in the proportions of items they use? Especially, do they differ in the extent to which they introduce chain-initiating reference into their texts? Second, does the proportion of INITIATING and NONINITIATING items change across contexts for all speakers equally? And third, regardless of the quantitative results, is the general pattern of response across contexts similar for all groups of speakers? The first two questions can be answered below. The last is approached in Section B.

NONINITIATING NGs, i.e., those which do not provide referents for other items, are used to about the same extent by all speakers. All speakers use these groups in about 9% of their narrative NGs, and about 14 to 15% of their cartoon and interview NGs. The differences are reliable across contexts, but are rather small for context effects. They account for about 18% of the total variance in the data.

Items which initiate referential chains are used differently across contexts and across speakers. These comprise only 2% of the nominal groups used in interviews, but 7 to 8% of the items used in narratives and cartoon texts. In addition, there is a small but significant tendency for TD speakers to rely on these less than other speakers do (4.1% versus 6 to 6.2%).

Table 18.   Percentage of Nominal Groups Which Do and Do Not Inititate Chains of Reference

| | NONINITIATING NGs | | |
| | Groups | | |
	TD	NTD	N
Cartoon	12.8	16.0	14.6
Narrative	10.2	8.2	8.3
Interview	14.4	12.7	17.4
	INITIATING NGs		
Cartoon	5.2^a	9.0	8.7
Narrative	5.6	8.5	7.6
Interview	1.5	2.2	2.2

ANOVA

		Groups	Contexts	Groups × contexts
	df	2,27	2,54	4,54
NONINITIATING:	F	<1	10.66^c	1.36
	$\hat{\omega}^2$	—	.18	—
INITIATING:	F	5.21^b	31.67^c	1.08
	$\hat{\omega}^2$	.06	.40	—

$^a p < .005$ for one-way ANOVA, $F(2,27) = 7.8$.
$^b p < .01$.
$^c p < .001$.

B. Discussion

The presentation of specific participants depends on a combination of the context into which a participant is to be introduced, and on who is speaking. When a PRESENTING group does not provide referents, then it is used in similar proportions by all speakers; but when it does provide needed information for other nominal groups, there are more variations in its use. To examine why and how these variations occur with one form of presentation and not with another, it is useful to compare the proportions of the two kinds of PRESENTING groups as they are used across contexts.

1. INITIATING/NONINITIATING Groups.   In the *task-based* contexts of cartoons and narratives, normal speakers use about 1 to 1.6 NONINITIATING items for every nominal group that initiates a referential chain. In *interviews*, they use many times that proportion—about nine NONINITIATING items for every INITIATING one. Thus, in task-based contexts, every other PRESENTING nominal group normally provides referents for nominal groups in the subsequent text; in the interview, such direct provision of referents occurs in only one of nine PRESENTING items. This demonstrates very clearly the profound effect that context has on normal presentation.

Examples of normal usage can be seen in examples (16) and (17):

(16) This is a man and a woman driving around a sharp curve of a mountain/ . . . /
      they're driving around the sharp curve of the road around the edge of the
      mountain/

(17) /the lift was actually, it consisted of a cable coming down and then just one
      bar, a wooden bar/ and you had to prop yourself on this/ and of course if you're
      in it for any length of time you know this was pretty painful/

Example (16) is taken from a cartoon description, in which: a man and a woman provide explicit referents in the verbal context for they; a sharp curve does this for the sharp curve; and a mountain for the mountain. In each of the INITIATING nominal groups (with solid underlines), participants are presented in the verbal context as if the listener had no prior knowledge of their identities and could not readily obtain such knowledge. We say that the groups are "INITIATING" because of the later occurrence of phoric groups (with broken underlines), referring directly back to the original referents. These later groups establish a connection between the participant being introduced and its subsequent occurrence.

Example (17) is taken from an interview in which two of the four nominal groups do not provide referents for subsequent items: a cable, and any length.[4] Evidently, these items provide background to the participant identified in "the lift." The NONINITIATING NGs seem to give detail and depth to the bare outlines of the event being described.

2. Schizophrenic Speakers. Schizophrenic speakers differ from normal speakers, with TD and NTD subjects showing unique patterns. The TD speakers used about double the normal proportions in task-based contexts (1:2.5) but are identical to normal speakers in interviews (1:9). And NTD speakers show a reverse pattern. In task-based contexts, they use about the same proportions as normal speakers (1:1.8) but in interviews they use markedly lower proportions (1:6). The last figure is interesting because it suggests that TD speakers behave normally in interviews and NTD speakers are different in some way. In the following pages, we study the texts from these two groups of schizophrenic speakers in some detail. This is necessary because, with only the bare proportions, one might conclude that TD speakers present information just as normal speakers do in interviews, and simply use more presentation in task-based contexts. This is not the case, as we see below.

a. TD in Task-Based Contexts. In structured contexts, TD speakers

---

[4]"A wooden bar" stands in apposition to "one bar" and in a sense both provide the referent for "this" which follows.

use about 2 to 2.5 NONINITIATING items for every INITIATING one, and this is about double the normal proportion. They do not use more NONINITIATING items than other speakers, so it seems that they are introducing fewer groups that provide referents than other speakers. There could be two reasons for this, one general to all verbal reference and one peculiar to INITIATING NGs. The general factor is this: TD speakers do not seem to use the verbal context to introduce participants to the same extent that other speakers do. Instead, they tend to depend on what is present in the physical situation, as:

(18)   /it's like he's caught in an avalanche/ or else he's been talking for so long that
         the snow just keeps falling on it/ it builds up in drifts/

In this cartoon description, the speaker relies on the situation when first mentioning three participants (he, the snow, it), by-passing three opportunities to use PRESENTING groups. At other times, speakers rely on a combination of the nonverbal situation and NONINITIATING groups. This is the case in (19) (NONINITIATING items are underlined; "it" is exophoric):

(19)   /I can't tell if it's snow or rain or cloud or fog or anything/

The second and more pervasive factor which accounts for the TD speaker's relatively high NONINITIATING proportion is reminiscent of the clinician's descriptions of concrete discourse on the one hand and vague and wooly discourse on the other. Thought-disordered speakers appear to underuse INITIATING groups relative to NONINITIATING groups because *most of their NONINITIATING groups are items intended for major roles in the discourse that have gone astray.* That is, it appears that the speaker *intended* to produce an INITIATING NG, introducing a primary participant and then referring back to the participant at a later point in the text but, this intention was thwarted.

One reason an intended initiation of a chain of reference is not realized is because of repetition: the speaker repeats the original nominal group with no clue to the listener that this information has already been presented. The cartoon description example (20) demonstrates this (NONINITIATING groups are given double underlines; INITIATING GROUPS are given single underlines):

(20)   /I see a woman in the middle of a snowbank/ I see a woman in a telephone
         booth in the middle of a snowbank going yackety yack yack yack/ and the
         snow is all piled up around her/ . . .

It is as if the speaker were signalling the listener: "Pay attention and store this away; this is new information you may need" and saying that again and again for the same items.

A second source of difficulty seems to be a kind of *miscalculation* of the presuming nominal group. In the following examples, the presuming groups fail to feed back directly to the PRESENTING items. This results in PRESENTING items that are single elements rather than initial links in a referential chain:

(21)   /the donkey was carrying salt/ he went through a river/ the river got full of salty water/ . . .

(22)   (In response to a request to re-tell the narrative)/there was an individual finding a way with one thing/ . . ./ it's something like that/

It is worth noting that the TD speaker does not always fail in the use of PRESENTING groups. Although these speakers fail to match normal speaker's proportions, they do follow the normal speaker's pattern of use. Like the normals, TD speakers use more INITIATING items in task-based contexts than in interviews. Thus, in broad outlines, the behavior of TD speakers is not different from that of other speakers.

b. TD speakers in Interviews. In interviews, TD speakers use the same proportion of INITIATING/NONINITIATING items as normal subjects. INITIATING groups are not a problem here because they are hardly ever used. We are seeing, therefore, a very low use of INITIATING items, which is the common practice, and a high use of NONINITIATING items.

This result is a little puzzling. If NONINITIATING groups are normally used to provide background information, and if TD speakers rarely use background information, how are TD speakers using all of the NONINITIATING groups that appear in their interviews? It seems again that these items are actually intended to serve as INITIATING groups in referential chains — to introduce participants that play major roles — but they fail for the same reasons that the TD speaker's INITIATING groups failed in task-based contexts. Items which could realize participants with major roles fail because they are repeated without any acknowledgment that they have been given before (23), and because they are not tied explicitly to subsequent nominal groups, as in (24) and (25) (NONINITIATING groups have double underlines):

(23)   /I've been listening to some Frank Sinatra, playing an album of Frank Sinatra upstairs/

(24)   /but there's a missing key to the missing key/ now what's that mean coming down/ and then there was a circle of, somebody described me as forgetful/ . . . . well keys are very important/ if you'd have to have, you'd have to have a key that fits the lock to open drawers, or what have you/ and someone also once described me as forgetful/ . . .

(25)   . . . /I remember going through the sea-aquarium, going just past the border and look at these here fish/ and I said to myself/ who the hell would want to be

a fish/ I said to them in my household[5] one day I think my next thing is I'll be
a fish/ you see I never had a sense of humor around my own family/ they
wouldn't accept me as I am/ . . .

In (24) "a key" and "a missing key" appear to encode the same participant, but both are PRESENTING. Similarly, "somebody" and "someone" in
(24) and "a fish" and "a fish" in (25) are PRESENTING items that could have
formed an identity chain.

   To summarize, in both task-based and interview contexts, TD speakers rarely use INITIATING groups appropriately. Very often when they use
a PRESENTING item, they do not successfully tie it to a phoric group. This
lack of successful tying means that we usually do not find discourse with
actions being carried through or with major participants moving
smoothly through several events. Instead, participants and events are
repeated and elements are connected indirectly (the latter are discussed
in detail in Chapter 6). In addition, TD speakers do not use NONINITIATING
groups as normal speakers do. They use little description in the verbal
context and so provide very little background information. Their NONINI-
TIATING items seem often to be INITIATING items that have failed. That is to
say, major participants which would be encoded in identity chains by
normal subjects are not part of a referential chain in TD subjects' discourse.

   c.   *NTD Speakers.* NTD speakers use NONINITIATING items as often as
normal speakers in cartoon and narrative contexts. In interviews, however, they seem to avoid them. Their transcripts show consequently the
lack of descriptive detail, as (26) and (27) demonstrate (NONINITIATING
items receive double underlines):

(26)   /we had, what did we do?/ we carried a lot of things with us/ and we met a lot
       of people/ a lot of different people/ we had a lot of good jam sessions going on
       and that, playing the guitar and that/ and things weren't too bad going out
       there/ it's quite it's quite a trip/[6] and I'd like to do it again/

(27)   (I: Can you tell me about a happy time?) /well when my son had his thirteenth
       Bar Mitzvah/ I was happy/ because we had a big affair/ and everybody was
       paying attention to me/ and he was happy too/ we both kissed him/ and he was
       the main attraction/ and we were all dressed up beautifully/ I guess that's all/

Although some NONINITIATING items are used, they tend to be used in
partitive constructions ("a lot") or are general nouns ("everybody,"
"things").

---

[5]Possessives neutralize the phoricity of the group they modify; "my household" may mean
"a house of mine" or "the house of mine" out of context; we code it as PRESENTING here as
it has no referent.
[6]The idiom neutralizes the phoricity of "a trip."

It is not clear why NTD speakers so rarely use NONINITIATING items in interviews. It might be that these are difficult to use successfully and therefore the speakers avoid using them in order to hide any difficulties from their listeners. (This could be similar to the data for GENERIC groups.) Or it may be that the level of difficulty is not an issue but speakers are simply less willing to reveal details of their personal experience and as a consequence, use relatively few NONINITIATING items. At any rate, NTD speakers are somehow avoiding using NONINITIATING items as descriptions, perhaps for the same reasons that they produce fewer clauses and fewer words per clause than other subjects, both schizophrenics and normals. It is possible that they are intentionally restricting their communications.

C. Summary

Both TD and NTD schizophrenic speakers differ from normal speakers in their manner of presenting new participants into their discourse.

1. TD Speakers. TD speakers rely less than normal speakers on items that initiate chains of reference. This is a statistically reliable but modest difference. However, in all contexts, there are strong qualitative differences in the way in which TD and normal speakers introduce participants. Essentially, the TD speaker's presentation often does not distinguish participants that take major roles from those that take minor roles in the events being described. Potential major role participants would normally be introduced through INITIATING NGs, items that initiate chains of reference in the text. However, these are often not used by TD speakers, because PRESENTING items are not followed in later clauses by phoric items that refer back to them. As a result, participants which could (and would in a normal subject's text) play major roles in the text are presented and are then never referred to directly again.

In addition, TD speakers often do not use PRESENTING items to introduce participants that could or should play minor roles in the text. Normally, such roles would be presented through the use of NONINITIATING NGs, items which do not initiate chains of subsequent reference. TD speakers use these items, but they use them to introduce potential *major role* participants, as described above. They rarely provide background descriptions through the use of minor role participants.

2. NTD Speakers. NTD speakers rely on about the same proportions of INITIATING and NONINITIATING items as normal speakers in task-

based contexts. In interviews, however, they use NONINITIATING items so
rarely that few participants which take minor roles are provided, and
their discourse texts lack descriptive detail.

Presuming Information from the Culture and from the Situation

When speakers use nominal groups which require referents, we say that they presume information. A group is considered *presuming* (or phoric) if it prompts the listener to ask, "What x?" or "Which x?" For example, in

(1)   *that guy* pulled a knife on me

the listener is obliged to ask "What guy?" The identity of the participant in *that guy* must be retrieved from the context of the utterance.

I. Text and Context

When we state that the speaker presumes information from a context shared with the listener, we are waving our hands over a vast domain. The domain includes all the evidence that must be invoked when one decides what is and what is not a text. For our purposes, this means deciding whether the discourse at hand is coherent within itself or if somehow something has changed. And the suspicion that somehow something has changed is often present when a listener encounters a schizophrenic speaker. Whether the speaker be normal or schizophrenic, however, the listener can be said to invoke two kinds of evidence to decide what is and what is not a text (cf. Halliday & Hasan, 1976, pp. 20–23). Listeners respond, we suppose, both to linguistic clues like the ones we are studying here—specific features that link a discourse together and form patterns of connection—and to nonverbal clues—to all they know

139

of the environment which bears on what is going on, what part the language is playing, and who is involved.

The general term *context* means here the *context of situation* in which a discourse is embedded. The concept was formulated by Malinowski (1923), elaborated by Firth (1951), and subsequently developed by Hymes (1967), Halliday (1978), Hasan (1979), and by many others (cf. Bates, 1977). It refers to all the extralinguistic features that have some bearing on the text itself. It does not refer to the fact that as this chapter is being written, it is a muggy August day in Toronto, Ontario; that sounds of a persistent telephone can be heard in the background; or that the writer is typing on a seven-year-old green Smith Corona. Context of situation refers only to those factors that affect the speaker's linguistic choices, such as the nature of the audience, the medium, the purpose of the communication, and so on.[1]

Thus, when we refer to the context of the discourse, we can mean many but not all characteristics of the total event in which the discourse functions. In the present chapter, we are concerned with the immediate (situational) and nonimmediate (cultural) context. In Section II, we shall focus briefly on what may be termed the *context of culture* (another of Malinowski's concepts). Roughly, this includes all events that are familiar in the life of a speaker–listener pair with a given sociocultural background. For the present subjects, this would include the circumstances they and their listeners share as North Americans, as Canadians, as residents of a particular large city, and so on. In Section III, we shall be concerned with the context of situation. This includes all events that are present in the immediate situation shared by speaker and listener, including the text itself and the nonverbal context. For example, this would include the conditions of speaker and listener facing each other from a distance of about 3 feet in a large room, across from a mirrored wall hiding a video-camera; and it would include the previous utterances that have been exchanged.

II. Presuming the Context of Culture

When a speaker indicates that the identity of a participant is recoverable from the *cultural context*, several possible distinctions could be made. One approach would be to use a dimension of immediacy, so that spatial and temporal events, which were not immediately present, were placed

[1]That is, the field, formality, role, and mode as outlined in Chapter 2.

into (approximately) ordered categories. For example, one could distinguish the present moment from the present day from the present month, season, year, and so on. This set of distinctions would be in the spirit of Weiner and Mehrabian's (1968) seminal work on the emotional distance speakers put between themselves and their listeners. This would be to adopt a "deictic" approach oriented toward the spatial, temporal, or social distance between a listener and the referent that must be retrieved. Alternatively, one can look at English and see how it classifies reference to the cultural context through its structure. The distinction which English makes is between HOMOPHORIC and UNIQUE reference. The HOMOœ PHORIC groups have a definite article in the deictic slot (e.g., the man, the Prime Minister) whereas UNIQUE groups are names consisting simply of a thing (e.g., John, Jupiter)[2].

We decided to classify reference to the context of culture as English structures this reference for two reasons. First, coding spatial, temporal, or social distance seemed too open to arbitrary classifications. Second, we believe that the contextual distinctions which matter in a language will be structured into that language and the way English classifies reference to the cultural context must not be ignored.

A. UNIQUE and HOMOPHORIC Reference

The feature CULTURAL CONTEXT in the REFERENCE network differentiates nominal groups as HOMOPHORIC or UNIQUE. These are summarized in Figure 7. UNIQUE reference is typically realized through proper names and involves assigning a name to concepts, individuals, or things in a community which members of the community must learn and share. For example, in

(2)   Snoopy is watching one of his butterflies go zinging by*

Snoopy presumes that the identity of the participant is already known through the culture which the speaker shares with the listener. To justify

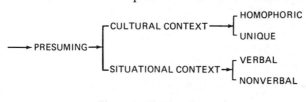

Figure 7. Phoric reference

[2]Names may include the definite article in a frozen colligation (e.g., The Hague).

this, one need only imagine that the listener rejects the presumed identity, as follows:

(3)   —Snoopy is watching one of his butterflies go zinging by*
        —Snoopy? Who's Snoopy?*
        —Snoopy? You don't know who Snoopy is? (etc.)*

HOMOPHORIC reference uses the definite article to mark out some object whose referent is accessible through shared membership in a community. Homophora is a gradient concept that may involve communities consisting of only a few people or including all speakers of the language. For example, in

(4)   I guess going on the roller coaster is my biggest thrill

the community sharing the knowledge of *the roller coaster* in a particular amusement park is very substantial but in

(5)   I remember going through the sea-aquarium just past the border

the community sharing knowledge of *the border* is likely to be larger still.

B. Analysis

Table 19 presents the percentages of nominal groups that are HOMOPHORIC and UNIQUE, along with the appropriate analyses of variance. The table shows that reference to the CULTURAL CONTEXT does not distinguish TD, NTD, and normal speakers from each other. For all speakers, there are reliable differences across contexts, primarily because the speakers do not make reference to the CULTURAL CONTEXT in narratives. The partic-

Table 19. Percentages of Nominal Groups Which Presume the Cultural Context

	Cartoon			Narrative			Interview		
	TD	NTD	N	TD	NTD	N	TD	NTD	N
HOMOPHORIC	2	2	2	0	0	0	3	4	2
(e.g., *The moon* is bright)									
UNIQUE	4	3	3	0	0	0	4	12	4
(e.g., *Mary* is here)									

ANOVA

		Groups	Contexts	Groups × contexts
	df	2,27	2,54	4,54
HOMOPHORIC:	F	<1	9.84^a	<1
	$\hat{\omega}^2$		.16	
UNIQUE:	F	<1	8.1^a	1.98
	$\hat{\omega}^2$		.13	

$^a p < .001.$

ular results for contexts are probably largely tied to the contexts used in this study. For example, we did not name any actors in the narrative, so there should be little UNIQUE reference in any case. This factor, in addition to the way in which narratives generally provide their own context (discussed in more detail in Section III) probably accounts for the lack of HOMOPHORIC and UNIQUE reference in narratives.

In the interview and in cartoon contexts, there is some small amount of reference to the CULTURAL CONTEXT. All speakers used a few appeals to HOMOPHORA(2–3%) and some UNIQUE reference (3% in cartoons and about 7% in interviews). This seems sensible, for in these contexts there were opportunities for the speakers to assume some shared community with their listeners.

C. Discussion

It is noteworthy that reference to the CULTURAL CONTEXT does not distinguish schizophrenic from normal speakers. This suggests that schizophrenic speakers, including those judged thought-disordered, can discriminate at least some important pragmatic features. Not one speaker seriously violated what seem to be constraints in the present narratives against appeals to the CULTURAL CONTEXT, and all speakers showed similar patterns of reference in cartoon and interview contexts.

However, let us be cautious in our generalizations from the analyses of the CULTURAL CONTEXT presented here. UNIQUE and HOMOPHORIC reference were insensitive to at least two possible failures by speakers. We did not distinguish instances in which (a) the speaker presumed a common culture that was not available to the listener, and (b) the speaker appeared to present more information than was appropriate, given the shared context with the listener.

Instances of (a) in which presumptions were not justified occurred in examples like (6):

(6)   you know I wanted Bert around

This is a case of UNIQUE reference to a context of culture in which the appeal is unsuccessful because the referent for Bert was unknown to the listener. Such instances were rare in the present data, but they might be more common in slightly different contexts and should be included in future analyses.

Instances of (b) in which too much information is given must be very tentative at this point, but might include the following:

(7)   I together with a little ten-year-old <u>S.P.</u> went for a walk to escape from some-
        thing evil

(8)   we moved from <u>50 J. Street</u> to <u>146 H.P. Avenue</u>

In both examples, the underlined nominal groups seem to give more information about the participants than is needed, given the very general
context of culture shared by the speaker and listener. It might have been
more appropriate not to identify the participants so fully.

D. Summary

1. Nominal groups which presume the CULTURAL CONTEXT are said to
realize either UNIQUE reference or HOMOPHORIC reference. The UNIQUE reference is typically realized through proper names. The HOMOPHORIC reference is realized through the definite article plus some Thing (at least),
which is recognizable through membership in a shared community (e.g.,
the moon, the roller coaster, the Queen's birthday).

2. Neither form of cultural reference distinguished among the three
groups of speakers studied here. However, it may be worthwhile in future studies to devise contexts eliciting more reference to the cultural context. Martin (1978) notes that young children have difficulty with names
and use more names in narratives as they get older. It would be interesting to check for a reversal of this development in schizophrenic discourse.

III. Presuming the Situational Context

A. Introduction

When speakers use a nominal group that makes reference to information located elsewhere, we say that the nominal group is presuming
(or phoric). When the information presumed is located in the culture, we
say that the context of culture is presumed. This was treated in Section
II. And when the information presumed is located in the situation in
which the utterance itself occurs, we say that the context of situation is
presumed. This is treated in the present section.

There are three ways in which nominal groups may presume the
context of situation: (a) through substitution and ellipsis,[3] (b) through
comparison, and (c) through definite reference to some identified participant in the situation.

---

[3] With substitution and ellipsis, the speaker presumes what might be called the content of a

Definite reference is far more common than comparative reference or substitution or ellipsis and it forms the focus of our study in the present section. Definite nominal groups require that the identity of a particular thing or class of things be retrieved from the context of the utterance. For example, if someone suddenly said

(12)   Here she comes now!*

she would be a definite nominal group with its referent in the nonverbal context of the situation. Alternatively one might say

(13)   Penny is always late. I hope she gets here soon.*

In this case, *she* would still be a definite nominal group, but the referent would be in the verbal rather than the nonverbal context.

In our introduction to reference in Chapter 4, we argued that every time speakers use a nominal group, they provide their listeners with clues for interpreting that group. With definite items, these clues are carried primarily by the class marked by pronouns, the definite article, demonstratives, and comparatives. In effect, every time speakers use a pronoun, the definite article, a demonstrative (e.g., this, that), or a comparative (e.g., another, bigger), they are instructing the listener to search for a referent in the situational context.

To claim that each nominal group carries an instruction to the listener is not to imply that the instruction need be very helpful. With most definite items,[4] the speaker only signals "Search elsewhere"; and does not indicate "Search the verbal context" or "Look right in front of you" or "You'll need a bit of inference here." Indeed the instruction seems much closer to a demand than a friendly guideline. The listener is informed that it is necessary to locate a particular referent and is not told where or how

---

nominal group but not the identity of the participant the group encodes. For example in

(9)   Susan saw some small papayas but wanted a big one.*

"a big one" presumes the content of "papayas" but does not refer to the same participants as "some small papayas." That is, the *identity* of the participant is not presumed, although the content of "papayas" is. For example, in

(10)   Susan saw some papayas but wanted a bigger papaya.*

the comparative group "a bigger papaya" presumes the identity of the smaller papayas. And in

(11)   Susan bought a papaya. I took the papaya to Henry.*

the definite group "the papaya" presumes the identity of "a papaya." Both groups refer to the same participant in the text.

[4]Some groups do give more help. Names point to the context of culture cited above. The demonstratives indicate distance if pointing to the nonverbal context; and "this" but not "that" can point to a referent which follows in the verbal context, so "that" in effect tells the listener to look to the preceding context when it is endophoric.

to do that. This surely constitutes a demand, and an "artful" speaker will presumably try to ease the listener's task by placing the demanded referents in accessible locations.

We distinguish four categories of referent location. Examples are given in Table 20. The categories are described in terms of *strategies* which the listener would need to recover the intended referents. The listener may recover referents from the explicit verbal context (endophoric retrieval) or from the explicit nonverbal context (exophoric retrieval) of the utterance. If no specific referent is provided by the speaker, listeners must somehow supply their own. This can be done by inference from a close semantic associate (bridging) or by the creation of a referent or the disambiguation of two or more likely referents (addition). These latter strategies are suggested by the work of Clark and Haviland (1974; Haviland & Clark, 1974).

The analysis of referent location for definite items is a fruitful approach to the comparison of schizophrenic and normal speakers. It allows us to conduct a detailed exploration of the speaker's art. In the present chapter, we study where normal speakers locate their referents and how these locations change with different contexts, and compare the locations of schizophrenic speakers' referring groups.

B. Psychological Processes in the Use of Definite Reference

By way of introduction, let us briefly suggest some of the psychological processes we may expect to be involved in the speaker's use of definite nominal groups. These items, as we shall see presently, are the predominant mode of reference in all speakers' productions in all the contexts studied here. They constitute about 60 to 80% of all nominal

Table 20. Retrieval Categories for Definite Reference[a]

Retrieval category	Location of referent	Example
Endophoric	Direct verbal context	A donkey was loaded with salt and he went to cross a river.
Exophoric	Nonverbal context	You are reading this sentence now.*
Bridging	Indirect verbal context	There's a house with two people standing in the door.
Addition	Unclear	A donkey was crossing the other river. A commuter and a skier are on a lift and he looks very cold.

[a] Definite nominal groups have solid underlines; their referents have broken underlines.
*Constructed example.

groups. Their popularity might be due to the efficiency which they bring to the communication process. They save the speaker from constantly having to re-present the same information, information that is often in a lengthy form. And they save the listener from having constantly to store information as if it were new. But once this is said, we can see a more important benefit to both speaker and listener. By presuming the specific identity of participants, definite groups have a potential to form referential links with other items in the discourse, and can help substantially to integrate the speaker's discourse. As a consequence, listeners may more readily decode and remember the discourse, and the speakers may more easily access their own productions and use them as a base for future utterances.

If definite nominal groups facilitate the integration of discourse by helping to frame a discourse structure, then the consequences of failing to use these items "artfully" should be serious. In the present chapter, we cannot say what would constitute a failure, because we do not study listeners directly. But we can lay the outlines for such a statement by examining how normal speakers use definite reference and determining whether schizophrenic speakers, and particularly TD speakers, act differently.

Broadly, what problems can we expect schizophrenic speakers to encounter in their use of definite nominal groups? For TD speakers, several problems should arise if our interpretation of earlier analyses are approximately correct. Three previous interpretations seem important here. In presenting new information, TD speakers seemed to have difficulty with linguistic processing. (1a) They did not manage to use INITIATING NGs very well, to establish identity chains in their texts. (1b) And they did not appear to use NONINITIATING NGs to provide background information, as other speakers did. Instead, they used explicit verbal description only occasionally and were more likely to use language to point more implicitly to the situation.[5] (1c) In addition, in effecting lexical cohesion and in depending on GENERIC items, these speakers again seemed to show evidence of reduced discourse organization at a semantic level, and increased dependence on phonological, lexical, and grammatical continuity.

If it is true that TD speakers do not fully develop their texts at a semantic level, then they should have at least three sorts of difficulties with definite reference. (2a) They should overuse unclear reference relative to

[5]For a discussion of reference in relation to explicit and implicit meaning, see Hawkins (1973).

other speakers, because they will have difficulty matching up definite items and their referents. This result is simply the other side of their failures with INITIATING NGs, and it will be surprising if it does not occur. (2b) They should rely on relatively low proportions of explicit verbal reference and should instead use high proportions of nonverbal reference (exophoric reference). This should occur in every context and not simply in particular contexts that promote nonverbal reference (i.e., not simply in cartoon contexts). Again, this is what we would expect from TD subjects' failure to use NONINITIATING groups as other speakers do. However, this is not a necessary result, and ,if it does occur, it will extend the observation in (1b). (2c) Bridging should be difficult for many speakers. Therefore, nominal groups should be found which form tenuous links to semantic associates, links which sometimes are judged to be bridged and often to require addition. This would follow from (1a) and (1c). If it occurs, it will extend the observation that TD speakers are not successful at discourse levels of semantic information processing.

Of course, there are alternative interpretations of some of the results sketched here. Result (2a), the overuse of unclear reference, could be accounted for in terms of a failure to access working memory, or an inability to consider the listener's needs. In discussion of the results, we shall consider some of the more tenable alternatives.

For schizophrenic speakers who are not thought-disordered, we have few expectations of differences from normal patterns. In the previous analyses, these NTD subjects behaved essentially as normal speakers did, only more conservatively. In general, they tended not to rely on items which TD speakers relied on extensively and/or misused. Perhaps, then, we might expect these speakers to underuse bridging if, in fact, TD speakers often misuse this category.

C. Analyses

Speakers presume participants in the utterance context very strongly and pervasively. In every context, definite nominal groups predominate. They constitute 80% of the NGs used in narratives, 64% of cartoons, and 58% of interviews. Table 21 gives the mean frequencies of definite NGs for each group and the percentage of definite/total NGs. An analysis of variance for the percentages is given in the bottom of the table. The differences in use across contexts are significant, and in fact account for a substantial 48% of the total variance in the data. There are no other reliable differences in the use of these items. This suggests that, taken as a whole category, definite reference is used about equally by all groups of speakers. This result supports the overall finding for reference with-

Table 21.   Mean Definite Nominal Groups per Speaker

Contexts	Groups TD	NTD	N	Total NGs (percentage)
Cartoon	121	90	125	64
Narrative	19	15	25	80
Interview	35	33	41	58

	ANOVA for percentage of Definite NGs/Total NGs		
	Groups	Contexts	Groups × contexts
df	2,27	2,54	4,54
F	2.95	45.0[a]	1.57
$\hat{\omega}^2$		48	

[a]$p < .001$.

in the verbal context reported in the cohesion analyses of Chapter 3.

D. Retrieval Analyses

Because definite NGs require specific referents in the situational context of the utterance, it is possible for coders to check whether the needed referents are actually provided. One can follow-up the speaker's instruction which says, effectively, "To understand me, search elsewhere," and ask: "Where?" The categories which are used for this follow-up are termed "retrieval" categories because they classify definite nominal groups according to where or how the listener must search in order to retrieve the referents which are required.

These analyses allow us for the first time to inquire systematically into the consequences for the listener of the speaker's use of reference. In studying PRESENTING groups in Chapter 5, we were able to pursue these consequences through *post hoc* analyses of the data. In Section II of the present chapter, we did not pursue the appeals to the cultural context in any depth, primarily because there were so few observations with which to work. But in the present analyses, there are many observations, and each nominal group requires a specific referent from the situational context. Consequently, we were able systematically to determine what the speaker's demands require of the listener.

1. Results. Every definite nominal group was classified according to the procedure needed to retrieve its referent. Four classifications were used: (a) *endophoric*, from the explicit verbal context of the situation; (b) *exophoric*, from the immediate nonverbal context; (c) *bridging*, from the implicit verbal context; and (d) *addition*, where the referent could not be definitely located in (a), (b), or (c). These analyses are based on about 20 nominal groups in narratives, 36 in interviews, and 112 in cartoons. For

30 speakers, this constitutes a data base for the retrieval analyses of about 5,040 observations.

2. Adequacy of the Subcategories. The retrieval categories account for substantial portions of the data variability and reveal substantial differences between groups of speakers and significant interaction effects. These results are given in Table 22, in which percentages of definite nominal groups falling into the various retrieval categories are shown along with the appropriate analyses of variance.

The bottom of Table 22 demonstrates the scope of the retrieval categories. First, the categories are described well by the treatment variables. In total, the treatment variables account for 60 to 73% of the data in three out of four categories. This means that no more than 40% of the variance in those categories is due to error. The single exception is bridging. In this category, one can account for only 16% of the variability in the data. However, this is still interesting because the major portion of the treatment effect is due to differences among groups of speakers. And this

Table 22.   Percentage of Definite Nominal Groups Which Fall Into Retrieval Categories

Retrieval categories	Context								
	Cartoon			Narrative			Interview		
	TD	NTD	N	TD	NTD	N	TD	NTD	N
Endophoric (direct verbal context)	55 [b]	73	74	69 [b]	79	86	46	43	46
Exophoric (nonverbal context)	38 [b]	21	18	5	3	1	42	50	43
Bridging (indirect verbal context)	4 [a]	5	7	8	4	10	3	3	7
Addition (context unclear)	2 [b]	1	—	17 [b]	14	2	9	3	4

ANOVA

		Groups	Contexts	Groups × contexts
	df	2,27	2,54	4,54
Endophoric:	F	4.19 [c]	62.8 [d]	2.66 [c]
	$\hat{\omega}^2$	.03	.54	.03
Exophoric:	F	1.87	90.1 [d]	3.13 [c]
	$\hat{\omega}^2$		.64	.03
Bridging:	F	5.99 [c]	4.68 [c]	1.17
	$\hat{\omega}^2$	.09	.07	
Addition:	F	11.18 [d]	23.35 [d]	4.93 [d]
	$\hat{\omega}^2$	.12	.45	.16

[a] $p < .05$ for one-way ANOVA, $F(2,27) = 4.26$.
[b] $p < .01$ for one-way ANOVA, $F(2,27) \geqslant 5.7$.
[c] $p < .05$.
[d] $p < .001$.

demonstrates a second point about retrieval categories: they reveal differences between speaker groups and/or interactions between speakers and contexts with sensitivity. The most striking example is with addition, in which group effects account for 12% of the total variability in the data, and interaction effects account for 16%. In both instances, the magnitude of these experimental effects exceeds that of our previous measures.

   3. Patterns of Retrieval Findings. Since retrieval categories account for substantial portions of variance in the data, and allow this in interesting detail, we shall examine the results for both individual categories and for the pattern of all retrieval categories across contexts. We first view the pattern across all speakers.

   a. Overall Data. If definite nominal groups carry an instruction from the speaker to the listener, then we shall want to ask how the listener should go about following such instructions. Table 22 provides some answers. In a task-based context like the narrative or cartoon task, the listener should first search in the explicit verbal context of the utterance. About 80% of all definite referents are normally located there. Failing this, and depending on the particular context, the listener should attend either to the nonverbal situation or attempt bridging to the verbal context. These categories account for as much as 10 to 20% of the normal speaker's referents. Finally, and only very rarely in normal discourse, the listener should try to create or disambiguate referents.

   This overview must be changed for other contexts and for other speakers. In the interview, normal speakers are just as likely to place their referents in the nonverbal situation as in the verbal context of the utterance (in about 45% of definite NGs, in each case). So a diligent listener would have to adjust his or her search priorities according to the context of situation. With schizophrenic speakers, the priorities have again to be adjusted. The TD speakers use the nonverbal situation as a source of referents almost as often as they use the verbal context. This is true not just in interviews but in cartoon tasks as well. Furthermore, TD speakers require addition fairly often, so listeners would have to be prepared to create referents when none are given. Finally, NTD speakers fall somewhere between the other two groups. Like normal speakers, they use a preponderance of verbal reference in structured contexts and a balance of verbal and nonverbal reference in the interview. But like TD speakers, these other schizophrenic speakers use definite NGs with unclear referents rather often.

   Having seen these data in overview, let us consider the retrieval categories themselves in more detail.

   b. Nonverbal and Direct Verbal Reference. Speakers use direct reference to the verbal context most frequently in task-based contexts (67–78% of all definite items) and least often in interviews (45%). Or, to say this almost in reverse, speakers refer to the nonverbal situation more often in the interview (45%) than in narratives (5%) or cartoon descriptions (26%). These results are true for all speakers. However, there are also some important variations in how speakers use nonverbal and direct verbal reference across contexts. Let us look first at how this is done with verbal reference.

Overall, TD speakers use significantly less verbal reference than other speakers. However, this is actually reliable only in task-based contexts. In both cartoons and narratives, TD speakers use about 10 to 20% less reference to the verbal context than other speakers. In interviews, all subjects use about the same proportions. As we would expect, results for nonverbal reference tend to be the inverse of verbal reference. The TD speakers use more exophoric reference than other speakers in cartoon descriptions and tend to use more in narratives. Again, in interviews all speakers use about the same proportions of exophoric reference.

In general, then, TD speakers use proportionately more reference to the nonverbal situation and less verbal reference than other speakers. This result is most evident in comparison with normal speakers in task-based contexts and is not seen at all in interviews. The NTD speakers tend to fall between the other two groups and are not reliably different from normals in any context.

Individual data. Analyses of individual speakers' behavior add to the group findings, allowing us to see in more detail how the different contexts are used. In cartoon contexts, TD speakers are clearly discriminable: 8 out of 10 speakers use low proportions of verbal reference and high proportions of exophoric reference, whereas few normal or NTD speakers show this pattern (2–3 subjects). In the narrative context, the results are similar: 8 out of 10 TD speakers use high proportions of reference to the nonverbal context, and no normal speakers do. NTD speakers fall between the other two groups (5 out of 10 subjects use proportions as high as those used by most TD speakers).

c. Indirect Reference. With indirect reference, the referent is a close semantic associate of the referring nominal group (as when "the door" is bridged from "house," or "the beer" from "picnic-basket"). Speakers use indirect reference to the verbal context slightly more often in narratives than in interviews (8% vs. 4%). This is a small effect, accounting for only 7% of the total variance in the data. However, speakers also differ among themselves and this difference accounts for 9% of the total variance, a rather substantial amount for a group effect. The difference reflects the fact that, in every context, normal speakers' use of bridging is almost double that of other subjects.

Analyses of individual speakers reveal that some discrimination of normal subjects is possible within each context. (a) In cartoons, 9 out of 10 normal speakers but only 3 to 5 schizophrenic speakers use high proportions of items that require bridging. (b) In narratives, every normal speaker and 8/10 TD speakers used at least some items that required bridging; but only 4 NTD speakers did this. (c) In the interview, although normal speakers could not be separated sharply from schizophrenic speakers, 5 normal speakers used more bridging than 19/20 of the schizophrenic speakers.

d. *Unclear Reference.* There are few nominal groups whose referents are not retrievable from the direct or nonverbal contexts of the situation (about 9 NGs per speaker in cartoon contexts, and 2 each in narratives and in interviews). However, the value of these few groups in discriminating between speakers and contexts is great. Normal speakers hardly ever require addition. They never require it in cartoons and require it in no more than 2% in narratives and 4% in interviews. In contrast, TD speakers rely on unclear reference in 2% of cartoons, in 9% of interviews, and in 17% of narratives. And in every context, NTD speakers fall between the other two groups. Individual speaker analyses suggest that the relationship between groups depends very delicately on the context in which the unclear referents are being used. In cartoon contexts, 8 out of 10 TD speakers use at least some unclear reference while only two of each of the other groups use any items of this sort. In narratives and in interviews, the three groups of speakers are indistinguishable.

E. Discussion of Retrieval Analyses

1. Sketching a Map for the Listener. As a way of introducing the discussion of retrieval categories, let us ask what the listener has actually to do in order to share the focus which definite nominal groups presume. In using definite reference, the speaker assumes that the listener knows or has easy access to some information. What must the listener do to gain that information? From the results presented above, we conclude that the listener must do different things with different speakers in different contexts. With speakers who are normal and who are engaging in some task other than talking (i.e., describing and interpreting cartoons, or retelling a narrative), listeners should search their memory of the recent discourse. This, however, is not the best tactic in an interview context. When speaker and listener are talking informally, listeners are just as likely to

154

Chapter 6

find referents in their representations of the nonverbal situation as in their memory of the previous verbal situation. In informal interviews then, the terrain of the search must be extended.

Without going beyond this approximate map, let us ask whether one can use it to discover the referent locations of the schizophrenic speaker. With an NTD speaker, the map will serve as a rough guide. But for TD speakers, the diligent listener must try a special transformation of scale:

(14)   Suppose that the TD speaker always behaves as a normal speaker who is in an informal speech context.

With TD speakers, the safest bet is to search equally often in the explicit verbal context and in the immediate nonverbal situation. This is true regardless of whether the putative context is talk-oriented or task-oriented. To be more precise, the proposed transformation will be helpful in *some* task-oriented contexts. In cartoon descriptions, for example, it is a fair guideline. In these contexts TD speakers require almost as much reference to the nonverbal situation as they do to the utterance itself (38% vs. 55%). In narratives, however, the proposed transformation seems misleading. Here, TD speakers used 69% endophoric reference and only 5% exophoric reference. These figures are hardly equivalent, and it would seem far wiser for the listener to assume a model of the normal speaker — to assume, that is, that in narrative contexts speakers almost never refer to the nonverbal situation. The problem with this conclusion is that it depends heavily on how one defines the situation. In the next section, we shall consider the possibility that schizophrenics define the situation more broadly than normal speakers.

   2.   Defining the Situation in Narratives. Our coders made an interestingly strict interpretation of unclear reference in narratives. Nominal groups were judged to require addition whenever a referent could not be found in the immediate verbal context or in the immediate nonverbal situation. That is, they treated the re-told narrative as context-independent of the input narrative. One may consider how strict a decision this is in light of the following examples from the first sentences of narratives (underlined items were coded as unclear NGs requiring addition):

(15)   a. well the donkey goes in the water with some salt on his back/
       b. well first he tried to carry salt/ and the salt melted in the water/
       c. well the farmer was going across the river with a donkey/
       d. the load was heavy because the elephant was carrying salt and that/

In (15), items (a) and (b), the referents do not seem "unclear" because the identities of the participants were given in the original version of the

narrative. On the other hand, some of the referents in (c) and (d) are obscure. Neither the farmer nor the elephant appear in the original narrative. In order to understand these items, one would have to create referents or make a rather heroic leap from the actual participants to the ones
presumed.[6]

In (15), there seems to be a difference between items (a) and (b) and
items (c) and (d): in the first two, the referent is easily accessible to the
hearer and in the last two, it is not. By treating the retold narrative as an
independent context, the coders were regarding reference to the original
narrative as neither exophoric nor endophoric. The reference is not exactly endophoric because it does not connect within-text events, the original narrative being defined as separate from the re-telling task. But it
would be possible to treat reference to the input narrative as "delayed"
exophora:[7] exophora to a just previous context. In a sense, the pattern of
reference found in the TD narratives resembles that of their cartoons [cf.
(a) to (d) in (16) below]. And it seems somewhat inconsistent to code a
phoric group as unclear in the narrative but as exophoric in the cartoon
task:

(16)   a. the memorials in the States down in uh/
        b. it looks like he's caught in an avalanche/
        c. the guy's looking at a bottle of whiskey or whatever it is/
        d. he has a mitt but he uses his bare hands/

Let us suppose for a moment that TD speakers are actually treating
the original narrative as part of the present situation. And let us expand
definition of exophoric reference to include what we may call "delayed
exophora", exophora to a just previous situation. With this expanded
definition, the addition category in narrative changes drastically. Table
23 presents the original values for exophoric and unclear NGs, (Analysis
I), and the revised values which assume that reference to the original
narrative is exophoric (Analysis II).

The table shows the consequences of a slight expansion in the definition of exophora. The proportion of unclear NGs for schizophrenic
speakers drops by about 60% and the proportion of exophoric NGs increases sharply. For TD speakers, 11% of the definite NGs are no longer
considered unclear but now fall easily into the category of exophoric ref-

---

[6]And notice that these new elements *are* presumed. It is not the case that the speaker
introduces a new participant, as in (e):
    e. there was a man about to cross the river*
[7]An alternative interpretation would be "delayed *endo*phora"; but this seems to give a very
narrow view of the speakers' treatment of the original narrative.

erence; for other schizophrenic speakers, 9% of the definite items change positions. The results for normal speakers are less dramatic. Only 2% of their definite NGs were judged to have unclear referents in the first place, so only that 2% can be considered in the reanalysis. What is interesting, however, is the fact that all of these 2% could be categorized under exophoric reference. For the schizophrenic groups, there were still some remaining items for which no referents could be identified. These constituted 6% of the definite NGs for TD speakers and 3% for NTD speakers.

Thus, expansion of the category of exophora to include the just-prior situation yields two results: (a) exophoric reference increases markedly for schizophrenic speakers but not for normals; (b) unclear reference drops to zero for normals but is still measurably large for schizophrenic speakers. These results suggest that much of the "unclear" reference in narratives was not unclear but simply classified in terms of normal subjects' interpretation of the retold narrative as an independent context in which the identity of participants could not be presumed.

It was suggested in (11) that one should use a model of a normal speaker engaged in talking rather than in a task as a guide to the referent locations of the TD speaker. This meant that one should look for referents in the nonverbal situation as well as in the explicit verbal context of the utterance. Our reanalysis of the narrative data supports this prescription. The general guideline for all contexts might be stated as follows:

(17)   Assume that the TD speaker will presume the identity of participants whenever possible.

Table 23.   Percentage of Exophoric and Unclear Reference in Narratives

	TD	NTD	N
Analysis I			
Exophoric NGs			
Personal reference	5	3	1
Situational reference	0	0	0
Unclear NGs	17[a]	14	2
Analysis II			
Exophoric NGs			
Personal reference	5	3	1
Situational reference	11[a]	9	2
Unclear NGs	6[b]	3	0

[a]Tests of independent proportions between groups show reliable differences between schizophrenic and normal speakers ($Z > 3.00; p < .001$).
[b]Tests of independent proportions show reliable differences between thought-disordered and normal speakers ($Z > 3.00; p < .001$).

Since TD subjects do not treat task-based contexts as context "free," as normal subjects do, this guideline provides an appropriate strategy for understanding about 60% of the otherwise unclear referents of the TD speaker.

There is something unfinished about this solution however. We have failed to note that all schizophrenic speakers act alike. The NTD speakers place their referents in the expanded situation just as often as TD speakers do. So, we must ask, is it really a wise strategy to suppose that these NTD speakers behave as normal speakers? In fact, it is correct to say that schizophrenic speakers who are not thought-disordered act somewhere between the other two groups. In task-based contexts, they refer to the nonverbal situation less frequently than normal speakers and more frequently than TD speakers. This is true in detail for both cartoons and narratives, as we shall see in the next section.

   3.   A Further Look at Exophora. How do the three groups of speakers actually invoke a shared focus with their hearers? To answer this, it is useful to study how exophoric reference is used in several contexts. Table 24 shows the percentage of exophoric nominal groups across three contexts, broken down into personal and situational reference.

Nominal groups with personal referents are those that identify speech roles in the situation. They identify the speaker (I, me, my ideas) and the listener (you, your friends) or listeners (both of you). They do not include the use of third person pronominals (she, their home) nor do they include the use of *you* in the sense of *everyone* or *anyone* (these instances along with *one* and the generalized *we*, are treated in Chapter 5). Nominal groups with *situational referents* are all other items that refer to the physical situation that is immediately present.

Table 24 shows that a different mix in personal and situational reference occurs in each context. Personal reference is used extensively in interviews, as one would expect, and is rarely used in the more task-oriented contexts. Situational reference is often used in cartoon contexts in which the speakers are asked to describe and interpret pictures that are in the immediate situation, but is normally not used in other contexts. The table also shows that schizophrenic speakers, especially TD subjects, tend to use more of both kinds of exophora—both situational and personal reference—than normal speakers. More precisely, schizophrenic speakers tend to use more of both kinds of exophora in task-based contexts. In the interview, all groups of speakers use about the same proportions. Let us now examine just what it is that the schizophrenic speakers are doing when they use higher proportions of exophora in structured contexts.

Table 24. Percentage of Exophoric NGs in Definite NGs

	Personal reference	Situational reference	Sum = exophoric NGs	Total definite NGs
Interview context				
TD	41	1	42	318
NTD	49	1	50	308
N	43	0	43	369
Cartoon context				
TD	11[a]	27[a]	38[a]	1061
NTD	3	18	21	755
N	6	12	18	1027
Narrative context				
TD	5	0 (11)[a]	5 (16)[a]	166
NTD	3	0 (9)	3 (12)	138
N	1	1 (2)	1 (3)	219

[a]Tests of independent proportions between groups show highly reliable differences ($Z > 3.00; p < .001$).
Note: Numbers in parentheses are estimates of delayed exophora from Table 23.

a. Exophora in Cartoon Contexts. Normal speakers characteristically give a detailed account of most elements in the cartoon pictures, as well as reporting what appears to be the central action or event of each cartoon. They use situational reference for about 12% of their definite nominal groups in this context and, in almost every case, they accompany their situational referents with identifying clauses and apposition. The examples in (18) are typical (exophoric elements are underlined):

(18) a. I see a boy standing there with a baseball mitt on a field/ and in the second sequence he's taken off his mitt to catch the ball/ . . .
      b. this is Mt. Rushmore in the U.S. pictured in outline/ a youngster in a car, a vacationing couple/ he is their son presumably or daughter/ waves to the figures in the rock high up in the mountains/ . . .

At the other extreme, TD speakers rarely describe elements outside of the central action. In fact, they hardly seem to "describe" the cartoons at all in the sense of giving a verbal account of separate elements and events. They are more likely to "point" to participants using pronouns and demonstratives to indicate their intended referents. They do this often, in 27% of their definite nominal groups and only occasionally accompany their pointing with extended endophoric reference or with more elaborate situational reference. The examples in (19) are typical:

(19) a. well they're all waving to that's Mt. Rushmore/ and there's[8] another mountain over there/ I guess that's where the Indians were/ they they are great men carved out of the mountains/

[8]"There" is stressed by the speaker, and so is regarded as exophoric.

   b. I presume this is a dog/ I presume this is a dog/ I presume that's a dog/ and
        that's something else/ I can't make it out/

In these examples, the pointing done by the underlined items is unambiguous, and it is easy to retrieve the intended referents from the situation. Occasionally, however, the referents are more difficult to access.
This may be because they are somewhat ambiguous as the speaker herself
acknowledges in the second clause (a) of (20), or because they require an
inferential step from the hearer, as in (b) of (20), where the dog in the
cartoon is taken for a lion:

(20)   a. this is simply outrageous/ I don't mean this/ this whole procedure is simply
            outrageous as far as this is concerned/ I suppose the most outrageous thing
            is that noise in the hallway/ . . .
        b. well it's not quite the Messianic time is it?/ the lion lies down with the man/
            it's not exactly like that/

Cases in which the identity of the phoric group was not directly retrievable from the cartoon occurred in only about 1% of the exophoric
items and were not classified separately. However, they are worth noting
because they show that situational reference can be confusing to the listener. In addition, TD speakers use a class of situational referents that is
difficult to characterize in terms of exophora. Exophora itself is not exactly the problem. What is troubling is that the speaker neither describes
the cartoon with verbal references nor points to it adequately with situational references. It seems instead that the cartoon is being described
more for the benefit of the speaker than for the benefit of the hearer. The
examples in (21) demonstrate this:

(21)   a. hello Charlie Brown/ he caught it/ and he forgot to get his glove/
        b. a ski lift/ what the hell does he think he's doing?/ 2-11-67 that's the date of
            it/ it's a good cartoon/

Again, examples like those given above were not very common. Perhaps four TD speakers used such interiorized accounts in one or two of
their ten descriptions.

The NTD schizophrenic speakers seem midway between the other
two groups in their use of exophora. They use little background description, as we noted in the discussion of PRESENTING groups in Chapter 5.
Like TD speakers, they tend to point nonverbally, and they tend not to
supplement their pointing with reference to the verbal context. However,
they use less reference to the nonverbal situation than TD speakers, and
they tend to point in a more descriptive or informative way than their
companion group. When these speakers refer to the nonverbal situation,
they are likely to use Deictics plus Qualifiers plus a descriptive Thing in

an elaborate pointing rarely used by TD speakers. The examples in (22) are representative (underlined items are exophoric):

(22) *a*. It's set in a little old-fashioned village/ or it's set back several hundred years/ the guy is in the stockade/ and so his hands and feet are sticking out/so one of the ladies is using his hands to roll the wool around/ so he's being put to some use even though he's a prisoner/

   b. the guy's looking at a bottle of whiskey or whatever it is/ and they're just staring at each other the bottle and the guy/

In cartoon contexts, then, we find significant differences in the use of situational referents by different groups. Thought-disordered speakers tend to point to participants in the situation and rarely supplement such pointing with identifying clauses and apposition. Normal speakers are less likely merely to point, and when they do point, they typically add on "redundant" endophoric reference. Nonthought-disordered speakers seem to take a middle path, using elaborated pointing and rarely using "redundant" endophoric reference.

b. Exophora in Narratives. In narratives, as we saw earlier, speakers do not refer to the nonverbal situation if the situation is defined strictly at the present moment. However, if the definition is expanded a bit to include the reading of the original narrative, then schizophrenic speakers use significantly more nonverbal reference than normal speakers (9–11% vs. 2% of the definite items). Although all schizophrenic speakers use about the same proportions of exophora in narratives, they use those proportions in different ways, and the pattern is strikingly similar to that seen in cartoon contexts. Thought-disordered speakers make strong presumptions about the hearer's information, normal speakers make almost none, and NTD speakers make some but supplement them with some helpful clues to the listener. For example, consider how speakers introduce the primary actor in the narrative, the donkey.

The TD speakers typically (8 out of 10) use the definite group *he*, giving their hearers virtually no additional clues to the referent. Other speakers never do this. The NTD schizophrenic speakers characteristically (7 out of 10) use definite items with a Deictic and identifying Thing—usually, *the donkey*—and occasionally use the PRESENTING nominal group *a donkey*. And normal speakers use PRESENTING groups in 9 out of 10 cases, scarcely ever requiring the hearer to retrieve the identity of the participant from their memory of the original narrative.

Thus, in the task-oriented contexts of narratives and cartoon descriptions, we find that TD speakers tend to use more referents to the nonverbal situation and fewer descriptive referring expressions (i.e., Deictic + Thing) than other speakers; and NTD speakers use referring expressions which are relatively elaborate, compared to TD speakers.

4. **Personal Reference.** There seems to be very little difference in the way in which the various groups of speakers use personal reference. In most cases, their use is restricted to "I see . . ." or "it seems to me" or other conventional sequences. What is indeed striking, however, is the powerful influence of context on the use of personal reference for all subjects. This suggests that efforts of earlier investigators (e.g., Lorenz & Cobb, 1954; Mann, 1944; White, 1949) to characterize the schizophrenic speaker's use of personal pronouns should be viewed with caution. One must always ask: What was the utterance context? Was it the same for patients and control subjects?

Table 24 indicates that, in task-oriented contexts, TD schizophrenic speakers tend to use more personal reference than normal speakers. However, (a) this is reliable only in one of the two task-based contexts (only in cartoon descriptions); (b) it is not true in either case for NTD speakers; and (c) it is not true for either TD or NTD schizophrenic speakers in interviews.

5. **Bridging and Addition: A Subtle Continuum.** How does a speaker form the subtle links of reference which carry a theme through from one clause to the next, from one sentence to the next, to form a cohesive text? We have so far explored some direct ways in which these bridges are formed. But now we come to a more delicate matter. How is it that the speaker carries us along indirectly, providing just the right balance of semantic information so that we move smoothly ahead instead of plunging into the next turn of discourse with only our imagination as a guide?

This question raises a central issue in the study of thought process disorder. In part, it asks the question posed by Blueler (1950) in his attempt to characterize the "looseness" of schizophrenic speech, and by Cameron (1938b) in his effort to account for "asyndesis"—the absence of "genuinely causal links" in schizophrenic discourse. It asks, roughly, how one forms an adequate semantic bridge. Of course, there are many ways to attack this question. One may focus on the nature of the explicit cohesive elements in the discourse, as we do generally in Chapter 5 and in the earlier portions of this chapter. One may study the thrust of predicative links, as Finn (1977) and Hobbs (1976) have urged, or characterize the central theme structure and its potential subthemes, as Bullwinkle (1977) and others have done. But in the present discussion, we approach the question of adequate links between clauses and sentences only with respect to the ties created by implicit reference. We raise this question in two forms. First we ask, how does one construct an adequate semantic bridge? And then we reverse the question and ask, when does an intended semantic bridge fail? With the first tack, we study examples of bridging: with the second, we study addition.

  a. Constructing an Adequate Semantic Bridge. Definite nominal groups sometimes seem to refer to nonexistent referents. For example, consider (23):

(23)   . . . /you can see they're like they're almost like a pattern with a flower/ they
      start from the middle and it's like a submerged ice cube/ that got frozen into
      the soil afterwards/ . . .

In this example, *it* seems not to have a prior referent, but if one looks far back in the text, there are possible candidates. It is as if, when one asks whether the referent for a pronoun is missing, the speaker could answer, "Yes, with an explanation." In almost every case in which a pronoun was coded as requiring addition, the referent seems to be ambiguous rather than missing. That is, it seems that with sufficient effort, the listener might make a guess at the intended referent.

  This brings us to the point that the referents for groups which require addition are not always irretrievable — they are just not *readily* retrievable. And so it seems fair to suppose that pronouns with referents which may or may not be present fit along a continuum of implicit referents that are easy to retrieve at one end and difficult to retrieve at the other. By categorizing an intended referent as bridged, the coders are in effect stating their certainty that the intended referent is item x ; by categorizing an item as requiring addition, they are stating their lack of certainty that any particular x is meant to serve as referent. The relative difficulty in making these judgments—compared to judgments about explicit referents—is reflected in the lower reliabilities for implicit categories, reported in Chapter 4.

  b. Considering the Composite Category. Since there is an arbitrariness to the decision that a nominal group's referent must be added or bridged, it is worth considering the two reference categories as a composite. This is done in Table 25. This table summarizes the proportions of bridging and addition in the total definite nominal groups used by each group of speakers and presents the composite proportions for those categories. The outstanding result is that TD speakers use twice the proportion of bridged + addition as their companion schizophrenic group. In both narratives and interviews, the two schizophrenic groups are at opposite extremes, with normal speakers in the middle. This consistency can be accounted for in terms of the following characterization:

(24)   *a*. TD speakers do not use bridging unless they also require relatively high
      proportions of addition from their listeners.

b. Normal speakers require high proportions of bridging and rarely demand addition.

c. NTD speakers require low proportions of both bridging and addition.

The description in (24) is useful because it allows us to distinguish each group of speakers from each other group, an accomplishment we cannot at all match if we look at either bridging or addition alone. Moreover, the pattern describes the individual speakers within each group. For both group means and individual measures, it suggests that the use of implicit verbal reference is an easy matter for normal speakers. They require implicit reference relatively often and rarely are obscure. However, for both groups of schizophrenic speakers, implicit verbal reference is a problem. Thought-disordered speakers seem unable to refer implicitly without also referring obscurely, as if the distinction for them between successful and unsuccessful bridging were shifting and unreliable. The NTD speakers can use bridging without also requiring high proportions of addition, but this is not without a cost. The cost seems to be one of restriction. The NTD speakers seem able to keep their unclear referent within bounds by attempting implicit reference only very rarely.

There seems to be, then, an excess on the part of TD speakers which contrasts with a restraint on the part of those schizophrenics who are not diagnosed as thought-disordered. Are these two findings related? Specifically, do TD speakers fail so often because they do not discriminate between easy and difficult referential links? And conversely, do NTD schizophrenics use low proportions of unclear reference because they are cautious about when or how they attempt to bridge the verbal context? We cannot answer these questions with any certainty, but is is tempting to suggest that the NTD speakers are using some rather strict editing procedures, procedures that are ignored by or not available to TD subjects. A

Table 25. Composite Values of Bridging and Addition in Two Verbal Contexts

	Bridging (percentage)	Addition[a] (percentage)	Total percentage	Total Definite NGs
	Context = interview			
TD	3	9	12[b]	166
NTD	3	3	6	138
N	7	4	11	219
	Context = narrative			
TD	8	6	14[b]	318
NTD	14	3	7	208
N	10	0	10	369

[a]Addition adjusted according to Analysis II, Table 23.
[b]Tests of independent proportions between groups show reliable differences between the two schizophrenic groups, $Z > 2.0$; $p < .05$.

similar interpretation is suggested by Sullivan's (1944) account of an inadequate "fantastic auditor" for some schizophrenic speakers, and by Cohen, Nachmani, and Rosenberg's (1974) "Impulsive Speaker" model of the schizophrenic speaker.

c. *Qualitative Differences in the Use of Indirect Reference.* In the quantitative analyses of indirect reference given above, we saw that NTD speakers differed from the other subjects. In effect, they looked least normal. Now, as we turn to qualitative analyses, the trend reverses. The NTD speakers behave essentially as normal speakers do, and it is TD speakers who are unique.

Let us consider some examples of bridging in normal and NTD speakers. Example (25) is taken from the narrative of a normal speaker (the bridged items have solid underlines, their referents have broken underlines):

(25)   there's a donkey carrying a couple of sacks of salt/ then he came to a river/ he
        was crossing the river/ and he fell into it/ with his cool refreshing water/ he
        decided to stay in for a few minutes/ he noticed that the load got lighter be-
        cause the salt had dissolved in the water/ and he decided the next day that he
        would try the same trick again/ . . .

Our classification of types of bridging is a tentative one and likely to be amended on the basis of further research. However, here we will note three broad types of bridging. The first depends on part-whole or implicational relationships between participants encoded as nominal groups. For example, once *house* is mentioned, the *roof, door, window,* etc., can be easily bridged. A very common example of this in our texts was bridging *the water* from *the river* or vice versa since rivers are full of (consist of) water. An example of an implicational bridge would be *the marriage* from *a divorce* since divorcées must have been married at one point. A second category includes spatial and temporal groups that are generally inferable in a situation. For example, *the ground* is inferable in an outdoor context; *the morning* is easily infered from someone sleeping. In (25), *the next day* is bridged from the fact that the action in the first five clauses obviously took place one day, though this time is not coded explicitly as a participant. The third category involves groups that refer to clauses or sets of clauses. *The load* in (25) is bridged from the first clause, from *a donkey carrying . . . sacks. The same trick* is bridged from the whole of the preceding clause. Because this third category involves an interpretation of the story on the part of the listener, we consider it a more sophisticated type of bridging than the first two categories.

Normal speakers use all three kinds of bridging in their narratives and interviews. And so do NTD schizophrenic speakers, as example (26) demonstrates (bridged items have solid underlines; their referents have broken ones):

(26)   a. . . . and my mother needed a sort of independence/ she'd always been extremely dependent on my father/ . . . I imagine that there were probably about ten happy years/ because she said/ you don't know what it was like during the beginning of the marriage/

b. . . . and the parents think they've had enough of nature/ and they try to take [the children] to England/ but on the way they get captured by the pirates/

c. . . . so when he went into the water the sponges filled up/ and he couldn't move/ and he was drowned because of the weight/

In example (26), the first type of bridging, implicational, is illustrated in (a); the second, spatial, in (b); and the third, inferential, in (c).

Examples like these were not common. It was common, as noted in the results section, for NTD speakers not to bridge at all in narratives and to bridge very little in interviews. However, when these subjects did refer indirectly to the verbal context, they seem to have been capable of making connections that were as complex and subtle as those made by normal speakers.

For TD speakers, with a single exception,[9] there are almost no examples of bridging of the third type in which an inference from whole clauses is required. Example (27) gives an instance of implicational bridging as having a key implies the lock it fits.

(27)   . . . / well keys are very important/ if you'd have to have, you'd have to have a key that fits the lock to open drawers or what have you/

Hopefully, these characterizations convey what seems to be the case for the content of bridged items: Normal and NTD speakers use rather sophisticated forms of bridging, linking definite nominal groups inferentially to clauses and sets of clauses, whereas TD speakers almost never use such forms.

6. A Note on Cartoon Contexts. There is a problem in coding addition and bridging in cartoon contexts. The problem arises because the

---

[9]One TD speaker differed from others in her group in two respects: she was able to require high proportions of bridging without also requiring high proportions of addition, and the bridging she did invoke was as developed and complex as that of any normal speaker. This is shown in the following excerpt from her interview:

. . . / and if a woman has a, conceives a child/ at a time when she's like perfectly happy with it then the baby, she doesn't have such painful labor/

cartoon pictures provide so very much information to the listener. There is so much information in the pictures that even a vague approximation will do to point the listener toward the speaker's intended referents. For example, listeners can easily find the referent for "it," "the dog," or perhaps even "the lion" if they are looking at a cartoon of a St. Bernard dog with a man. So it is actually very difficult to produce unclear referents for simple pictures. One must either misidentify a participant (e.g., refer to a male as *her*) or identify a participant ambiguously (e.g., refer to *him* when there are two males in the cartoon). With bridging, there is a related problem. Because participants are physically present in the cartoon pictures, one cannot determine whether the nominal groups describing those participants are bridging previous verbal referents or are simply being introduced exophorically. Example (28) demonstrates this problem in an excerpt from a TD speaker (bridged items have solid underlines; the referent has broken ones):

(28) Santa Claus, coming down off the chimney/ came down through it/ he lifts the sled and the reindeer/

Our coders were instructed to code an item as bridged if it possibly referred indirectly to the verbal context, and as endophoric if it possibly referred directly to the verbal context. This resulted in a strong coding bias toward the verbal context. Whenever an item could be interpreted as exophoric or endophoric, we erred in the direction of the verbal context and probably underestimated the extent of reference to the nonverbal situation.

We know of no way at present of resolving the referential ambiguity of phoric groups other than in this mechanical way. All that can be said in favor of our coding bias is that normal subjects share the bias when encoding their own texts, preferring endophoric to exophoric reference. At any rate, we are probably underestimating the true proportion of addition and overestimating the true proportion of bridging in the cartoon task. For this reason, we did not include the cartoon data in the reanalyses of bridging and addition presented above.

F. Summary

1. Explicit Reference
   a. Normally, to find most referents for definite nominal groups, the listener should search the explicit verbal context of the utterance.
   (1) This is true if the discourse is task-based.

      (2) If the discourse is talk-based, the listener should search both the nonverbal and the verbal context.

  b. With TD speakers, strategy (2) is appropriate for the listener. That is, in all contexts the listener should follow guidelines for a normal speaker in talk-based contexts.

  c. If the speaker is schizophrenic but not thought-disordered, strategies (1) and (2) are fairly adequate. To be more successful in locating referents, the diligent listener should slightly overuse strategy (2), using it occasionally in talk-based contexts.

  d. In task-based contexts, the details of direct reference depend on the speaker.

      (1) Normal speakers describe participants with primary reference to the verbal context. When they refer to the nonverbal situation, it is generally to the cartoon as pictures rather than to participants and events. The exophoric reference is part of an identifying clause which contains groups that spell out the identity of the exophoric group (e.g., "*this* is Mt. Rushmore in the U.S. pictured in outline").

      (2) TD speakers rarely describe but often "point" with their words, using pronouns and demonstratives and omitting the thing which would clarify their reference (e.g., "*it* is rising"; "*that*'s not funny").

      (3) NTD speakers rarely describe but when they "point" they use more experiential content encoded in the thing (such as *the guy* instead of *he*, and *this old village* instead of *it*).

  e. The use of personal reference (I, my friends) depends on both context and speaker.

      (1) All speakers use the same proportions of personal reference in interviews.

      (2) In cartoon contexts, TD speakers use more personal reference than normal speakers.

      (3) NTD speakers do not differ from normal speakers in any of the three contexts.

2. The Continuum from Indirect to Unclear Reference

  a. About 10% of all definite items presume unclear or indirect referents. TD speakers use about twice as many such items as other schizophrenic speakers.

  b. Different groups of speakers show different patterns of use for indirect and unclear reference.

(l) Normal speakers rely on high proportions of bridging and little or no addition.

(2) TD speakers do not rely on bridging unless they also require high proportions of addition.

(3) NTD speakers require little bridging and little addition.

c. The quality of bridging differs in different groups.

(1) Normal and NTD speakers bridge from part/whole and implicational associates of definite nominal groups and inferentially from a clause or set of clauses.

(2) TD speakers bridge primarily from part/whole or implicational associates.

d. The generalizations in (1) to (3) are made for contexts with a primarily verbal base, i.e., narratives and interview. They are not intended to apply to contexts with a pictorial base such as cartoons.

The Discourse of Schizophrenic Speakers: A Discussion

I. Introduction

In Chapter 1 we suggested that the diagnosis of thought disorder involves a double inference. The clinician procedes from a personal experience of confusion to infer that the patient is confused. The inference is made to account for the listener's experience. Next, from the conclusion that the patient's speech is confusing, the clinician infers that the patient's thought must be confused. This inference is an effort to account for the speaker's behavior.

In later chapters, we tried to describe the middle premise of the double inference—the patient's speech. What is it, we asked, that confuses a listener so that he or she speculates about the speaker's thought process? To answer, we attempted to discover how the language use of "confusing" speakers (those judged to show thought disorder) differed from that of other speakers. Our aim was to characterize some of the ways in which the schizophrenic speaker creates, or fails to create, coherent discourse. To do this, we used a method of successive approximations. Each chapter described in more detail aspects of language we studied in earlier chapters. In Chapter 3, we began by asking how speakers form their narratives and interviews into cohesive productions. We found two kinds of differences among the groups. In narratives, schizophrenic speakers relied less on cohesive tying than normal speakers. For NTD speakers, this could be largely attributed to the speakers' relatively low productivity, but for TD schizophrenics, productivity could not account for the data, and we could not explain the low cohesion scores. Next, in interviews, many TD speakers relied heavily on lexical cohesion, and this co-occurred with uses of language which we did not see in the samples from other speakers: sequences of clauses with parallel grammatical and phonological (including rhythm and intonation) structures; topicalization which seemed to follow lexical ties; and, occasionally, singing.

In Chapters 4 to 6, we tried to make these results clearer. A REFERENCE analysis was used to distinguish the ways in which English speakers can present new information and presume old information in their talk. Where specific old information was presumed, items were divided into retrieval categories according to what the listener needed to do to find the information required. Three results emerged from these analyses. First, schizophrenic speakers frequently did not encode participants in the verbal context but depended instead on the nonverbal situation. Second, TD speakers relied strongly on lexical cohesion whereas, NTD speakers did not. And finally, TD speakers failed in several ways to create referential ties in their discourse, both in the presentation of new participants and in the presumption of old ones.

In the present chapter we discuss the results of these analyses from several perspectives. First, we consider why TD speakers sometimes fail to produce coherent discourse. This takes us, in Section II, to summary descriptions of the three groups of speakers through discriminant function analyses. In Section III, it leads us to question how the distinctive uses of language by TD and NTD speakers bear on their ability to use language. In Section IV, we consider other strategies for studying the discourse of schizophrenic speakers and review the limitations of the approach we have used here.

II. Discriminating among the Groups of Speakers

In order to summarize the quantitative results of reference and retrieval analyses, we forced the three groups of speakers to be as distinct as possible. Seven measures in each context were subjected to stepwise discriminant function analyses. The measures were those that had been most sensitive to group differences in the univariate analyses reported in Chapters 5 and 6. The seven measures for three contexts gave a total of 21 discriminating variables: the four retrieval categories (endophora, exophora, bridging, and addition), the two presenting categories (INITIATING and NONINITIATING groups), and GENERIC items in cartoon, narrative, and interview contexts.

Table 26. Speaker Classifications Based on Stepwise Discriminant Function Analyses

	Cartoon texts			
Percentage correctly classified		Percentage misclassified		
		As TD	As NTD	As N
TD	90	x	10	0
NTD	30	40	x	30
N	70	0	30	x

Discriminating variables: INITIATING items, addition, bridging

	Narratives			
TD	80	x	10	10
NTD	60	30	x	10
N	100	0	0	x

Discriminating variables: addition, GENERICS, bridging

	Interviews			
TD	60	x	20	20
NTD	80	20	x	0
N	70	10	20	x

Discriminating variables: GENERICS, addition, NONINITIATING, and bridging

	All Texts			
TD	100	x	0	0
NTD	100	0	x	0
N	90	10	0	x

Discriminating variables: Total = 11, Top 5 are: addition (narrative), INITIATING (cartoon), bridging (cartoon), GENERICS (interview & cartoon)

The analyses for each of the contexts and overall contexts are summarized in Table 26.

Overall contexts, 11 of the 21 variables contribute significantly to the differentiation of groups. When all 11 variables are used, 29/30 speakers can be correctly classified. All TD and NTD and nine out of ten normal speakers are correctly classified.

This is precisely what we want in overview — the smallest number of variables which will give the best discriminating power among the three groups. This overall analysis does not actually reveal which variables are maximally sensitive in the individual contexts. It only indicates which ones account for most, and then next most, and next most, of the remaining variability among the groups. So the first several variables are interesting, and those remaining are simply taking up the leavings of the major variables. Therefore, let us note the first five: (1) addition in narratives; (2) INITIATING groups in cartoons; (3) bridging in cartoons; and (4) and (5) are GENERICS in interviews and narratives, respectively.

Table 26 also summarizes the results for individual contexts. In every case, the discriminating variables include bridging and addition in combination with GENERICS and/or INITIATING/NONINITIATING groups. The particular combination of successful variables depends on the context.

Normal speakers rely relatively often on implicit reference. Their implicit referents are almost always accessible through bridging and rarely require addition. However, more addition is required in the interview than in task-based contexts. When these speakers present new participants in the text, they initiate chains of reference and they also use noninitiating groups. The balance depends on the context: in task-based contexts, these speakers rely about equally on INITIATING and NONINITIATING groups; in interviews, they initiate chains of reference less often and rely more on NONINITIATING groups. Occasionally, they use GENERIC items.

The TD speakers also rely on high proportions of implicit reference, but their referents are frequently inaccessible to the listener. About once every two or three times that they use implicit reference, their referent is obscure. This is true if there is a verbal base to the context. If there is an image base, as in cartoon descriptions, then there are fewer unclear references. In introducing new participants, these speakers rarely initiate chains of reference. However, they use NONINITIATING groups in about the same proportions as normal speakers do. In addition, they use GENERIC items relatively often in interviews and narratives.

Finally, NTD speakers rarely rely in implicit reference. This is true in general, and especially in interview contexts. In interviews, NTD speakers rarely require bridging or addition, and rarely use NONINITIATING groups. And, unlike other schizophrenic subjects, they rarely use GENERIC items.

III. Implications of the Results for the Language Abilities of Schizophrenic Speakers

Why do some schizophrenic speakers produce coherent discourse but others do not? There are two parts to this question, as we have argued in Chapter 1. The first part concerns the listener's judgment of coherence; the second concerns the causes of the speaker's behavior.

What prompts a listener to assess some discourse samples as coherent and others as incoherent? Our initial work on this question appears in an earlier paper (Rochester, Martin, & Thurston, 1977) and is summarized in Chapter 2. It involves a statistical assessment of judges' evaluations as they relate to TD and NTD use of various cohesive strategies. What is needed now is more systematic experimentation with normal listeners to assess the effects of the strategies used by TD and NTD and normal speakers. For example, our statistical study suggests that the general schizophrenic reliance on nonverbal context is not disruptive to listeners, but that the use of ambiguous referents is. One would like to know what it is that gets disrupted — storage processes, comprehension, anticipation of new information? When a chain of inference is called for by the speaker, what does the listener require to arrive at the correct (i.e., intended) interpretation? Hobbs (1976) suggests that the listener is continually evaluating the salience of participants, based on the context in which the discourse is occurring. But if context for normal speakers means primarily "foregoing verbal context" and if for schizophrenic speakers it means "nonverbal and verbal context," then there may be many miscalculations of salience by normal listeners. Such errors could contribute to comprehension failures but might be easily remedied. Other problems might be less easily solved. Hobbs's (1976) work and that of Garrod and Sanford (1978) offer some valuable models of listener processes that could be tested in connection with schizophrenic speaker strategies.

The second part of the question of coherence concerns the speaker's abilities to use language. It will occupy us for the remainder of the present chapter. In Table 27, the three distinctive characteristics of discourse which distinguished our three groups of speakers are summarized.

The table indicates that reference to the nonverbal situation, the presentation of new and presumption of old information, and a reliance on lexical cohesion distinguish the groups of speakers. The last two categories distinguish TD subjects from all other speakers, both schizophrenic and normal. This summary suggests two points about the language abilities of young, relatively intact TD speakers like those studied here. First, it indicates that there are certain identifiable language uses that TD speakers cannot manage very well, but that are within the capabilities of NTD schizophrenic speakers. Discriminant function analyses distinguish every TD speaker from every NTD speaker on the basis of this usage, so it appears that TD and NTD schizophrenic patients can be discriminated purely on the basis of their language. Secondly, the summary indicates that the distinction between TD and other speakers is at a highly developed level of language use—and not at the level of word salad or neologisms or speech blocking. For the patients studied here, there is a clear problem in the use of language, but it is not a simple problem.

Table 27.   Some Characteristics of Schizophrenic Discourse

TD schizophrenics	NTD schizophrenics	Normals
1. There is a bias away from verbal encoding, with high exophoric reference in task-based contexts.	(Similar to TD schizophrenics). Bias away from verbal.	(Different from TD schizophrenics). Bias toward verbal.
2. There are problems with systems which present and presume information.	(Different from TD schizophrenics). Limited use of presumptional systems.	(Different from TD schizophrenics). Presumption is not a problem.
a. In presenting information, major role participants may not initiate chains of reference, but minor role participants may.	a. Minor role participants are not presented.	a. Major role participants initiate chains of reference; minor role participants do not.
b. In presuming information, indirect reference is accompanied by ambiguous or obscure reference.	b. Indirect reference is rare.	b. Implicit reference is made without obscure reference.
3. Lexical features are important sources of discourse links.	(Different from TD schizophrenics). Little reliance on lexical ties.	(Different from TD schizophrenics). Moderate reliance on lexical ties.
a. There is high lexical cohesion in interviews.	a. There is low lexical cohesion in interviews.	
b. There is high use of GENERIC groups in interviews.	b. There is low use of GENERIC groups.	

The fact that the TD speaker appears to have an identifiable language problem that is not simple has led us to speculate that TD speakers might have occasional problems in encoding their speech at the level of discourse, but not at the level of expression (sound or writing) nor at the level of lexicogrammatical form. Such encoding difficulties need not always occur, but could vary according to the interpersonal and cognitive demands made on the speaker in different discourse contexts. In the next section, we present this formulation in more detail and discuss how well it accounts for the data in the preceding chapters and in the literature at large. Later, we consider whether hypotheses of hemispheric assymetries of function are useful in predicting shallow encoding in some but not all schizophrenic speakers.

A. Depth of Processing and the TD Speaker

In 1972, Craik and Lockhart proposed a framework for memory research which offered two interesting arguments. They claimed that the ability of a subject to remember could be understood as a by-product of the kind of analysis that the subject performed on the materials to be remembered; and they argued that the persistence of the memory depended on the "depth" to which the materials had been analyzed. The notion of depth was not developed in any detail but seemed to imply a series of linguistic analyzers that operated in a fixed order: from phonological to structural to semantic, in which the subject's role is that of a listener asked to remember lists of words.

The first argument was part of what has come to be called "the new look" in experimental studies of memory. Essentially, it proposes that what the subjects "do" in their mental operations is critical and that what is presented to them in the form of experimental materials is secondary. A similar argument has been made recently by Levy and Trevarthen (1977) in their studies of elementary language processes in split-brain patients. They note that it is not the nature of the stimuli that determines hemispheric dominance but rather the nature of the central processing requirements demanded. For both sets of investigators, what is important is *how* the subject processes the materials at hand—rather than the nature of the materials themselves.

Craik and Lockhart's second argument suggests that what the subject is doing in memory tasks is performing perceptual and cognitive analyses to various "depths" so that the materials to be remembered are processed more or less fully. Deeper processing, they hypothesize, will lead to a longer lasting memory trace. This notion has been tested in experiments in which subjects are asked to make various judgments about words exposed briefly on a tachistoscope. The subjects' ability to remember the words depends strongly on the nature of the judgment they are asked to make. Questions concerning a word's meaning were followed by higher recall than questions concerning either the word's sound or the physical characteristics of the printed form (Craik & Tulving, 1975, Expts, I–IV).

Craik and Lockhart's original formulation implied that a stimulus is processed through a fixed series of analyzers, from phonological to structural to semantic; that the system stops processing once the analysis relevant to the experimental task is carried out; and that judgment time might serve as an index of the depth of processing reached. The investigators have subsequently revised these and other assumptions (cf. Craik, 1975; Craik & Tulving, 1975; Lockhart, Craik, & Jacoby, 1975). One revision of the original formulation states that a more satisfactory concept than "depth" is the notion of a minimal encoding which can be elaborated by further structural, phonemic, and semantic encoding. The difference in formulation is that where "depth" implied operations carried out in a fixed sequence, "elaboration" implies that there are many different ways of encoding the basic perceptual core of the event. Encoding elaboration is said to depend on the breadth of analysis carried out. Regardless of the descriptive term adopted, however, the critical feature of the theory is that retention depends on the nature of the encoding operations performed.

This view of human information processing suggests that the subject is a potentially active strategist who implements a variety of perceptual/ cognitive operations as they are required. It is a concept that has been very useful to investigators of schizophrenic memory processes. Koh (1978; Koh, Kayton, & Peterson, 1976) for example reports that young schizophrenic subjects fail to organize lists of words, but when encoding and organization are induced in the input stages of recall tasks, the schizophrenic patients recall as readily as normal controls. Koh suggests, on the basis of this finding and several others, that young, nonpsychotic schizophrenics suffer from a "deficit in executive control" in memory tasks that require extensive elaboration of the stimulus materials (typically, word lists). Similarly, Traupmann (Traupmann, 1976; Traupmann, Berzofsky & Alpert, 1975) suggests that schizophrenic subjects "fail to implement active strategies for processing information to the cognitive depth necessary to support recall" (1976, p. 1). And Larsen and Fromholt (1976) report that schizophrenics' recall deficit could be eliminated if subjects were actively engaged in sorting words to be recalled into self-determined categories.

All the memory studies cited are based on word lists or word strings. And in all, the schizophrenic subjects showed improvements when they were actively engaged in the processing. It may be, therefore, that when schizophrenic patients are not so engaged, they fail to process verbal materials actively to the same depth or degree of elaboration as normal subjects. The schizophrenic subjects are capable of processing word lists, the studies suggest, but they do not do so spontaneously.

We would like to use a version of the "depth of encoding" hypothesis to account for the occasional failure of TD speakers to produce coherent discourse. Using a framework of Halliday's systemic theory (see Chapter 4), we assume that the speaker processes meanings into expressions by making choices within a number of language systems. The systems can be roughly represented in terms of cognitive operations needed to make decisions at the level of phonological/written expressions, lexicogrammatical forms, and semantic meanings within the text (between sentences). Fawcett (1972a, b) has attempted a detailed version of a cognitive model for systemic theory. Here, we simply postulate the existence of separate levels of decision-making at the strata of textual meaning, wording, and expression. This is not a sufficient formulation, but it seems a necessary beginning to outlining the competence and difficulties of the TD speaker.

B. Stratal Slips

If we use the metaphor of separate strata of decision-making for textual meaning, wording, and expression, we can distinguish the choices speakers make with regard to phonological similarities from those they make about relationships within the sentence or clause, and both of those from decisions made at the level of meaning within text. Encoding at each stratum can be more or less complete or "deep," and encoding across the strata can be "wide" so as to include all strata, or "narrow," so that only one or two of the three available classes of decisions are made.

We suppose that the fully competent adult speaker can use all strata of decision-making and does so to produce coherent texts. As the speaker becomes less competent to process meanings into expressions—that is, is a child, or is an adult placed under high stress or fatigue, or is in some other way given less control over language processing—he or she begins to fail in certain orderly ways to produce coherent discourse. The first failures occur at the level of sentence-to-sentence links and may be seen in a lack of topic direction, in failures to establish major and minor role actors and clear event lines, and in a lack of certain kinds of cohesion between clauses. Later failures would include the earlier ones and, in addition, involve mistakes at the lexicogrammatical stratum of language use. In this case, one would see the use of neologisms, inadequate grammatical forms, and the use of inappropriate wordings of various kinds. However, the intonation patterns and pausing and other prosodic features of normal speech would be more or less intact. Finally, a complete breakdown in language operations would be signaled by the speaker's inability to match intonation patterns or select rhyming words when asked.

This speculative account allows us some predictions of what one might expect as the language processing of adult speakers becomes increasingly impaired. We use the notion of "stratal slips" to summarize this view of the speaker as failing at successive levels of language operations. There are two ways in which stratal slips can be seen in analyses of discourse: They can be seen *within-text*, as cohesive links change from conjoining clauses on the basis of their semantic (propositional) content to tying on the basis of lexicogrammatical forms; and then to tying on the basis of intonation contours or rhymes. Stratal slips can be seen *outside-of-text* as connections within the text are reduced, and connections between the text and the situation increase. The baseline for performance must, of course, depend on the context of situation, on the social class and age of the speaker, and such other factors as the speaker's role and the register of the discourse. But if these factors are similar for a group of speakers, then the speakers should use similar proportions of verbal and nonverbal encoding. If they do not, and if there are substantial differences in the proportions of within-text references, there may be important differences in the abilities of the speakers to encode verbally. This sort of argument is evidently more inferential than one based on within-text links, because it relies primarily on an absence of verbal coding rather than an excess of certain kinds of linkages. Nevertheless, by considering evidence both within-text and outside-of-text, we can build an inferential base for the concept of stratal slips in the processing of TD speakers.

C. Evidence for Stratal Slips

1. Within-Text. There are two sorts of within-text evidence which suggest that TD speakers are restricted in the breadth of their language processing. First, many TD speakers rely on very high proportions of lexical cohesion in interviews. Second, TD speakers exhibit a lack of control over systems for presuming information in English. These data are reviewed in turn.

a. Lexis. Data from the preliminary cohesion analyses in Chapter 3 suggest that language processing is very active in TD speakers but occurs at a reduced level of semantic encoding. Many TD speakers in interviews depended strongly on lexical ties to the neglect of other forms of cohesion. As we discussed in Chapter 3, lexical ties seem to require less extensive integration of textual information than other forms of cohesion. This is particularly true when the ties are accomplished through repetition of lexical items across clauses, rather than through the use of synonyms or general categories. Other forms of cohesion generally require the semantic encoding of participants and events at the level of the clause, sentence, or discourse—beyond the individual lexical item.

Since most of the TD speakers, but none of the other schizophrenic speakers, relied on high proportions of lexical ties, there seems to be a limitation in linguistic processing that is unique to TD speakers. And since most of the TD lexical ties were word repetitions, a further restriction is suggested.

Nöth (1978) provides a more detailed study of the kinds of lexical ties that schizophrenic speakers use to form texts. In a reanalysis of data reported by other investigators (e.g., Maher, 1968; Woods, 1938), she demonstrates that schizophrenic speakers sometimes give the illusion of coherent discourse by tying clauses together on the basis of the phonetic similarity or the lexical meaning of individual words, rather than depending on the more extended semantics of the clause, sentence, or discourse unit. She identifies several kinds of associations between lexical items which "only simulate textual coherence." These include *paradigmatic* associations in which words are related in terms of their lexical meanings but do not follow syntactically, *homophone* associations (e.g., *meat* and *meet*) in which textual coherence is simulated through similar word sounds but does not occur at the level of meaning, and *paraphone* associations in which phonetically similar words are used in adjacent clauses/ phrases (e.g., I was *a glass bowl/* I didn't say *grass in the hole* either/). Nöth argues that these lexical associations interfere with the actual comprehensibility of the text by giving the illusion of meaningful ties when, in fact, only limited lexical or phonological similarities exist.

In addition, a number of clinical researchers and linguists have described the tendency of "schizophasic" speakers to chain together lexical items and to produce texts in which topics are determined on the basis of lexical and phonological features, rather than in terms of the larger discourse unit. For example, Chaika (1974a) suggests that schizophrenic speakers may not be able to match semantic features to words in the lexicon; Piro (cited by Arieti, 1974) proposes that verbal signs and their cognitive and emotional meanings become dissociated; and Arieti (1974) reports that his schizophrenic patients frequently separate words from their meanings. Arieti cites one patient who experienced "long strings of meaningless words" which "poured into his head when he would lie awake early in the morning" (p. 107). With regard to topicalization according to lexical and/or phonological ties across clauses, both Chaika (1974a; 1977) and Lecours and Vanier-Clément (1976) have described a similar phenomenon in detail.

Thus, in the present study and in a number of other descriptions of "thought-disordered" or "schizophasic" speech, there is evidence that texts are sometimes integrated through limited lexical chaining rather than through the use of more elaborate semantic ties. And, anecdotally in the present study and more systematically in other descriptions, it appears that such speakers sometimes rely on phonological tying of clauses to connect their discourse. The data from lexical analyses, then, suggest that TD or "schizophasic" speakers are actively processing at a lexico-grammatical level, but that the extent of their textual encoding is sometimes restricted. Rather than processing at the level of discourse or sentence propositions, these speakers sometimes process at the level of individual lexical meanings or sounds.

b. *Discourse: Systems for Presuming Information.* Although TD speakers form extensive lexical links in their texts, they frequently fail to tie their sentences together in a meaningful way, so it sometimes "looks as though ideas of a certain category . . . were thrown into one pot, mixed, and subsequently picked out at random, and linked with each by mere grammatical form or other auxilliary images" (Bleuler, 1950, p. 16). In several analyses, there was evidence that TD speakers do not establish chains of reference through their texts to the same extent and in the same manner as other speakers.

Initiating Chains of Reference. In Chapter 5, we found that TD speakers are less likely than other subjects to initiate chains of reference in texts. This is evident in structured texts—narratives and cartoon descriptions—in which speakers introduce new participants. That is, speakers in these contexts normally mention "a donkey" or "a St. Bernard" before describing more of what "the donkey" or "he" or "it" does. Schizophrenic TD speakers are less likely than others to provide such referential chains (e.g., a donkey . . . he) through their texts for two reasons. First, they (and NTD schizophrenic speakers as well) often do not encode information in the verbal context to the same extent as normal speakers. This is discussed in more detail below. Second, TD speakers seem to have a problem in matching initial and subsequent references to a given participant. This is not the case for NTD schizophrenics or for normal subjects and is therefore a relatively distinctive TD problem.

What is it that is problematical for the TD speaker in establishing referential chains through a text? There were some hints in our data that some potential referential chains failed because they missed linking a participant with its intended referent (e.g., the donkey was carrying *salt*/ . . . / the river got full of *salty water*/). It is possible that speakers were unable to maintain an adequate representation of their initial productions in a short-term memory storage, or at least could not use such representations in planning later productions. This hypothesis (given in more detail in Rochester, 1978b) is one of several accounts of how speakers may fail to initiate referential chains through their texts. Fawcett (1972a, b) and Hobbs (1976) offer alternative models. All three models, however, suggest that the establishment of referential chains through a text is a complex language skill that requires both the integration of information across clauses and the short-term storage of the speaker's own verbal productions.

A second factor that was responsible for the TD speakers' failures to initiate chains of reference was the repetition of participants. Repetition of nominal groups (e.g., I see *a woman* in the middle of a snowbank/ I see *a woman* in a telephone booth . . .) means that the original presentation of a participant is not followed by a phoric group that refers back to it (e.g., a woman . . . her). Consequently, no referential chain can be initiated, and a potential cohesive link between clauses is not realized. We have speculated (Rochester, 1978b) that such occurrences represent the use of too much information on the part of TD speakers and hence argue against notions of TD speaker as intentionally misleading the listener. Too much information, coupled with a miscalculation of referential ties, seems to point again to a failure to integrate recently stored verbal events with the productions being planned. Again, however, the details of the model seem less significant than more general aspects of the behavior as a complex linguistic process. The fact that TD speakers occasionally fail to render adequately their reference chains seems to point to some restrictions in their ability to perform high-level semantic encoding.

Bridging as a Form of Presumption. Bridging is one strategy for presuming information from the verbal context. It allows the speaker to create within-text linkages. As we saw in Section II, TD speakers do not require bridging of their listeners unless they also require high proportions of addition. In contrast, normal speakers require relatively high proportions of bridging and little addition. If bridging and addition are thought of as points on a continuum of indirect reference (cf. discussion in Chapter 6), then it appears that both NTD and normal speakers use this form of ref-

erence successfully and TD speakers do not. They do not, that is, manip-
ulate the presuming information in a manner that is helpful to listeners.
This suggests, again, that TD speakers may not be in control of the system
of presumption in English.

The notion that the use of bridging requires some skill from the
speaker is supported by Martin's (1978) observations of children. He reports that younger children (6–7 year olds) were significantly less likely
to require bridging in their narratives than older children (8–11 year olds).
This suggests children may learn to control this kind of presumption in
texts.

It is possible, therefore, that TD speakers' failures to use nondirect
reference successfully indicate a lack of control of the presumptional system. And, as we suggested above, this can be considered in terms of an
encoding hypothesis as follows: to bridge successfully, the speaker must
provide for inferences from the propositions underlying the bridged element. This requires deep semantic information processing which TD
speakers sometimes seem to lack.

2. Text-to-Situation. There are two kinds of text-to-situation evidence which indicate that TD speakers are restricted in the breadth of
their language processing. First, an examination of the way in which TD
subjects use structurally complex items (nominal groups) suggests that
complexity depends more on the situational context than on any particular ability of the speakers. Second, a study of how TD speakers introduce new participants suggests that presentations depend strongly on
the situational context of the discourse and do not reflect any general
features of the TD speaker's ability. In both cases, it seems that TD speakers avoid encoding in the verbal context when the wider situational context provides needed identifications. This suggests that TD speakers are
capable of structurally complex verbal encoding and of introducing new
participants, but for some reason, choose not to exercise these capabilities
when they need not. The evidence for this is presented below.

a. Structure. In Chapter 4, we found that all subjects used nominal
groups of about the same complexity in interviews, but that in task-based
contexts TD speakers produced less complex items. One could interpret
these data as evidence that TD speakers are frequently unable to produce
complex constructions. However, there are arguments against this interpretation. First, in every context, TD speakers produced some nominal
groups that were as complex as any produced by normal speakers.
Hence, the TD speakers were capable of producing structurally complex
items. Second, if TD speakers were having difficulty producing complex

items, they should have produced fewer complex items than normal subjects in all contexts. Instead, as we have mentioned, this occurred only in task-based contexts. Third, and perhaps most importantly, not only did TD speakers produce fewer complex items than other subjects in task-based contexts, but they *decreased* the complexity of their presenting nominal groups whereas other speakers showed corresponding *increases*. The proportion of complex nominal groups for TD subjects drops significantly from about 5% in interviews to less than 1% in narratives; and the drop in cartoon contexts is also large, but not reliable. For other subjects, there are *increases* of up to 4 to 6%. This suggests that the TD speakers were actively responding to context differences rather than simply unable to produce many complex items.

Taken together, the data suggest that TD speakers in the present study were as capable as normal speakers in their ability to encode meanings with nominal group structures, but that they were influenced by the context to restrict their encoding of participants in some circumstances. It appears that when the situation provided the identity of participants, the TD speakers tended not to engage in complex encoding. Thus, in narrative retellings and in cartoon descriptions, the TD speakers produced less complex nominal groups than other speakers; but in interviews, TD speakers did not differ from other subjects.

This conclusion agrees with the observations in the literature that schizophrenic speech is rarely agrammatical (e.g., Cohen, 1978; Gerson, Benson, & Frazier, 1977). It is also consistent with studies of schizophrenic listeners by Gerver (1967), Truscott (1970), and others cited in Chapter 1. However, our conclusion must be regarded as tentative at this point. Our data are observational and are restricted to nominal groups. We have not examined complexity at other syntactic levels, not have we tested the speakers' ability to produce complex items on demand, to discriminate different complex items, to recognize such items, and so on (see Dennis & Whitaker, 1976, for a model of how such testing could be conducted). The general limitations of naturalistic studies in inferring speakers' abilities are in force here and must restrict our ability to generalize beyond the present data. However, within those restrictions, it is remarkable that all the results for structural analyses can be accounted for in terms of strong links that TD speakers make between their presentation of participants and the situational context. It appears that the wider context of the utterance has a powerful influence on the form of the TD speaker's discourse, and that its effect is less influential on NTD and normal subjects.

b. Situation. Normally, texts in narrative and cartoon tasks were relatively independent of the situational context, and those in interviews were not. TD speakers, however, did not produce self-contextualizing discourse to the same extent as other subjects. These speakers were more dependent than others on information retrievable from the nonverbal context or a preceding verbal one. They were less likely than others to treat their own presentations as part of a distinct contextual configuration.

In interviews, it is normal to form situation-text ties and schizophrenic speakers' practice of relying on exophoric reference is not distinctive. However, in task-based contexts, at least in the rather formal contexts provided here, normal speakers' discourse is relatively independent of the contextual configuration, and text-situation links are rare indeed. In these contexts, therefore, reference to oneself (or to the listener) is not the normal practice and tends to stand out. The TD speakers use about double the normal proportion of personal reference in cartoon texts, and about five times the normal proportion in narratives. But these proportions are not high in any case (11% of definite nominal groups in cartoons and 5% in narratives). *They are distinctive because of the context,* not because of the act of personal reference in itself. The NTD speakers tend to use more personal reference than normals and less than TD speakers in the task-based contexts. Presumably, this reflects the NTD tendency to use more situation-text ties than normals and less than TD speakers.

In their strong dependence on the surrounding contextual configurations, TD speakers resemble younger children as opposed to older children and working class as opposed to middle class adults. Martin (1978) found that 6 to 7 year olds were significantly more likely than older (8 to 11 year olds) children to identify participants exophorically when they are introduced. And Schatzman and Strauss (1955) were perhaps the first of many (cf. Robinson & Rackstraw, 1972) to report that working class adults do not give detailed expositions of the context but seem to assume that the listener is "watching the same film." In contrast, the middle-class speakers supply the listener with context, setting the stage for events to be related.

The common element in the three groups of speakers who do not meet the ideal of low self-contextualization may be a lack of elaborate encoding in the verbal context. In TD speakers, younger children and working-class children and adults, there is evidence that the speakers are *able* to use presenting items but choose not to do so when the participants are already provided by the context of situation. One can say that the speakers who use low self-contextualization select different options from their companion groups for the same contextual situation (cf. Martin, 1978). In this sense, the former use the language system differently from the latter. One may also say, at a more psychological level, that speakers who rely little on self-contextualization are choosing not to encode verbally when there is an option not to do so.

The latter interpretation would be consistent with the interpretation of TD speakers' use of complex items, suggested above. That is, TD speakers seem not to present complex nominal groups when the participants to be encoded are already present in the situational context; and TD speakers (and younger children and working-class adults) do not encode participants in the verbal context when the identity of the participants is already available to the listener through the context of situation. With regard both to complexity of nominal groups and to presumption, then, it seems that TD speakers may choose not to encode verbally, when this is an option.

To conclude, there is evidence from analyses of structural complexity and from analyses of reference that TD speakers depend less on their own verbal context and more on the "situational" context than other subjects. The "situation" may be the nonverbal situation provided by pictures in the cartoon task, or may be the previous verbal context provided by the original telling of the narrative. In both cases, the TD speaker does not reintroduce participants into his or her own discourse, if the participants have already been given elsewhere. This reliance on some other context does not in itself support our hypothesis of the TD speaker as a shallow language processor, but it does demonstrate that TD speakers tend not to encode in the verbal context, when they can avoid it. It therefore suggests that there is a tendency away from elaborate encoding in the verbal context for TD speakers, in contrast to other speakers, both schizophrenic and normals.

IV. Some Hypotheses to Account for Discourse Failure

To claim that the TD speaker occasionally fails to encode meanings to the level of discourse, or fails to encode meanings in a self-contained verbal context, makes us ask "Why?" In this section, we review some of the hypotheses that attempt to answer this question.

Let us first, however, consider one point that is prior to such hypotheses. We have been assuming that all the phenomena which we can describe for speakers are actually language phenomena, and this may very well be incorrect. In fact, the "depth of processing" formulation that we have adopted never explicitly attempts to deal with language operations but claims to be a general proposal for human information processing. The implication of this proposed generality is that, when we see failures at the level of discourse, we are actually viewing problems in complex information processing. And, in the absence of statements to the contrary, we must assume that the schizophrenic subject who is considered thought-disordered would be equally impaired in making complex discriminations in melodies, in spatial analyses, and in other nonverbal, nonserial tasks.

This is probably not an overstatement of the position, since Koh (1978) has attempted some studies of spatial memory in schizophrenic subjects and has never claimed to be tapping language-specific memory skills. Indeed, it seems fair to cite the strong position taken by Salzinger, Portnoy, & Feldman (1978, p. 35) as a possible hypothesis in this connection. These investigators argue that "the oft-reported peculiar schizophrenic language . . . is not itself the underlying problem" that the schizophrenic speaker has to encounter. Rather, language is useful to the investigator because it is "an ideal index of any general behavioral difficulty."

We find that the Salzinger et al. hypothesis and the general position taken by students of memory processes are problematic for efforts to understand the role of language processes in the "thought-disordered" patient. The problem, as we mentioned in Chapter 1, is that by making one's hypothesis very general, one cannot test the possibility that there are impairments peculiar to one system which do not hold for other systems. However, there is also a risk in narrow hypotheses focused on language at the expense of more general information processing strategies.

In the present studies, we have maintained such a narrow focus, attempting to describe language use only and ignoring other aspects of functioning. We believe that this approach is probably necessary as a beginning step. However, it does seem essential to add onto studies of language processing simultaneous studies of other aspects of cognitive and perceptual functioning, so that one can assess the extent to which incoherent discourse cooccurs with disrupted functioning in other domains. At the present time, we simply do not know whether TD speakers would also show impairment in general information processing operations, or in only some sorts of cognitive operations that involve serial processing or linear inference. As we shall see in the following pages, these questions become very interesting as one tries to discover what might be responsible for the occasional incoherent productions of the schizophrenic speaker.

A. Language versus Thought as the Essential Problem in "Thought-Disorder"

We observed in Section III that the TD speakers examined in the present study appear to have an identifiable language problem, but that it is not a simple problem. The TD speakers, as we have seen, show a profound sensitivity to context. In addition, they seem able to make decisions at the level of lexicogrammatical form: there were no substantial differences between TD and other speakers is the complexity of nominal groups, and in the entire sample of TD speech we could find only three items that might be called neologisms. Finally, although only anecdotally, the TD speaker's intonational patterns seemed to be appropriate to the sentence structures and contexts they were using, so that one did not find, say, a falling intonation with a yes/no question structure.

The observation that the language use problem is not a simple one is consistent with recent reports in the literature which describe young "schizophasic" patients. For example, Cohen (1978, p. 1) comments that "as cryptic or disorganized as schizophrenic speech may sound, it rarely (if ever) includes hard instances of agrammatism or word-finding deficits." And Gerson, Benson, & Frazier (1977, p. 968) observe that distortion of syntax, "almost a hallmark of aphasia," is rarely found in schizophrenia. These comments, plus similar observations by Lecours and Vanier-Clément (1976) and DiSimoni, Darley, and Aronson (1977) indicate that it is unlikely that TD speakers are suffering from a temporary or episodic aphasia. For the TD speakers to undergo even brief aphasic periods, one would expect that the lower strata of speech production systems—from the phonological/written to the lexicogrammatical—would show evidence of disruption. We have not seen evidence of such disruption, nor do the reports cited above suggest that there is likely to be such evidence in young patients who have not been isolated.

The suggestion that TD speakers may be in some sense aphasic has been made by Fish (1957), by Chapman (1966), and by Chaika (1974a, 1977), among others. It seems to be prompted by observations that there are specifiable problems in the TD (or "schizophasic") speaker's use of language. Those who find no problems at the level of morphology and syntax reject these interpretations and argue that the problem exists at the level of thought, rather than language. As we noted in Chapter 3, Lecours and Vanier-Clément conclude that there is not a language disorder in schizophrenia but rather a thought disorder. Schizophasic discourse is rule-governed, they claim, at the level of phonemes, morphemes, and generally syntax, but it is rule-deviant at the level of concepts ("paradigmatic relations"). Similar arguments are made by Brown (1973), Fromkin (1975), and Gerson et al. (1977).

The conclusion that the problem in thought disorder or "schizophasia" exists at the level of thought, not language, involves an assumption about the scope of a language system. The conclusion implies a system of language that is unable to account for language use beyond the clause or sentence. This is the case for standard transformational theory. Thus, for Fromkin and others who follow a version of this theory, problems beyond the level of the clause must be beyond the level of language. From within the framework of such a theory, there is no way to dispute the assertion that the problems encountered by TD speakers are not based in a language system. However, if one embraces a wider theoretical system that postulates linguistic rules at the level of discourse—rules about the linkages among clauses and among sentences—then the problems encountered by TD speakers can be conceptualized as language problems. The system we have followed here is based on Halliday's (1970, 1973, 1978) systemic models and permits a wider view.

Since the question of whether thought disorder is language-based seems to be a matter of which linguistic theory one adopts, one might argue that the question itself is meaningless. This may be so, but at the present time there are some reasons for keeping the issue alive. The reasons essentially bear on the question of etiology. For one thing, there is a growing body of literature to suggest that at least one aspect of the problem of schizophrenia is a consequence of a dysfunction of the brain hemisphere dominant for language. Some of the studies localize this even further by singling out the left temporal lobe as the source of dysfunction. Such hypotheses directly implicate language functioning and make it important to determine whether, in fact, one can identify specific impairments in schizophrenic patients that do not appear in other psychiatric patients or in normal speakers.

Other reasons for considering the question of language impairment relate to etiological factors indirectly, because they bear on the question of diagnosis. There have been a few recent studies of mania which suggest that "thought-disorder" in mania and in schizophrenia are not differentiable states. One study has explicitly examined the discourse of manic patients and reports results that are closely comparable to the findings presented here. As we discuss in the following pages, this may indicate that the "thought-disordered" or "schizophasic" state tells us more about psychosis than about schizophrenia, and that inferences about schizophrenia based on "schizophasic" speakers may be misleading.

Finally, the question of language impairment in schizophrenia allows us to study the course of schizophrenic episodes in minute detail, and may consequently allow us to understand what distinguishes schizophrenic patients who show no signs of incoherent speech (NTD subjects in this study) from those whose discourse is disrupted.

In the next section, we briefly review the arguments for lateralization of function in schizophrenia and consider how the present findings fit with those arguments. Following that, we discuss the question of diagnosis of schizophrenia from the symptoms presented by "thought-disordered" patients. As will be evident, the hypothesis of some sort of left-hemisphere dysfunction in young, acute schizophrenic patients seems to account for a wide variety of our results and lays out some interesting predictions for future studies. In addition, there is some speculative support for this hypothesis from analyses of the discourse of NTD speakers. However, the data from studies of mania suggest that we must be cautious in supposing that we are studying schizophrenia, in the absence of comparable studies of other psychiatric groups and probably also in the absence of groups with known neurological lesions.

B. Evidence of Lateralized Dysfunction in Schizophrenia

In 1969, two reports appeared which suggested that there might be a malfunctioning of the left hemisphere in schizophrenia. In a paper urging investigation of sensory factors in psychopathology, Peter Venables described some unpublished data for click thresholds. In normal subjects, he reported, the left ear was more sensitive, but in schizophrenics the laterality was reversed. Moreover, the extent of the reversal was said to be related to "the degree of incoherence of speech shown by the patient." Venables proposed that such results might point to a malfunctioning of the hemisphere associated with verbal processing.

It was also in 1969 that Pierre Flor-Henry's important survey of 100 cases of temporal-lobe epilepsy appeared. Among the several findings, there was evidence of a preponderance of epilepsy involving left foci among psychotics, and particularly among schizophrenics. Flor-Henry reported that 43% of all schizophrenics had left-sided foci, 47.5% had bilateral foci, and 9.5% had right-sided foci. In the control group of epileptic patients with no psychotic symptoms, 50% showed right-sided foci. Flor-Henry suggested that patterns of neuronal activity in the dominant temporal lobe and limbic system are fundamentally responsible for the schizophrenic syndrome.

Subsequently, John Gruzelier and his colleagues examined schizophrenic patients for evidence of impairment in the left hemisphere (Gruzelier, 1978; Gruzelier & Hammond, 1976; Gruzelier & Venables, 1974). Three of the investigations measured skin-conductance levels and showed a reduced general responsiveness in the left hand of schizophrenic subjects by comparison with their right hand. Gruzelier interpreted these results as evidence of a reduced ipsilateral (i.e., left hemisphere) response. However, Shimkunas (1978) argues congently against this interpretation and for the contralateral mediation of the electrodermal response. According to Shimkunas's analysis, the Gruzelier *et al.* results show a *heightened* general arousal in the left hemisphere of acute schizophrenics.

In recent years, several investigators have reported lateralization effects cooccurring with schizophrenic symptomatology. There have been studies of the effects of chlorpromazine on lateralization of tones (Gruzelier, 1978), studies of schizophrenic adults and their children on tests with right-hemisphere factor loadings (e.g., comprehension, similarities, vocabulary) (Gruzelier, 1978); investigations of handedness (Fleminger, Dalton, & Standage, 1977; Gur, 1977; Oddy & Lobstein, 1972); an inquiry into the relation between laterality variables and concordance for schizophrenia (Boklage, 1977); and studies of responses to verbal and spatial stimuli in the right and left visual fields (Gur, 1978). The evidence in support of left-hemisphere dysfunction in schizophrenia has been reviewed by Flor-Henry and Gruzelier (in press).

Most of the laterality studies cited above have been interpreted as offering support for a left-hemisphere impairment that is either causally related to or cooccurs with schizophrenic symptoms. However, it is also possible that those functions of schizophrenic patients mediated by the left hemisphere are largely intact, but that, under some circumstances, right-hemisphere functioning supervenes. This interesting alternative is suggested by Witelson's (1976, 1977) work with dyslexic children. She reports that the various data for deficient left-hemisphere processing of those children—including poor performance on linguistic tasks and on tasks which require sequential processing, and impaired recall of dichotic stimulation similar to that of patients with known temporal lobe dysfunction—have masked the issue of right-hemisphere processing. In her studies of right-hemisphere specialization in dyslexic subjects, she finds support for a right-hemisphere superiority. Wherever possible a spatial, parallel, holistic mode of processing seems to predominate in her dyslexic subjects. For example, the dyslexic subjects were superior to other subjects in touch tasks and were faster in learning Chinese logographs than normal controls. Witelson concludes that in dyslexic children there is little good evidence for dimished left-hemisphere specialization for language, but substantial support for a right-hemisphere superiority.

The possibility that "thought-disordered" or "schizophasic" patients are operating with largely intact left hemispheres but dominant right hemispheres raises some interesting questions that have not been considered widely. For one thing, it suggests that the common practice of comparing right- and left-hemisphere mediated functions within a subject may be misleading. The problem comes when investigators find that right-hemisphere functioning is superior to left functioning on a task in which left functioning would normally be superior, and then conclude that *left*-hemisphere functioning is inadequate. The conclusion might just as well be that *right*-hemisphere functioning is predominant. For example, Gur (1978) compared schizophrenics and matched controls on verbal and spatial tachistoscopic tests and found reliable differences between groups on the verbal test. The schizophrenics were superior in recognizing nonsense syllables in their left visual field, compared to their performance in the right visual field. The reverse was true for normal subjects where the expected left-hemisphere superiority occurred. Gur concludes that there is evidence of a left-hemisphere dysfunction in schizophrenia. Given the data, she might just as well conclude that there is right-hemisphere facilitation. That is at least a tenable hypothesis.

A second question to be considered is how we might test the functional specialization of the right and left hemispheres in schizophrenia. In Chapter 1, we suggested that very little is known about the memory processes of schizophrenic patients, because most of the experimental tests have used verbal stimuli and the few which used spatial stimuli often had very complicated verbal instructions. We do not know whether schizophrenic subjects would be superior to other psychiatric subjects or normals on such right-hemisphere tasks as remembering faces, identifying logographs, or recalling emotionally toned words if the task instructions were kept simple. This is a question that will need some specially designed new tests, as well as a sensitivity to the problems of fatigue and medication usual in testing patient populations.

Another question raised by the possibility of right-hemisphere dominance is the consideration that the left hemisphere of schizophrenic patients may be largely intact in its functioning. The data from the present study seem to fit this description better than they fit a hypothesis of left-hemisphere impairment. If we suppose a left-hemisphere impairment, it would seem that schizophrenic patients should show signs of aphasia and other characteristics of left-hemisphere or left-temporal lobe disorder. But our data suggest that in order to behave as a TD subject, a speaker *requires an operational left hemisphere.* Specifically, as we noted earlier in this chapter, TD speakers produce syntactically complex nominal groups, rarely use neologisms and produce a profusion of familiar lexical items. In left-temporal lobe aphasias, one would expect to see extensive disruptions in syntax and in the use of lexical items (cf. Buckingham & Kurtesz, 1976). Moreover, our TD subjects sometimes relied on rhyming to tie their text together. There is evidence that rhyming requires adequate left-hemisphere functioning and apparently cannot be accomplished by the right hemisphere in adults (Levy & Trevarthen, 1977; Weinstein & Lyerly, 1976). Finally, the TD speakers' reliance on high levels of lexical cohesion in interviews indicates that they are tying their clauses together on the basis of lexical meanings. Although patients with nonfunctional left hemispheres can read and understand simple single words (Gazzaniga & Sperry, 1967; Zaidel, 1976), it seems that the semantic interpretation of lexical items of any complexity requires an adequately functioning left hemisphere.

In brief, it is difficult to conceive of certain of the behaviors of TD speakers occurring without the fairly extensive involvement of their left hemispheres. But how then are we to account for their unusual reliance on lexical ties, for their several failures to present new information and presume old information in a coherent manner, and for the general tendency of schizophrenic speakers to rely on the situational context of the discourse? Moreover, there is fairly clear evidence of left-temporal abnormalities in the power spectra of the "resting" EEGs of schizophrenics (Flor-Henry, 1976) and of heightened activation of left-hemisphere functioning (Gur, 1978; and perhaps in the Gruzelier electrodermal data, as interpreted by Shimkunas, 1978). These results suggest that a hypothesis couched purely in terms of right-hemisphere function is bound to be inadequate, and that it is necessary to suppose *some* impairment in the left-hemisphere processes of schizophrenic patients. The data showing heightened activation of left-hemisphere processes indicate that the impairment in functioning may be related to some excessive activation of these processes.

Shimkunas (1978) has proposed a model of schizophrenic thought that incorporates the sort of hypothesis which seems to be needed at this point. He combines the notions of an overactivated left hemisphere with a highly arousable right hemisphere into the following formulation: in schizophrenic patients with a diagnosis of thought disorder, there is an overloaded left hemisphere which functions in parallel with a potentially highly arousable right hemisphere. The processing strategies of the two hemispheres cannot be resolved and integrated because the interhemispheric transfer operations are defective.

There is little that we can say about right-hemisphere functioning, as we indicate above. Shimkunas suggests that evidence of right-hemisphere dominance will be seen primarily in chronic patients, once continued overactivation of the left hemisphere has resulted in a shutdown of operations or, in Roland Fischer's terms (1971), a "jammed computer." There is also little to be said from the present study about problems in interhemispheric transfer of information. We did not study this in any systematic way. Perhaps one could argue that the cartoon task represented a test of the speaker's ability to proceed from images into words, and therefore gives some evidence of the TD speakers' abilities to use the results of such transfer. However, there were so many other factors operating to differentiate cartoon contexts from other contexts—the speaker's relation to other participants, the purpose, topic, and orientation to the nonverbal situation, and so on (see Chapter 1)—that we shall not attempt to comment on this.

There is a variety of evidence from the present study to support Shimkunas's notion that in young, relatively acute schizophrenic patients, left-hemisphere processes are overactivated to the point that those processes are eventually immobilized. We do not see evidence of immobilization, it seems, but there does seem to be evidence of restricted functioning at the level of discourse production. As we suggested in Section III, there seem to be occasional "stratal slips" by TD speakers in which functioning at the lexicogrammatical stratum is maintained, but functioning at the level of discourse meaning is impaired.

To review briefly, the hypothesis of an overworked left hemisphere receives support from (a) cohesion analyses, indicating that processing is very active in TD speakers but frequently occurs at the level of lexical cohesion to the relative neglect of other forms of textual integration; (b) reference analyses, indicating that TD speakers are less likely than other speakers to initiate chains of reference in texts. The notion of limited operation in the left hemisphere leading to some dominance by the right hemisphere receives some support from *(c)* analyses of nominal group complexity, which may indicate that TD speakers rely strongly on the situational context for encoding the identities of participants, and *(d)* reference analyses, which show that TD speakers tend not to encode participants in the verbal context when there is an option provided through the wider situational context of the utterance.

There is, then, evidence to support the hypothesis that TD schizophrenic speakers may be operating with an overworked left hemisphere and, possibly, a potentially dominant right hemisphere. This suggests what the impairment may be. However, there is also evidence that very clearly indicates that the left hemisphere of TD speakers must be operating at a relatively complex level of encoding during much of their discourse production. Such evidence comes from our own studies of reference within the text and from the work of Cohen and his colleagues (e.g. Cohen, 1978; Cohen *et al.*, 1974) of reference between the situation and the text.

In our own work, each time we cite a supposed restriction in TD speakers' left-hemisphere processing, we must acknowledge that this is an "occasional" failure. The need for such a caution seems to be as important as the fact that TD speakers fail to use reference or cohesion or complex nominal groups as normal and NTD speakers do. As we indicate at the end of Chapter 5, TD speakers sometimes do initiate referential chains in their discourse. It is also true that TD speakers match the normal speakers' *pattern* of use for referential chains by initiating significantly more chains in task-based contexts than in the interview. These instances of successful establishment of chains of reference argue strongly for some extensive linguistic competence in TD speakers. Zaidel (1976, 1977) has shown that there is a relative "immaturity" of the disconnected right hemisphere for short-term sequential recall of verbal material. Consequently, the TD speakers' occasional facility in establishing referential chains through their texts seems to imply that the linguistic processing of their left hemisphere must be continuing, even though it may not be fully adequate at all times.

In a related series of studies, Cohen and his colleagues have studied how acute schizophrenic speakers form situation-text referential links. At first, the schizophrenic speaker provides an adequate description of the situational stimulus (a colored disk). The description refers to the stimulus disk in a way that allows a listener to select that particular disk from an array of several others. However, as the discriminability of the disk to be selected decreases, and as the time spent in describing it increases, the schizophrenic speaker's references become less and less adequate. Where a normal speaker says, for example, "Both are salmon-colored. This one, however, has more pink," a matched acute schizophrenic speaker gives the following description: "Make-up. Pancake make-up. You put it on your face and they think guys run after you. Wait a second! I don't put it on my face and guys don't run after me. Girls put it on them" (cited in Cohen, 1978, p. 17).

Cohen notes that the single most distinctive feature of his subjects' longer utterances was a tendency for responses "to lose their connection to the referent" and for references to the situational stimuli to be replaced by "a bewildering variety of intraverbal associations" (Cohen, 1978, pp. 17–18). What is interesting is that as the referential links to the situation become less adequate, the acute schizophrenic speakers' productions do not show signs of halting but rather seem to grow more profuse at some lower level of processing. For extended descriptions and for descriptions of stimuli in highly similar arrays, there are lexical and phonological linkages among clauses and some semantic links within text, but few links between the schizophrenic subject's descriptions and the situational stimuli (cf. Cohen, 1978, Appendix). The high productivity of "intraverbal associations" seems to support a hypothesis of an overactive left hemisphere. With increased anxiety, Cohen notes, these verbal associations increase. This account fits with Shimkunas's (1978) hypothesis that increased arousal leads to a limitation in the schizophrenic subject's left-hemisphere-mediated processing, due to cognitive gating of the sort postulated by Silverman (1964, 1972) and Fischer (1971).

To sum up, data from studies of lexical and phonological linkages in discourse, from studies of nominal group complexity, and from studies of referential links within text and between text and situation suggest that schizophrenic speakers sometimes fail to produce coherent discourse. However, with every failure there is evidence of processing that seems to require the superior linguistic skills of the left hemisphere. The two factors—the occasional failures and the pervasive evidence of linguistic skill—suggest that schizophrenic speakers who are diagnosed as "thought-disordered" or "schizophasic" are relying on left-hemisphere processing that is occasionally restricted to a shallow level of phonological or lexicogrammatical analysis.

If one conceives of the language system as a series of coding levels or "strata," one can imagine a "stratal slip" by TD and other "schizophasic" speakers from the level of discourse to the level of lexicogrammatical form. Occasionally, in interviews and other situations in which the interpersonal contact is close and there may be intensified emotional arousal, the stratal slip may extend to the phonological level. In this case, lexical items might be linked phonologically rather than semantically. This can also occur in extended discourse, as Cohen (1978) and Salzinger, Portnoy, and Feldman (1978) suggest. Nevertheless, in all these instances, we would seem to be viewing the outcome of left-hemisphere operations— and not the results of a totally "jammed" or nonfunctioning brain.

C. "Thought Disorder" and the Diagnosis of Schizophrenia

Is "thought disorder," in the sense of incoherent discourse described in the present study, diagnostic of schizophrenia? As we indicated in Chapter 1, we cannot answer this question in the present study, because we did not perform a cross-sectional analysis of diagnostically different groups of speakers. However, there are two sources of indirect evidence that bear on this question, and we consider them in turn. First, we ask who were the NTD speakers, and why did these schizophrenic subjects give no indication of disrupted speech to our clinical and lay judges? Then we review results which suggest that in mania there are discourse failures similar to those we have described in TD schizophrenic speakers.

1. The NTD Speakers. Schizophrenic speakers who were not judged thought-disordered constitute a valuable study group in their own right. They were distinctive in several ways. First, they produced fewer clauses and fewer words per clause than other subjects over all contexts. Second, in interviews, they used significantly smaller proportions of lexical ties and GENERIC groups than TD speakers. Third, there was a trend for NTD speakers to introduce very few nominal groups that were not later presumed. Most participants which were introduced provided referents for later nominal groups so that, in effect, participants were not introduced unless they played a major role in the textual development. And finally, NTD speakers made fewer indirect references (bridged and unclear items) than other subjects. However, when they did require inferences from their listeners, the implied referents were almost always easy to find.

What is striking about these results is their frequent contrast with the TD outcomes. It is not the case, as we had expected, that NTD speakers fall somewhere between normal and TD speakers on most measures.

Rather, NTD speakers were often so different from TD speakers that there was almost no overlap between the two groups' scores.

It is not clear how one should interpret the NTD data. The primary problem is in knowing how to identify these NTD speakers. They do not differ reliably from TD subjects on parameters, such as hospitalization, drug dosage, education, and social class, but this does not preclude some important differences. One possibility is that the NTD group includes those schizophrenic patients who are more sensitive to drugs and hence are showing a faster improvement in their symptomatology. Another possibility which may be complementary to the first is that NTD speakers are more cautious in their productions than TD speakers, intentionally restricting their discourse in areas where TD speakers' productions seem aberrant.

The relationship between thought disorder and drugs has been formulated by some workers. One interesting proposal is a "dual process" model of schizophrenia (e.g., Kay & Singh, 1979; Namyslowska, 1975). The cognitive problem in schizophrenia, it is suggested, has two components: one is a drug-resistant component that involves difficulty in abstract thinking and does not change with neuroleptic treatment; and the other is a drug-sensitive component that involves "thought disorganization" and loose associations. The latter is said to be related to increased arousal and rapidly amenable to neuroleptic treatment. Cognitive disorders seen in schizophrenia are supposed to represent the complex actions of these two components.

There is evidence from a variety of sources that supports the notion of a drug-sensitive component of schizophrenia which involves language-related functions. Most impressively, Gruzelier (1978) reports regular improvement in the right-ear (left-hemisphere) auditory discriminations of schizophrenic subjects over the course of chlorpromazine treatment; and he reports increasingly poorer performance for those subjects over the course of placebo administration. This suggests that left-hemisphere processes in schizophrenics are probably responsive to phenothiazine treatment, and implies that language processes should improve as time on such treatment increases. This is consistent with anecdotal reports that a schizophrenic patient's "thought disorder" will disappear after about 3 to 6 weeks of phenothiazine treatment.

The clinical impression of remission of signs of formal thought disorder with phenothiazines has been confirmed in a clinical study by Harrow, Himmelhoch, Tucker, Hersch, and Quinlan (1972), indicating that "idiosyncratic thinking" is responsive to antipsychotic medication in acute patients. Also, Oltmanns, Ohayon, and Neale (1978) report that chronic schizophrenic patients taken off antipsychotic medication are more distractable than other chronic patients. Since distractability (on a digit span test) appears to be correlated with formal thought disorder, this result lends some indirect support to the possible relationship between incoherent language and the action of antipsychotic medication. Finally, Fink's (1974a, b) studies indicate that speech becomes more cryptic, more repetitive, and more "defensive" (with less personal reference, more qualification, more past tenses) with phenothiazine medication, and more diverse, with greater imagery and less "defensive" with psychotomimetics like LSD and mescaline. Again, disturbed language use seems to become more restrained with the continued administration of phenothiazines.

Thus, from the anecdotal comments, from the somewhat scanty experimental data, and from the speculative connection between arousal and TD language use, we can suggest that NTD speakers might be schizophrenic patients who were especially responsive to medication. If so we would expect them to be more "cryptic" — and they were, producing fewer clauses than TD subjects. They should use less personal reference than TD speakers, and they do. And perhaps, if we may infer from Fink's description of "defensive" language behaviors that NTD speakers should avoid language use which proves problematic for TD speakers, NTD speakers should produce very few GENERIC items and rely only minimally on lexical cohesion in interviews, and they do.

Let us now pursue Gruzelier's results and suppose for a moment that NTD speakers actually were TD speakers whose overly activated left-hemisphere functions had been slowed down through phenothiazine medication. There is some support for this in Levy's (1968) study of sentence structure in the discourse of four schizophrenic speakers. He measured the proportion of subordinate propositions to total propositions to obtain a "subordination index" which reflected the structural complexity of discourse. In the first 48 hours after the administration of chlorpromazine, the subordination index dropped significantly and then, following symptomatic recovery, it increased above the pretreatment levels. Levy notes that this seems to be a contradictory effect: an apparent drop in linguistic competence followed by a clear improvement. However, Gruzelier's work suggests that chlorpromazine may reduce left-hemisphere overactivation. If this interpretation of his findings is correct, then one would expect to find lowered productivity at the lexicogrammatical level. This would mean that medicated patients should use fewer lexical items

and less syntactically complex constructions as the overactivation decreases. Our data confirm the lowered lexical production, and Levy's
point to a reduced syntactic complexity. Upon symptom remission, normal left-hemisphere operations would be restored. Schizophrenic subjects should then show no differences from normal subjects in lexical and
syntactic forms, once the subjects were equated on potentially confounding variables, such as education and social class.

In addition, if chlorpromazine and other medications in the phenothiazine class act to reduce left-hemisphere overactivation, we would expect NTD speakers to carry out complex discourse operations compe-
tently. The NTD speakers should be able to initiate chains of reference in
text to the same extent that normal speakers do, and they should be able
to refer indirectly to participants without at the same time referring obscurely. These expectations are approximately confirmed—with an interesting restriction. The NTD speakers were able to initiate chains of reference in text, but they almost never did this for participants that took minor roles. Instead, they introduced only major role participants and then
(correctly) referred back to those introductions, establishing referential
chains. In addition, the NTD speakers did refer indirectly without referring obscurely—but their indirect references (through bridging) were
very rare indeed.

In discussing these results in Chapters 5 and 6, we suggested that the
NTD speakers might be somehow cautious, avoiding those discourse
forms that were especially problematic for the TD speaker. This also
seemed to account for the NTD speakers' lack of GENERIC items and very
low proportions of lexical cohesion relative to both TD and normal subjects. Caution seems a fair guess, but perhaps we should also add that the
NTD speaker's restricted use of some discourse forms is reminiscent of
the behavior of younger children learning to use complex discourse devices. Slobin (1973) and Thieman (1975) report that younger children use
full sentence forms in preference to contractions and sentence deletions.
These full forms are not really preferable, because the contracted forms
contribute to the unity of texts by making various parts of the discourse
interdependent (as in ellipsis, discussed in Chapter 3). But it seems that
overspecified discourse devices are strategies that are used when the discourse task becomes too complex for the speaker. Russell and Snow
(1977) suggest this on the basis of their observations that such devices
occur only in cases in which the language task is structurally very complex and decrease as the age of elementary school children increases.

It seems possible that the NTD subjects' neglect of minor roles and indirect reference may be a reflection of some difficulty in performing the complex language processing operations needed to realize these discourse features. This is not to say that the NTD speakers are not capable of performing these operations occasionally, but it may be that such performance is difficult or stressful in some way. At this point, we know that NTD speakers resemble younger children in their use of overspecified devices, but we do not know why. Unlike the children, NTD speakers seem to have some control over their occasions for using such devices. However, we do not know whether it is caution or stress or some other factor that dictates the NTD speaker's neglect of contracted and indirect forms in favor of overspecified ones. By making a choice in favor of the latter strategy, the NTD speakers sacrifice some integration in their talk, and gain some certainty that they will not be misunderstood. These results are straightforward, but whether the NTD speaker acts with such results in mind is something which we cannot discover from the present studies.

There are several other questions raised in considering NTD speakers which we cannot answer adequately at the present time. We do not know how antipsychotic medication effects are related to language changes in the schizophrenic patients, nor how these two variables are affected by brain changes that may accompany the medication treatment. Fink has proferred some interesting hypotheses, but there are as yet no systematic studies of language use to test them. We also know very little about the course of "thought disorder" in acute schizophrenia. Harrow and his colleagues (Harrow, Hakavy, Bromet, & Tucker, 1973; Harrow & Quinlan, 1977) have made some important beginnings, and Kantorowitz and Cohen's (1977) studies of chronic patients are also valuable. But as Cohen (1978) points out, there is a great need for longitudinal studies of the same group of patients over time in order to describe adequately if and how the features of their symptomatology change.

Finally, the NTD speakers force us to consider again the status of "thought disorder" as a construct. The dual process model of schizophrenia states that "thought disorder" is characteristic of all psychosis and not peculiar to schizophrenia (Harrow & Quinlan, 1977 and Koh, 1978 also make this argument). If this is correct, then the present observations about TD speakers tell one nothing about schizophrenia but rather are descriptive of psychosis. In this case, it is the NTD speakers who would be the characteristic schizophrenic patients. The TD speakers might at best reveal the acute psychotic process and might reveal nothing about a distinctive schizophrenic syndrome.

2. Manic Patients. The possibility that TD speakers are not distinctively "schizophrenic" seems even more likely when one considers the available data comparing manic and thought-disordered schizophrenic patients. Andreasen (in press), in particular, has addressed this issue with detailed descriptions of various language symptoms. Because her work is based on the clinical categories, it is difficult to compare it directly to the findings reported here. Durbin and Marshall (1977), however, have analyzed the discourse productions of manic patients, and their results do afford us some direct comparisons. They found that manic patients, like the TD patients in the present study, preserve a "basic linguistic competence as regards phonology, the retrieval of proper lexical items, and the generation of complex and grammatical sentences" (p. 217). But between sentences, manic patients made a great number of errors in "semantic anaphora." That is, they did not provide explicit links between sentences in sequence. The authors conclude that frequently, when the speaker is manic, "it is not possible for a listener to supply the processes which would recover enough old information for the discourse to be meaningful" (p. 217).

This conclusion seems similar to our observation that TD speakers use high proportions of unclear reference, relative to other speakers, and often fail to initiate chains of reference in their texts. And in general, Durbin and Marshall's observation that the listener cannot supply "enough old information" seems to correspond to our observation that persons listening to a TD speaker must search for identifications which are promised but not provided. In addition, when Durbin and Marshall reinterviewed four of their six subjects upon remission of mania, they found that none of the subjects made errors in semantic anaphora. Although we did not systematically test patients in remission, it is our impression that for TD speakers as well the distinctive language symptoms disappear.

Thus, observations of NTD speakers in the present study and comparisons of the present findings for TD speakers with those reported for manic speakers suggest that the language disorders seen in schizophrenic subjects may not be unique to schizophrenia, but rather may characterize an acute psychotic process general to mania and schizophrenia.

This tentative conclusion is supported by the results of a study of selective attention in normal subjects and in schizophrenic and manic patients. Oltmanns (1978) tested the effects of distractor items on word-span and digit span tests. He found that schizophrenic subjects' recall was deficient on words presented early in a list, suggesting that irrelevant words may interfere with the schizophrenic's ability to recode relevant items in short-term memory into a more lasting form. To some extent, this was true for manic patients as well. Moreover, both manic and schizophrenic patients were abnormally distracted, even at slower rates of item presentations. This may mean that both patient groups do not seem able to take advantage of the extra time to actively select and rehearse relevant items. Finally, both groups made more intrusive errors. Oltmanns concludes on the basis of this and other evidence that manic and schizophrenic patients have similar problems in selective attention. These appear to be problems in initiating active information processes, such as rehearsal, coding, and some forms of memory search. It is not that schizophrenics (and perhaps manics) code inappropriately or rehearse irrelevant stimuli, he concludes, but that they are less efficient than normal subjects in actively processing relevant stimuli.

Oltmanns's account of the schizophrenic subject as a shallow or passive processor of information is consistent with many of the results reported in the present study. The fact that he suggests extending this account to manic patients implies again that manic and schizophrenic subjects may be using similar kinds of processing strategies not only with word and digit lists, but also in producing discourse.

If this conclusion is supported by further studies, a new set of questions will have to be asked. We shall need to determine whether the hypothesis of an overactivated left hemisphere, so tenable for TD schizophrenic speakers taken alone, is at all conceivable for other acutely psychotic patients. It seems likely that it will not fit for psychotically depressed individuals (see Flor-Henry, 1976), but then the language data do not suggest that these patients should resemble schizophrenic patients. Thus far, it is only manic patients who should fit the model for thought disorder that describes schizophrenic patients. In addition, we shall have to ask about the commonalities between mania and acute schizophrenia. It is possible that at given point in time, manic patients and TD schizophrenics show similar language disturbances but that the course of these disturbances is distinct, and, therefore, the syndromes cannot be equated (see Carlson & Goodwin, 1973).

D. Summary

Section I reviewed the results of the preceding chapters and Section II presented discriminant function analyses of the reference and retrieval categories. We found that TD, NTD, and normal speakers could be accurately separated into groups, and that the quantitative results of *(a)* GENERIC groups, *(b)* PRESENTING groups that either initiate or do not initiate referential chains, and *(c)* indirect reference were required to make these discriminations. Section III presented an overview of the results and some tentative conclusions as follows: (1) TD speakers seem capable of using complex structural elements but choose not to when the information to be encoded is provided by the situational context; (2) TD speakers rely heavily on lexical cohesion and use relatively high proportions of GENERIC groups in interviews; (3) TD speakers do not establish chains of reference through their texts to the same extent and in the same manner as other speakers. These results seem best described in terms of a shallow information processing hypothesis that portrays TD speakers as occasionally failing to use sufficiently elaborate verbal encoding strategies. In Section IV, a variety of hypotheses to account for the TD speakers' discourse failures were considered. The most promising seemed to be Shimkunas's (1978) proposal of left-hemisphere overactivation in acute patients, coupled with an easily aroused right hemisphere. Finally, the findings for NTD speakers were considered, and it was hypothesized that these speakers are schizophrenic patients who are more responsive to phenothiazine medication than the TD patients.

Appendix 1. Identification Information for Subjects

Group	Subject number	Age	Sex	Education (yrs.)	I.Q."	Occupation	Socioeconomic status of parents"
TD	1	18	M	11	96	Student	M = Occupational therapist
	2	18	F	11	116	None	F = Stage manager
	3	28	M	13	97	Clerk	F = Professor
	4	31	M	11	92	Orderly and TV repairman	F = Shoe repairman
	5	19	M	12	112	Student	F = Judge
	6	21	M	14	99	Student	F = Physician
	7	20	F	10	Invalid	Telephone operator	F = Decorator
	8	36	F	18	Invalid	Proof-reader	M = Teacher
	9	24	F	16	Invalid	Teacher	F = Director
	10	18	M	10	106	Student	F = Salesman
NTD	1	18	M	9	Invalid	Student	F = Grocery store owner
	2	20	M	13	108	Clerk	F = Certified public accountant
	3	23	M	16	113	Student	F = Personnel president of firm
	4	37	M	15	104	Filmmaker	F = Professor of chemistry
	5	23	M	11	111	Housekeeper	F = Farmer
	6	22	M	15	120	Student	F = Teacher
	7	23	F	13	Invalid	Student	M = Engineer
	8	41	F	10	Invalid	Housewife	M = Textile store owner
	9	32	F	8	92	Housewife	F = Hired man
	10	19	F	15	113	Student	F = Lawyer

(Continued)

Appendix 1. (*Continued*)

Group	Subject number	Age	Sex	Education (yrs.)	I.Q.[a]	Occupation	Socioeconomic status of parents[c]
N	1	22	M	18	123	Student	F = Lawyer
	2	46	M	16	131	Writer	M = Waitress
	3	22	M	15	111	Salesman	F = Bakery store owner
	4	19	M	12	117	Warehouseman	F = Construction worker
	5	18	F	13	113	Student	F = Rabbi
	6	43	M	18	115	Teacher	M = Teacher
	7	18	F	13	N/A[b]	Student	F = Postal clerk
	8	48	F	12	124	Housewife	F = Electrical engineer
	9	48	F	11	N/A	Nurses' Aid	F = Machinist
	10	28	M	15	N/A	TV Technician	M = Musician

[a]Estimated WAIS equivalents from the Shipley-Hartford Scale, according to Paulson and Lin (1970).
[b]N/A = not available.
[c]Socioeconomic status of highest status or living parent, estimated according to Blishen, Jones, Naegele, and Porter (1968).

Appendix 2. Identification for Subjects Who Were Patients

Group	Subject Number	Grid test[a]		Hospitalization		Medication[c] (cpz/day)	Final diagnosis
		I Score	C Score	Previous number	Est. duration[b] (months)		
TD	1	573	−.41	1	2.4	3,000	Acute
	2	720	+.49	0	5.5	0	Chronic undifferentiated
	3	264	+.37	6	2.8	600	Acute
	4	466	+.21	4	1.5	400	Acute
	5	439	+.25	0	3.5	400	Acute
	6	529	−.20	0	2.5	160	Paranoid schizophrenic
	7	271	−.15	2	2.7	2,000	Schizoaffective
	8	519	+.02	1	1.6	1,300	Catatonic schizophrenic
	9	602	+.38	1	1.8	300	Acute
	10	745	−.25	1	2.5	480	Chronic
NTD	1	567	+.27	0	1.5	800	Simple
	2	522	+.38	1	1.2	1,000	Acute
	3	438	−.19	1	2.6	1,000	Acute
	4	635	−.27	0	1.0	80	Acute
	5	802	+.44	1	2.2	100	Acute
	6	540	+.19	3	1.1	600	Chronic
	7	478	−.31	2	4.5	2,000	Simple
	8	364	−.16	4	1.9	800	Paranoid schizophrenic
	9	443	+.23	1	1.6	800	Chronic
	10	431	−.11	0	0.5	600	Acute

[a]Bannister-Fransella Grid Test of Schizophrenic Thought Disorder (Bannister & Fransella, 1967).
[b]Including present stay.
[c]Chlorpromazine equivalents, estimated according to Hollister (1970).

References

Aaronson, D., Lorinstein, I.B., & Shapiro, H. *Cognitive and linguistic aspects of sentence coding.* Paper presented at the 42nd meeting of the Eastern Psychological Association, New York, N.Y., April 1971.

Anderson, S.W. Ballistic control of rhythmic articulatory movements in natural speech. In D.R. Aaronson & R. Rieber (Eds.), Developmental psycholinguistics and communication disorders. *Annals of the New York Academy of Sciences,* 1975, *263,* 236–243.

Andreasen, N.C. Do depressed patients show thought disorder? *Journal of Nervous and Mental Disease,* 1976, *163*(3), 186–192.

Andreasen, N.C. I. The clinical assessment of thought, language, and communication disorders: The definition of terms and evaluation of their reliability. *Archives of General Psychiatry,* In press. (a)

Andreasen, N.C. II. The diagnostic significance of disorders in thought, language, and communication. *Archives of General Psychiatry,* In press. (b)

Andreasen, N.C., & Powers, P.S. Overinclusive thinking in mania and schizophrenia. *British Journal of Psychiatry,* 1974, *125,* 452–456.

Antinucci, F., & Parisi, D. Early language acquisition: A model and some data. In C. Ferguson & D. Slobin (Eds.), *Child language development.* New York: Holt, Rinehart & Winston, 1973.

Arieti, S. *Interpretation of schizophrenia* (2nd edition). New York: Basic Books, 1974.

Astrachan, B.M., Harrow, M., Adler, D., Brauer, L., Schwartz, A., Schwartz, C., & Tucker, G. A checklist for the diagnosis of schizophrenia. *British Journal of Psychiatry,* 1972, *121,* 529–539.

Bär, E.S. Semiotic studies in schizophrenia and senile psychosis. *Semiotica,* 1976, *16*(3), 269–283.

Bartko, J.J., & Carpenter, W.T. On the methods and theory of reliability. *The Journal of Nervous and Mental Disease,* 1976, *163,* 307–317.

Bates, E. Pragmatics and sociolinguistics in child language. In D. Morehead & A. Morehead (Eds.), *Language deficiency in children: Selected readings.* Baltimore: University Park Press, 1977.

Benson, D.F. Psychiatric aspects of aphasia. *British Journal of Psychiatry,* 1973, *123,* 555–556.

Benson, J.D., & Greaves, W.S. *The language people really use.* Agincourt, Ontario: The Book Society of Canada (Linguistics for Canadians), 1973.

Berry, M. *Introduction to systemic linguistics I. Structures and systems.* London: Batsford, 1975.

Berry, M. *Introduction to systemic linguistics II. Levels and links.* London: Batsford, 1977.

Bleuler, E. *Dementia praecox; or the group of schizophrenias*. New York: International Universities Press, 1950. (Originally published, 1911).

Blishen, B.R., Jones, F.E., Naegele, K.D., & Porter, J. (Eds.). *Canadian society: Sociological perspective*. Toronto: Macmillan of Canada, 1968.

Bloomfield, L. *Language*. New York: Henry Holt, 1933.

Blumenthal, A.L. *Language and psychology: Historical aspects of psycholinguistics*. New York: Wiley, 1970.

Boklage, C.E. Schizophrenia, brain asymmetry development, and twinning: Cellular relationship with etiological and possibly prognostic implication. *Biological Psychiatry*, 1977, *12*, 19–35.

Boland, T.B., & Chapman, L.J. Conflicting predictions from Broen's and Chapman's theories of schizophrenic thought disorder. *Journal of Abnormal Psychology*, 1971, *78*(1), 52–58.

Bransford, J.D., Barclay, J.R., & Franks, J.J. Sentence memory: A constructive versus interpretative approach. *Cognitive Psychology*, 1972, *3*, 193–209.

Brown, R. Schizophrenia, language and reality. *American Psychologist*, 1973, 28, 395–403.

Buckingham, H.W., & Kurtesz, A. *Neologistic jargon aphasia*. Amsterdam: Swets & Zeitlinger B.V., 1976.

Bullwinkle, C. *Levels of complexity in discourse for reference disambiguation and speech act interpretation*. Cambridge, Mass.: M.I.T. Artificial Intelligence Laboratory Memo, 1977.

Butterworth, B. Hesitation and semantic planning in speech. *Journal of Psycholinguistic Research*, 1975, *4*, 75–88.

Cameron, N. A study of thinking in senile deterioration and schizophrenic disorganization. *American Journal of Psychology*, 1938, *51*, 650–665. (a)

Cameron, N. Reasoning, regression and communication in schizophrenics. *Psychological Monographs*, 1938 (Whole No. 221). (b)

Cameron, N. Experimental analysis of schizophrenic thinking. In J.S. Kasanin (Ed.), *Language and thought in schizophrenia*. Berkeley: University of California Press, 1944.

Cancro, R. Psychological differentiation and process-reactive schizophrenia. *Journal of Abnormal Psychology*, 1969, *74*, 415–419.

Carlson, G.A., & Goodwin, F.K. The stages of mania. *Archives of General Psychiatry*, 1973, *28*, 221–228.

Carpenter, M.D. Sensitivity to syntactic structure: Good versus poor premorbid schizophrenics. *Journal of Abnormal Psychology*, 1976, *85*(1), 41–50.

Carswell, E.A., & Rommetveit, R. *Social contexts of messages*. New York: Academic, 1971.

Chaika, E. A linguist looks at "schizophrenic" language. *Brain and Language*. 1974, *1*, 257–276. (a)

Chaika, E. *Linguistics and psychiatry*. Paper presented at the LSA Summer Meeting, Amherst, Mass., July 1974. (b)

Chaika, E. Schizophrenic speech, slips of the tongue, and jargonaphasia: A reply to Fromkin and to Lecours and Vanier-Clément. *Brain and Language*, 1977, *4*, 464–475.

Chapman, J.D. The early symptoms of schizophrenia. *British Journal of Psychiatry*, 1966, *122*, 225–251.

Chapman, L.J., & Chapman, J.P. *Disordered thought in schizophrenia*. Englewood Cliffs, N.J.: Prentice-Hall, 1973.

Chapman, L.J., Chapman, J.P., & Daut, R.L. Schizophrenic inability to disattend from strong aspects of meaning. *Journal of Abnormal Psychology*, 1976, *85*(1), 35–40.

Chapman, L.J., Chapman, J.P., & Miller, G.A. A theory of verbal behavior in schizophrenia. In B.A. Maher (Ed.), *Progress in experimental personality research* (Vol. 1). New York: Academic, 1964.

Charniak, E. Organization and inference in a frame-like system of common knowledge. In

R.C. Schank & B.L. Nash-Webber (Eds.), *Theoretical issues in natural language processing*. Cambridge, Mass.: Bolt, Beranek, & Newman, Inc., 1975.

Chomsky, N. *Syntactic structures*. The Hague: Mouton, 1957.

Chomsky, N. *Aspects of the theory of syntax*. Cambridge, Mass. MIT Press, 1965.

Chomsky, N., & Miller, G.A. Introduction to the formal analysis of natural languages. In R.D. Luce, R.R. Bush, & E. Galanter (Eds.), *Handbook of mathematical psychology* (Vol. 2). New York: Wiley, 1963.

Clark, H.H. Word associations and linguistic theory. In J. Lyons (Ed.), *New horizons in linguistics*. Baltimore, Md.: Penguin, 1970.

Clark, H.H. The language-as-fixed-effect fallacy: A critique of language statistics in psychological research. *Journal of Verbal Learning and Verbal Behavior*, 1973, *12*, 335–359.

Clark, H.H., & Haviland, S.E. Psychological processes as linguistic explanation. In D. Cohen (Ed.), *Explaining linguistic phenomena*. Washington, D.C.: Hemisphere, 1974.

Cohen, B.D. Referent communication disturbances in schizophrenia. In S. Schwartz (Ed.), *Language and cognition in schizophrenia*. New York: Erlbaum, 1978.

Cohen, B.D., Nachmani, G., & Rosenberg, S. Referent communication disturbances in acute schizophrenia. *Journal of Abnormal Psychology*, 1974, *83*(1), 1–13.

Cohen, J. A coefficient of agreement for nominal scales. *Educational Psychological Measurement*, 1960, *20*, 37–46.

Coleman, E.B. Approximations to English: Some comments on the method. *American Journal of Psychology*, 1963, *76*(2), 239–247.

Collins, A.M., Brown, J.S., & Larkin, K.M. Inference in text understanding. In R. I. Shapiro, B.C. Bruce, & W.F. Brewer (Eds.), *Theoretical issues in reading comprehension*. Hillsdale, N.J.: Erlbaum, 1978.

Craik, F.I. *Depth of processing in recall and perception*. Paper presented at the 6th International Symposium on Attention and Performance, Stockholm, 1975.

Craik, F.I., & Lockhart, R.S. Levels of processing: A framework for memory research. *Journal of Verbal Learning and Verbal Behavior*, 1972, *11*, 671–684.

Craik, F.I., & Tulving, E. Depth of processing and the retention of words in episodic memory. *Journal of Experimental Psychology: General*, 1975, *104*(3), 268–294.

Cromwell, R.L., & Dockeki, P.R. Schizophrenic language: A disattention interpretation. In S. Rosenberg & J. Koplin (Eds.), *Developments in applied psycholinguistic research*. New York: Macmillan, 1968.

Del Castillo, J.C. The influence of language upon symptomatology in foreign-born patients. *American Journal of Psychiatry*, 1970, *127*(2), 160–162.

Dennis, M., & Whitaker, H.A. Language acquisition following hemidecortication: Linguistic superiority of the left over the right hemisphere. *Brain and Language*, 1976, *3*, 404–433.

DiSimoni, F.G., Darley, F.L., & Aronson, A.E. Patterns of dysfunction in schizophrenic patients on an aphasia test battery. *Journal of Speech and Hearing Disorders*, 1977, *42*, 498–513.

Durbin, M., & Marshall, R.L. Speech in mania: Syntactic aspects. *Brain and Language*, 1977, *4*, 208–218.

Ellis, J., & Ure, J. Registers. In A.R. Meetham *et al.* (Eds.), *Encyclopedia of linguistics: Information and control*. Oxford: Pergamon, 1969.

Ellsworth, R.B. The regression of schizophrenic language. *Journal of Consulting Psychology*, 1951, *15*, 387–391.

Fawcett, R. P. *Systemic functional grammar in a cognitive model of language*. Paper presented at the meeting of the Linguistic Association of Great Britain; Sheffield, November 1972. (a)

Fawcett, R.P. *Generating a sentence in systemic functional grammar*. Paper presented at the

Meeting of the Linguistics Association of Great Britain; Sheffield, November 1972. (b)

Fairbanks, H. The quantitative differentiation of samples of spoken language. *Psychological Monographs*, 1944, *56*, 19–38.

Feigl, H. Validation and vindication: An analysis of the nature and the limits of ethical arguments. In W. Sellars & H. Hospers (Eds.), *Readings in ethical theory*. New York: Appleton-Century-Crofts, 1952.

Feldstein, S., & Jaffe, J. Schizophrenic speech fluency: A partial replication and hypothesis. *Psychological Reports*, 1963, *13*, 775–780.

Fillenbaum, S. On the use of memorial techniques to assess syntactic structures. *Psychological Bulletin*, 1970, *73*, 231–237.

Fine, J.H. *Text in context: Systemic grammar and conversational analysis in the study of children's dialogues*. Unpublished doctoral dissertation, Cornell University, Utica, N.Y., 1977.

Fink, M. Brain function, verbal behavior and psychotherapy. *Comprehensive Psychiatry*, 1974, *15*, 257–266. (a)

Fink, M. Induced seizures and human behavior. In M. Fink, S. Kety, A. McGaugh, & T.A. Williams (Eds.), *Psychology of convulsion therapy*. Washington, D.C.: V.H. Winston, 1974. (b)

Finn, P.J. Can rules be devised to make implicit intersentence case relationships explicit? In W.J. Russell (Chair.), *Discourse linguistic symposium*. Presented at the meeting of the American Educational Research Association, New York, N.Y., 1977.

Firth, J.R. *Papers in linguistics 1934–1951*. London: Oxford University Press, 1951.

Fischer, R. A cartography of the ecstatic and meditative states. *Science*, 1971, *174*, 897–904.

Fish, F.J. The classification of schizophrenia: The views of Kleist and his co-workers. *Journal of Mental Science*, 1957, *103*, 443–463.

Fleminger, J.J., Dalton, R., & Standage, K.F. Handedness in psychiatric patients. *British Journal of Psychiatry*, 1977, *131*, 448–452.

Flor-Henry, P. Psychosis and temporal lobe epilepsy. A controlled investigation. *Epilepsia*, 1969, *10*, 363–395.

Flor-Henry, P. Lateralized temporal-limbic dysfunction and psychopathology. In S.R. Harnad, H.D. Steklis, & J. Lancaster (Eds.), *Origins and evolutions of language and speech*. Annals of the New York Academy of Sciences (Vol. 280). New York: The New York Academy of Sciences, 1976.

Flor-Henry, P., & Gruzelier, J.H. *Hemispheric asymmetries of function and psychopathology*. New York: Elsevier, in press.

Fodor, J.A. Can meaning be an *rm*? *Journal of Verbal Learning and Verbal Behavior*, 1965, *4*, 73–81.

Frake, C.O. Plying frames can be dangerous: Some reflections on methodology in cognitive anthropology. *The Quarterly Newsletter of the Institute for Comparative Human Development*, 1977, *1*, 1–7.

Francis, H. Social class, reference and context. *Language and Speech*, 1975, *18*, 193–198.

Frederiksen, C.H. Representing logical and semantic structure of knowledge acquired from discourse. *Cognitive Psychology*, 1975, *7*, 371–458.

Freedman, A.M., Kaplan, H.I., & Sadock, B.J. *Modern synopsis of comprehensive textbook of psychiatry* (2nd ed.). Baltimore: Williams & Wilkins, 1976.

Fromkin, V.A. A linguist looks at "A linguist looks at 'schizophrenic language.' " *Brain and Language*, 1975, *2*, 498–503.

Garrett, M., Bever, T., & Fodor, J. The active use of grammar in speech perception. *Perception and Psychophysics*, 1966, *1*, 30–32.

Garrod, S., & Sanford, A. Anaphora: A problem in text comprehension. In R. N. Campbell & P.T. Smith (Eds.), *Recent advances in the psychology of language: Formal and experimental approaches* (Vol. 4b). New York: Plenum, 1978.

Garvey, C., Caramazza, A., & Yates, J. Factors influencing assignment of pronoun antecedents. *Cognition*, 1974/75, *3*(3), 227–243.

Gazzaniga, M.S., & Sperry, R.W. Language after section of the cerebral commisures. *Brain*, 1967, 131–148.

Gerbner, G. Preface. In G. Gerbner, O.R. Holsti, K. Krippendorff, W.J. Paisley, & P.J. Stone (Eds.), *The analysis of communication content*. New York: Wiley, 1969.

Gerson, S.N., Benson, D.F., & Frazier, S.H. Diagnosis: Schizophrenia versus posterior aphasia. *American Journal of Psychiatry*, 1977, *134*(9), 966–969.

Gerver, D. Linguistic rules and the perception and recall of speech by schizophrenic patients. *British Journal of Social and Clinical Psychology*, 1967, *6*, 204–211.

Gleason, H.A. Contrastive analysis in discourse structure. *Georgetown University Monograph Series on Language and Linguistics*, Washington, D.C.: Georgetown University Press, 1968.

Goldman-Eisler, F. *Psycholinguistics: Experiments in spontaneous speech*. New York: Academic, 1968.

Goldman-Eisler, F. Pauses, clauses, sentences. *Language and Speech*, 1972, *15*, 103–113.

Goldstein, K. The significance of special mental tests for diagnosis and prognosis in schizophrenia. *American Journal of Psychiatry*, 1939, *96*, 575–587.

Goldstein, K. Methodological approach to the study of schizophrenic thought disorder. In J.S. Kasanin (Ed.), *Language and thought in schizophrenia*. Berkeley: University of California Press, 1944.

Goldstein, K., & Scheerer, M. Abstract and concrete behavior: An experimental study with special tests. *Psychological Monographs*, 1941, *53*(2, Whole No. 239).

Gottschalk, L.A., & Gleser, G.C. Distinguishing characteristics of the verbal communications of schizophrenic patients. In D. McRioch & E.A. Weinstein (Eds.), *Disorders of communication*. Baltimore, Md.: Williams & Wilkins, 1964.

Gottschalk, L.A., & Gleser, G.C. *The measurement of psychological states through the content analysis of verbal behavior*. Berkeley: University of California Press, 1969.

Gottschalk, L.A., Hausmann, C., & Brown, J. S. A computerized scoring system for use with content analysis scales. *Comprehensive Psychiatry*, 1975, *16*, 77–90.

Gottschalk, L.A., Winget, C.N., & Gleser, G.C. *Manual of instructions for using the Gottschalk-Gleser content analysis scales*. Los Angeles: University of California Press, 1969.

Greenfield, P.M., & Smith, J.H. *The structure of communication in early language development*. New York: Academic, 1976.

Gregory, M. Aspects of varieties differentiation. *Journal of Linguistics* 1967, *3*(2), 177–198.

Grof, S. *Realms of the human unconscious*. New York: Viking, 1976.

Grosjean, F., Grosjean, L., & Lane, H. *The patterns of silence: Performance structures in sentence production*. Unpublished manuscript, 1978. (Available from the Department of Psychology, Northeastern University.)

Gruzelier, J.H. Bimodal states of arousal and lateralized dysfunction in schizophrenia: Effects of chlorpromazine. In L.C. Wynne, R.L. Cromwell, & S. Matthysse (Eds.), *The nature of schizophrenia: New approaches to research and treatment*. New York: Wiley, 1978.

Gruzelier, J.H., & Hammond, N. Schizophrenia: A dominant hemisphere temporal-limbic disorder? *Research Communications in Psychology, Psychiatry, and Behavior*, 1976, *1*, 33–72.

Gruzelier, J.H., & Venables, P.H. Two-flash threshold, sensitivity and B in normal subjects and schizophrenics. *Quarterly Journal of Experimental Psychology*, 1974, *26*, 594–604.

Gur, R.E. Motoric laterality imbalance in schizophrenia. *Archives of General Psychiatry*, 1977, *34*(1), 33–37.

Gur, R.E. Left hemisphere dysfunction and left hemisphere overactivation in schizophrenia. *Journal of Abnormal Psychology*, 1978, *87*, 226–238.

Gutwinski, W. *Cohesion in literary texts.* The Hague: Mouton, 1976.

Haley, J. An interactional description of schizophrenia. *Psychiatry,* 1959, *22,* 321–332.

Halliday, M.A.K. Notes on transitivity and theme in English: Part 1. *Journal of Linguistics,* 1967, *3,* 37–81. (a)

Halliday, M.A.K. Notes on transitivity and theme in English: Part 2. *Journal of Linguistics,* 1967, *3,* 199–244. (b)

Halliday, M.A.K. Language structure and language function. In J. Lyons (Ed.), *New horizons in linguistics.* Baltimore, Md.: Penguin, 1970.

Halliday, M.A.K. *Explorations in the functions of language.* London: Edward Arnold, 1973.

Halliday, M.A.K. Text as semantic choice in social contexts. In T. van Dijk & J. Petofi (Eds.), *Grammars and descriptions: Studies in text theory and text analysis.* Berlin & New York: de Gruyter (Research in Text Theory #1), 1977.

Halliday, M.A.K. *Language as a social semiotic: The social interpretation of language and meaning.* London: Edward Arnold, 1978.

Halliday, M.A.K., & Hasan, R. *Cohesion in English.* London: Longman, 1976.

Harrow, M., Himmelhoch, J., Tucker, G., Hersch, J., & Quinlan, D. Overinclusive thinking in acute schizophrenic patients. *Journal of Abnormal Psychology,* 1972, *79,* 161–168.

Harrow, M., Harkavy, K., Bromet, E., & Tucker, G. A longitudinal study of schizophrenic thinking. *Archives of General Psychiatry,* 1973, *28,* 161–168.

Harrow, M., & Quinlan, D. Is disordered thinking unique to schizophrenia? *Archives of General Psychiatry,* 1977, *34*(1), 15–21.

Hasan, R. *Text vs. sentence: Basic questions of textlinguistics* (Part II). Hamburg: Helmut Buske Verlag, 1979.

Haviland, S.E., & Clark, H.H. What's new? Acquiring new information as a process in comprehension, *Journal of Verbal Learning and Verbal Behavior,* 1974, *13,* 512–521.

Hawkins, P.R. Social class, the nominal group and reference. In B. Bernstein (Ed.), *Class, codes and control, Vol. II.: Applied studies towards a sociology of language.* London: Longman, 1973.

Henderson, A.I. Time patterns in spontaneous speech — cognitive stride or random walk? A reply to Jaffe *et al. Language and Speech,* 1974, *17,* 119–125.

Hirsch, S.R., & Leff, J.P. *Abnormalities in parents of schizophrenics.* New York: Oxford University Press, 1975.

Hobbs, J.R. *A computational approach to discourse analysis.* Research Report #76–2. Department of Computer Science, City College, City University of New York, December 1976.

Hollister, L.E. Choice of antipsychotic drugs. *American Journal of Psychiatry,* 1970, *127,* 186–190.

Holmes, V.M. & Forster, K.I. Detection of extraneous signals during sentence recognition. *Perception and Psychophysics,* 1970, *7*(5), 297–301.

Holmes, V.M. & Forster, K.I. Click location and syntactic structure. *Perception and Psychophysics,* 1972, *12,* 9–15.

Hörmann, H. *Psycholinguistics. An introduction to research and theory.* New York: Springer-Verlag, 1971.

Hymes, D. Models of the interaction of language and social setting. *Journal of Social Issues,* 1967, *23,* 8–28.

Ianzito, B., Cadoret, R., & Pugh, D. Thought disorder in depression. *American Journal of Psychiatry,* 1974, *131*(6), 703–707.

Ingram, D. Transitivity in child language. *Language,* 1971, *47,* 888–910.

Jaffe, J. Markovian communication rhythms: Their biological significance. In M. Lewis & L.

Rosenblum (Eds.), *Interaction, conversation, and the development of language.* New York: Wiley, 1977.

Jaffe, J., & Feldstein, S. *Rhythms of dialogue.* New York: Academic, 1970.

Jacobson, R. Discussant of "Factors and forms of aphasia" by A.R. Luria. In A.V.S. de Reuck & M. O'Connor (Eds.), *CIBA Foundation symposium on disorders of language.* Boston: Little, Brown, 1964.

Jarvella, R.J. Syntactic processing of connected speech. *Journal of Verbal Learning and Verbal Behavior,* 1971, *10,* 409–416.

Kantorowitz, D., & Cohen, B.D. Referent communication in chronic schizophrenia. *Journal of Abnormal Psychology,* 1977, *86* 1–9.

Kay, S.R., & Singh, M.M. Cognitive abnormality in schizophrenia: A dual process model. *Biological Psychiatry,* 1979, *14,* 155–176.

Kleist, K. Schizophrenic symptoms and cerebral pathology. *Journal of Mental Science,* 1960, *106,* 246–255.

Koh, S.D. Remembering of verbal materials by schizophrenic young adults. In S. Schwartz (Ed.), *Language and cognition in schizophrenia.* New York: Erlbaum, 1978.

Koh, S.D., Kayton, L., & Peterson, R.A. Affective encoding and consequent remembering in schizophrenic young adults. *Journal of Abnormal Psychology,* 1976, *85*(2), 156–166.

Kraepelin, E. *Dementia praecox and paraphrenia* (R.M. Barclay, trans.). Edinburgh: E & S Livingstone, 1919.

Krippendorff, K. Introduction. In G. Gerbner, O.R. Holsti, K. Krippendorff, W.J. Paisley, & P.J. Stone (Eds.), *The analysis of communication content.* New York: Wiley, 1969.

Labov, W. The study of language in its social context. *Studium Generale,* 1970, *23,* 30–87.

Labov, W. *Sociolinguistic patterns.* Philadelphia: University of Pennsylvania Press, 1973.

Labov, W., & Waltezky, J. Narrative analysis: Oral versions of personal experience. In J. Helm (Ed.), *Essays on the verbal and visual arts.* Seattle: University of Washington Press, 1967.

Lackner, J.R. Observations on the speech processing capabilities of an amnesic patient: Several aspects of H.M.'s language function. *Neuropsychologia,* 1974, *12,* 199–207.

Laffal, J. The contextual associates of sun and god in Schreber's autobiography. *Journal of Abnormal and Social Psychology,* 1960, *61,* 474–479.

Laffal, J. *Pathological and normal language.* New York: Atherton, 1965.

Laing, R.D. *The politics of experience.* New York: Pantheon, 1967.

Larsen, S.F., & Fromholt, P. Mnemonic organization and free recall in schizophrenia. *Journal of Abnormal Psychology,* 1976, *85,* 61–65.

Lawson, J.S., McGhie, A., & Chapman, J. Perception of speech in schizophrenia. *British Journal of Psychiatry,* 1964, *110,* 375–380.

Lecours, A.R., Vanier-Clément, M. Schizophasia and jargonaphasia: A comparative description with comments on Chaika's and Fromkin's respective looks at "schizophrenic" language. *Brain and Language,* 1976, *3,* 516–565.

Lenneberg, E.H. *Biological foundations of language.* New York: Wiley, 1967.

Lesgold, A.M. Pronominalization: A device for unifying sentences in memory. *Journal of Verbal Learning and Verbal Behavior,* 1972, *11,* 316–323.

Levy, J., & Trevarthen, C. Perceptual, semantic and phonetic aspects of elementary language processes in split-brain patients. *Brain,* 1977, *100,* 105–118.

Levy, R. The effect of chlorpromazine on sentence structure of schizophrenic patients. *Psychopharmacologia,* 1968, *13,* 426–432.

Levy, R., & Maxwell, A.E. The effect of verbal context on the recall of schizophrenics and other psychiatric patients. *British Journal of Psychiatry,* 1968, *114,* 311–316.

Lewinsohn, P.M., & Elwood, D.L. The role of contextual constraint in the learning of language samples in schizophrenia. *Journal of Nervous and Mental Disease,* 1961, *133*, 79–81.

Lindsley, J.R. Producing simple utterances: How far ahead do we plan? *Cognitive Psychology,* 1975, *7*, 1–19.

Lockard, R.B. Reflections on the fall of comparative psychology: Is there a message for us all? *American Psychologist,* 1971, *26*, 168–179.

Lockhart, R.S., Craik, F.I.M., & Jacoby, L.L. Depth of processing in recognition and recall: Some aspects of a general memory system. In J. Brown (Ed.), *Recognition and recall.* London: Wiley, 1975.

Lorenz, M., & Cobb, S. Language patterns in psychotic and psychoneurotic subjects. *Archives of Neurology and Psychiatry,* 1954, *72*(6), 665–673.

MacKay, D.G. Spoonerisms: The structure of errors in the serial order of speech. *Neuropsychologia,* 1970, *8*, 323–350.

Maher, B.A. Schizophrenia: Language and thought. In B.A. Maher (Ed.), *Principles of psychopathology.* New York: McGraw-Hill, 1966.

Maher, B.A. Schizophrenia. *Psychology Today,* 1968, *1*, 30–33.

Maher, B.A. The language of schizophrenia: A review and interpretation. *British Journal of Psychiatry,* 1972, *120*, 3–17.

Maher, B.A., McKean, K.O., & McLaughlin, B. Studies in psychotic language. In P.J. Stone, R.F. Bales, Z. Namenworth, & D.M. Ogilvie (Eds.), *The general inquirer: A computer approach to content analysis.* Cambridge, Mass.: MIT Press, 1966.

Malinowski, B. The problem of meaning in primitive languages, Supplement 1 to C.K. Ogden & I.A. Richards, *The meaning of meaning.* London: Kegan Paul, 1923.

Mann, M.B. The quantitative differentiation of samples of spoken language. *Psychological Monographs,* 1944, *56*, 41–74.

Maratsos, M.P. *The use of definite and indefinite reference in young children.* London: Cambridge University Press, 1976.

Marks, L.E., & Miller, G.A. The role of semantic and syntactic constraints in the memorization of English sentences. *Journal of Verbal Learning and Verbal Behavior,* 1964, *3*, 1–5.

Martin, J.R. *Learning how to tell.* Unpublished doctoral dissertation, University of Essex, 1978. (Available from University Microfilms International, 18 Bedford Row, London, WCIR 4EJ, #78–70,018.)

McGhie, A. Attention and perception in schizophrenia. In B.A. Maher (Ed.), *Progress in experimental personality research* (Vol. 5). New York: Academic, 1970.

McGhie, A., & Chapman, J. Disorders of attention and perception in early schizophrenia. *British Journal of Psychiatry,* 1961, *34*, 103–116.

Miller, G.A. Some psychological studies of grammar. *American Psychologist,* 1962, *17*, 748–762.

Miller, G.A. Some preliminaries to psycholinguistics. *American Psychologist,* 1965, *20*, 15–20.

Miller, G.A., & Chomsky, N. Finitary models of language users. In R.D. Luce, R.R. Bush, & E. Galanter (Eds.), *Handbook of mathematical psychology* (Vol. 2). New York: Wiley, 1963.

Miller, G.A., & Isard, S. Some perceptual consequences of linguistic rules. *Journal of Verbal Learning and Verbal Behavior,* 1963, *3*, 217–228.

Miller, G.A., & Selfridge, J.A. Verbal context and the recall of meaningful material. *American Journal of Psychology,* 1950, *63*(2), 176–185.

Minsky, M. A framework for representing knowledge. In P.H. Winston (Ed.), *The psychology of computer vision.* New York: McGraw-Hill, 1975.

Namyslowska, I. Thought disorders in schizophrenia before and after pharmacological treatment. *Comprehensive Psychiatry,* 1975, *16*(1), 37–42.

Neale, J.M., & Cromwell, R.L. Attention and schizophrenia. In B.A. Maher (Ed.), *Progress in experimental psychology* (Vol. 5). New York: Academic, 1970.

Nöth, W. Disturbances of associations in schizophrenia. *Orbis*, 1978, *26*(2), 163–187.

Nuttall, R.L., & Solomon, L.F. Prognosis in schizophrenia: The role of premorbid social class, and demographic factors. *Behavioral Science*, 1970, *15*, 255–264.

Oddy, H.C., & Lobstein, T.J. Hand and eye dominance in schizophrenia. *British Journal of Psychiatry*, 1972, *120*, 331–332.

Olson, G.M., & Clark, H.H. Research methods in psycholinguistics. In E.C. Carterette & M.P. Friedman (Eds.), *Handbook of perception (Vol. 7) Language and speech*. New York: Academic, 1976.

Oltmanns, T.F. Selective attention in schizophrenic and manic psychoses: The effect of distraction on information processing. *Journal of Abnormal Psychology*, 1978, *87*(2), 212–225.

Oltmanns, T.F., Ohayon, J., & Neale, J.M. The effect of anti-psychotic medication and diagnostic, criteria on distractibility in schizophrenia. In R. Wynne, R. Cromwell, & S. Matthysse (Eds.), *Nature of schizophrenia: New findings and future strategies*. New York: Wiley, 1978.

Paulson, M.J., & Lin, T. Predicting WAIS I.Q. from Shipley-Hartford scores. *Journal of Clinical Psychology*, 1970, *26*, 453–461.

Payne, R.W. An object classification test as a measure of overinclusive thinking in schizophrenic patients. *British Journal of Social and Clinical Psychology*, 1962, *1*, 213–221.

Payne, R.W. *Attention, arousal and thought disorder in psychotic illness*. Paper presented at the Biometrics Research Workshop in Objective Indicators of Psychopathology; New York, N.Y., 1968.

Payne, R.W. Cognitive defects in schizophrenia: Overinclusive thinking. In J. Hellmuth (Ed.), *Cognitive studies* (Vol. 2). New York: Brunner/Mazel, 1971.

Pavy, D. Verbal behavior in schizophrenia: A review of recent studies. *Psychological Bulletin*, 1968, *70*, 164–178.

Perry, J.W. *Roots of renewal in myth and madness: The meaning of psychotic episodes*. San Francisco: Jossey-Bass, 1976.

Poulsen, D., Kintsch, E., Kintsch, W., & Premack, D. *Children's comprehension and memory for stories*. Unpublished manuscript, University of Colorado, 1978.

Quirk, R., Greenbaum, S., Leech, G., & Svartvik, J. *A grammar of contemporary English*. London: Longman, 1972.

Rattan, R.B., & Chapman, L.J. Associative intrusions in schizophrenic verbal behavior. *Journal of Abnormal Psychology*, 1973, *82*, 169–173.

Raeburn, K.M., & Tong, J.E. Experiments on contextual constraint in schizophrenia. *British Journal of Psychiatry*, 1968, *114*, 43–52.

Reber, A.S. On psycho-linguistic paradigms. *Journal of Psycholinguistic Research*, 1973, *2*, 289–320.

Reed, J.L. Schizophrenic thought-disorder: A review and hypothesis. *Comprehensive Psychiatry*, 1970, *11*, 403–432.

Reilly, F.E., Harrow, M., & Tucker, G.J. Language and thought content in acute psychosis. *American Journal of Psychiatry*, 1973, *130*, 411–417.

Reilly, F., Harrow, M., Tucker, G., Quinlan, D., & Siegel, A. Looseness of associations in acute schizophrenia. *British Journal of Psychiatry*, 1975, *127*, 240–246.

Riegel, K.F. Subject-object alienation in psychological experiments and testing. *Human Development*, 1975, *18*, 181–193.

Riegel, K.F. The temporal structure of dialogues. In W. Haas (Ed.), *Dialogue*. Columbia, South Carolina: Hornbeam Press, in press.

Robinson, W.P., & Rackstraw, S.J. *A question of answers* (Vol 1). London: Routledge & Kegan Paul, 1972.

Rochester, S.R. The significance of pauses in spontaneous speech. *Journal of Psycholinguistic Research,* 1973, *2,* 51–81.

Rochester, S.R. Reference as a speech art: An argument for studying the listener. In R.N. Campbell & P.T. Smith (Eds.), *Recent advances in the psychology of language: Formal and experimental approaches* (Vol. 4B). New York: Plenum, 1978. (a)

Rochester, S.R. Are language disorders in acute schizophrenia actually information processing problems? In L.C. Wynne, R.L. Cromwell, & S. Matthysse (Eds.), *The nature of schizophrenia: New approaches to research and treatment.* New York: Wiley, 1978. (b)

Rochester, S.R., & Gill, J.R. Production of complex sentences in monologues and dialogues. *Journal of Verbal Learning and Verbal Behavior,* 1973, *12,* 203–210.

Rochester, S.R., Harris, J., & Seeman, M.V. Sentence processing in schizophrenic listeners. *Journal of Abnormal Psychology,* 1973, *3,* 350–356.

Rochester, S.R., Martin, J.R., & Thurston, S. Thought process disorder in schizophrenia: The listener's task. *Brain and Language,* 1977, *4,* 95–114.

Rochester, S.R., Thurston, S., & Rupp, J. Hesitations as clues to failures in coherence: Studies of the thought-disordered speaker. In S. Rosenberg (Ed.), *Sentence production: A handbook of theory and practice.* New York: Erlbaum, 1977.

Rommetveit, R. *Words, meanings, and messages.* New York: Academic, 1968.

Rommetveit, R. *On message structure: A framework for the study of language and communication.* London: Wiley, 1974.

Rosenberg, S.D., & Cohen, B.D. Speakers' and listeners' processes in a word-communication task. *Science,* 1964, *145,* 1201–1203.

Rosenberg, S.D., & Cohen, B.D. Referential processes of speakers and listeners. *Psychological Review,* 1966, *73,* 208–231.

Rosenberg, S.D., & Tucker, G.J. *Verbal content and the diagnosis of schizophrenia.* Paper presented at the 29th Annual Meeting of the American Psychiatric Association, Florida, May 1976.

Russell, W.J., & Snow, D.D. Discourse processes in elementary school children. In W.J. Russell (Chair.), *Discourse linguistics symposium.* Presented at the meeting of the American Educational Research Association, New York, N.Y., 1977.

Sachs, J.S. Recognition and memory for syntactic and semantic aspects of connected discourse. *Perception and Psychophysics,* 1967, *2,* 437–442.

Sachs, J.S. Memory in reading and listening to discourse. *Memory and Cognition,* 1974, *2,* 95–100.

Sacks, H. An initial investigation of the stability of conversational data for doing sociology. In D. Sudnow (Ed.), *Studies in social interaction.* New York: The Free Press, 1972.

Salzinger, K., Portnoy, S., & Feldman, R.S. Experimental manipulation of continuous speech in schizophrenic patients. *Journal of Abnormal and Social Psychology,* 1964, *68,* 508–518.

Salzinger, K., Portnoy, S., & Feldman, R.S. Communicability deficit in schizophrenics resulting from a more general deficit. In S. Swartz (Ed.), *Language and cognition in schizophrenia.* New York: Erlbaum, 1978.

Salzinger, K., Portnoy, S., Pisoni, D.B., & Feldman, R.S. The immediacy hypothesis and response-produced stimuli in schizophrenic speech. *Journal of Abnormal Psychology,* 1970, *76,* 258–264.

Schatzman, L., & Strauss, A. Social class and modes of communication. *American Journal of Sociology,* 1955, *60,* 329–338.

Seeman, M.V. Analysis of psychotic language—A review. *Diseases of the Nervous System,* 1970, *31,* 92–99.

Seeman, M.V. Therapist-induced speech disorder. *Psychotherapy Theory, Research and Practice*, 1975, *12*, 175–178.

Seeman, M.V., & Cole, H.J. The effect of increasing personal contact in schizophrenia. *Comprehensive Psychiatry*, 1977, *18*, 283–293.

Shakow, D. Segmental set: A theory of formal psychological deficit in schizophrenia. *Archives of General Psychiatry*, 1962, *6*, 17–33.

Shimkunas, A. Hemispheric asymmetry and schizophrenic thought disorder. In S. Schwartz (Ed.), *Language and cognition in schizophrenia*. New York: Erlbaum, 1978.

Siegel, A., Harrow, M., Reilly, F., & Tucker, G. Loose associations and disordered speech patterns in chronic schizophrenia. *Journal of Nervous and Mental Disease*, 1976, *162*(2), 105–112.

Siegman, A.W. Cognition and hesitation in speech. In A.W. Siegman & S. Feldstein (Eds.), *Of speech and time: Temporal speech patterns in interpersonal contexts*. Hillsdale, N.J.: Erlbaum, In press.

Silverman, J. The problem of attention in research and theory in schizophrenia. *Psychological Review*, 1964, *71*, 352–379.

Silverman, J. Stimulus intensity modulation and psychological dis-ease. *Psychopharmacologia*, 1972, *24*, 42–80.

Silverman, J. *On the sensory bases of transcendental states of consciousness*. Paper presented at a scientific conference sponsored by the Smithsonian Institute and the Drug Abuse Council, Washington, D.C., 1975.

Singer, M.T. Family transactions and schizophrenia: I. Recent research findings. In J. Romano (Ed.), *The origins of schizophrenia*, Amsterdam: Excerpta Medica, 1967.

Singer, M.T., & Wynne, L.C. Differentiating characteristics of parents of childhood schizophrenics, childhood autistics, and young adult schizophrenics. *American Journal of Psychiatry*, 1963, *120*, 234–243.

Singer, M.T., & Wynne, L.C. Thought disorder and family relations of schizophrenics. IV. Results and implications. *Archives of General Psychiatry*, 1965, *12*, 201–212.

Singer, M.T., Wynne, L.C., & Toohey, M.L. Communication disorders and the families of schizophrenics. In L.C. Wynne, R.L. Cromwell, & S. Matthysse (Eds.), *Nature of schizophrenia: New approaches to research and treatment*. New York: Wiley, 1978.

Slobin, D.I. Cognitive prerequisites for the development of grammar. In C.A. Ferguson and D.I. Slobin (Eds.), *Studies of child language develoment*. New York: Holt, Rinehart & Winston, 1973.

Stolz, W., & Tiffany, J. The production of "child-like" word associations by adults to unfamiliar adjectives. *Journal of Verbal Learning and Verbal Behavior*, 1972, *11*, 38–46.

Stone, P.J., Bales, R.F., Namenworth, Z., & Ogilvie, D.M. The General Inquirer: A computer system for content analysis and retrieval based on the sentence as a unit of information. *Behavioral Science*, 1962, *7*, 484–498.

Stone, P.J., Dunphy, D.C., Smith, M.S., & Ogilvie, D.M. *The General Inquirer: A computer approach to content analysis*. Cambridge, Mass.: MIT Press, 1966.

Storch, A. The primitive archaic forms of inner experiences and thought in schizophrenia. *Nervous and Mental Diseases Monograph*, 1924 (36).

Suchotliff, L.C. Relations of formal thought disorder to the communication deficit in schizophrenia. *Journal of Abnormal Psychology*, 1970, *76*(2), 250–257.

Sullivan, H.S. Peculiarity of thought in schizophrenia. *American Journal of Psychiatry*, 1925, *82*, 21–86.

Sullivan, H.S. The language of schizophrenia. In J.S. Kasanin (Ed.), *Language and thought in schizophrenia*. New York: W.W. Norton, 1964. (Originally published in 1944.)

Taber, C. *The structure of Sango narrative*. Hartford, Conn. Hartford Seminary Foundation (Hartford Studies in Linguistics, 17), 1966.

Taylor, W.L. "Cloze procedure": A new tool for measuring readability. *Journalism Quarterly*, 1953, *30*, 415–433.

Thieman, T.J. Imitation and recall of optionally deletable sentences by young children. *Journal of Child Language*, 1975, *2*, 261–269.

Thorndyke, P.W. The role of inferences in discourse comprehension. *Journal of Verbal Learning and Verbal Behavior*, 1976, *15*, 437–446.

Titchener, E.B. *Experimental psychology* (Vol. 2). New York: Macmillan, 1905.

Traupmann, K.L. Effects of categorization and imagery on recognition and recall by process and reactive schizophrenics. *Journal of Abnormal Psychology*, 1975, *85*(4), 307–314.

Traupmann, K. Differential deficit: Psychometric remediation is not acceptable for psychometric artifact. *The Quarterly Newsletter of the Institute for Comparative Human Development*, 1976, *1*, 2–3.

Traupmann, K.L., Berzofsky, M., & Alpert, M. *Process schizophrenics suboptimally implement active memory encoding strategies.* Paper presented at the Annual Meeting of the American Psychological Association; Chicago, Ill., 1975.

Truscott, I.P. Contextual constraint and schizophrenic language. *Journal of Consulting and Clinical Psychology*, 1970, *35*, 189–194.

Tucker, G.J., & Rosenberg, S.D. Computer content analysis of schizophrenic speech: A preliminary report. *American Journal of Psychiatry*, 1975, *132*(6), 611–616.

Turner, R.J., Raymond, J., Zabo, L.J., & Diamond, J. Field survey methods in psychiatry. *Journal of Health and Social Behavior*, 1969, *10*(4), 289–297.

Venables, P.H. Sensory aspects of psychopathology. *Neurobiological Aspects of Psychopathology*, 1969, 132–141.

Vetter, H.J. *Language behavior in schizophrena: Selected readings in research and theory.* Springfield, Ill.: Charles C Thomas, 1968.

Vigotsky, L. [Thought in schizophrenia] (J. Kasanin, trans.). *Archives of Neurology and Psychiatry*, 1934, 31, 1063–1077.

Vigotsky, L. *Thought and language.* Cambridge, Mass.: MIT Press, 1962.

Voloshinov, V.N. *Marxism and the philosophy of language.* New York: Academic, 1973.

Weckowicz, T.E., & Blewett, D.B. Size constancy and abstract thinking in schizophrenic patients. *Journal of Mental Science*, 1959, *105*, 909–934.

Weiner, M., & Mehrabian, A. *Language within language: Immediacy, a channel in verbal communication.* New York: Appelton-Century-Crofts, 1968.

Weinstein, E.A., & Lyerly, O.G. Personality factors in jargon aphasia. *Cortex*, 1976, 12, 122–133.

Werner, O., Lewis-Matichek, G., Evans, M., & Litowitz, B. An ethnoscience view of schizophrenic speech. In M. Sanches & B. Blout (Eds.), *Sociocultural dimensions of language use.* New York: Academic, 1975.

White, M.A. A study of schizophrenic language. *Journal of Abnormal and Social Psychology*, 1949, *44*, 61–74.

Whitehorn, J.C., & Zipf, G.K. Schizophrenic language. *Archives of Neurology and Psychiatry*, 1943, *49*, 831–851.

Winer, B.J. *Statistical principles in experimental design.* New York: McGraw-Hill, 1971.

Winograd, T. Understanding natural language. *Cognitive Psychology*, 1972, *3*, 1–191.

Witelson, S.F. Abnormal right hemisphere specialization in developmental dyslexia. In R. Knights & D. Bakker (Eds.), *The neuropsychology of learning disorders: Theoretical approaches.* Baltimore, Md.: University Park Press, 1976.

Witelson, S.F. Developmental dyslexia: Two right hemispheres and none left. *Science*, 1977, *195*, 309–311.

Woods, W.L. Language study in schizophrenia. *Journal of Nervous and Mental Disease*, 1938, *87*, 290–316.

Woodward, J.A., & Goldstein, M.J. Communication deviance in the families of schizophrenics: A comment on the misuse of analysis of covariance. *Science*, 1977, *197*, 1096–1097.

Wynne, L.C. Schizophrenics and their families: Research on parental communication. In J.M. Tanner (Ed.), *Developments in psychiatric research*. London: Hodder & Stoughton, 1977.

Wynne, L.C., & Singer, M.T. Thought disorders and the family relations of schizophrenics: I. A research strategy. *Archives of General Psychiatry*, 1963, *9*, 191. (a)

Wynne, L.C., & Singer, M.T. Thought disorders and the family relations of schizophrenics: II. Classification of forms of thinking. *Archives of General Psychiatry*, 1963, *9*, 199–206. (b)

Zaidel, E. Auditory language comprehension in the right hemisphere following cerebral commissurotomy and hemispherectomy: A comparison with child language and aphasia. In E. Zurif & Caramazza (Eds.), *The acquisition and breakdown of language: Parallels and divergencies*. Baltimore, Md.: Johns Hopkins Press, 1976.

Zaidel, E. Unilateral auditory language comprehension on the Token Test following cerebral commissurotomy and hemispherectomy. *Neuropsychologia*, 1977, *15*, 1–18.

Index

Addition, 146
Anaphoric reference. *See also* Endophoric reference
  definition of, 53
  in mania, 53–54, 201
Andreasen, Nancy C.
  Bleulerian descriptions of thought disorder, 3, 39–41, 43
  thought disorder in psychotic states, 52–53
Aphasia. *See also* Schizophasia
  and schizophrenia language, 41, 100–101, 192
  and thought disorder, 6, 187–189
Asyndesis, 161

Behaviorism
  assumptions about, 10
  clinicians, influence on, 10
  experimental tradition, influence on, 24
  neobehaviorism, 12
  psycholinguistics, influence on, 9, 11
  and schizophrenic language, 12
Biology, 16, 21
Bleuler, Eugen
  donkey narrative, 64
  frame of reference, 81
  and origin of term schizophrenia, 2
  schizophrenia, criteria for, 4, 28, 39–40, 59
  sentence tying, 180
  on speech and thought, 1 n
Bloomfield, Leonard, 11
Bridging. *See also* Indirect reference; Retrieval categories
  and addition, 161–166

Bridging *(Cont.)*
  in children, 182
  definition of, 146
  as a form of presumption, 181

Cameron, Norman, 1, 10, 59
Carpenter, Mary, 20–22, 113
Cartoon task description, 62–64
Chaika, Elaine
  schizophrenia and episodic aphasia, 6, 99–100, 187
  schizophrenia and lexical features, 91, 179–180
  schizophrenia and sound features, 92–180
  schizophrenic speaker, analysis of a, 3, 41–43
Chains of reference. *See* Referential chains
Chapman, Loren J. (and Jean P. Chapman)
  literature, review of, 8, 12
  schizophrenia and word meanings, 92
  thought disorder, 6
Chomsky, Noam, 10, 15, 48
Circumstantiality, 6. *See also* Loose associations
Clark, Herbert H.
  psycholinguistic measures, 14–15, 47
  psycholinguistic theory, 23, 47–48
  strategies of referring, 146
Classifier, function in nominal group, 107–108
Clause length, 86–88. *See also* Independent clause
"Click" experiments, 20, 22
Clinical studies, 38–45
Cognitive gating hypothesis, 193, 195

223